PLANTING TEETH

A Namibian Story

WOLSAK
& WYNN

Cover image: © Costas Anton Dumitrescu/Shutterstock
Cover and interior design: Ingrid Paulson
Author photograph: Charles Earle
Typeset in Whitman and Directors Gothic
Printed by Ball Media, Brantford, Canada

The publisher gratefully acknowledges the support of the Canada Council for the Arts, the Ontario Arts Council and the Canada Book Fund.

Wolsak and Wynn Publishers, Ltd.
280 James Street North
Hamilton, ON
Canada L8R 2L3

LIBRARY AND ARCHIVES CANADA CATALOGUING IN PUBLICATION

Midgley, Peter, 1965–, author
Counting teeth : a Namibian story / Peter Midgley.

ISBN 978-1-894987-89-9 (pbk.)

1. Midgley, Peter, 1965– —Travel—Namibia. 2. Namibia—Description and travel.
3. Namibia—History. 4. Namibia—Biography. I. Title.

DT1536.M53 2014   916.88104'42   C2014-904078-4

For my daughters, who at different times have shared Namibia with me.

"The death rattle of the dying and the shrieks of the mad . . . they echo in the sublime stillness of infinity."

—*Unknown German soldier, recalling the*
Wars of Resistance in Namibia

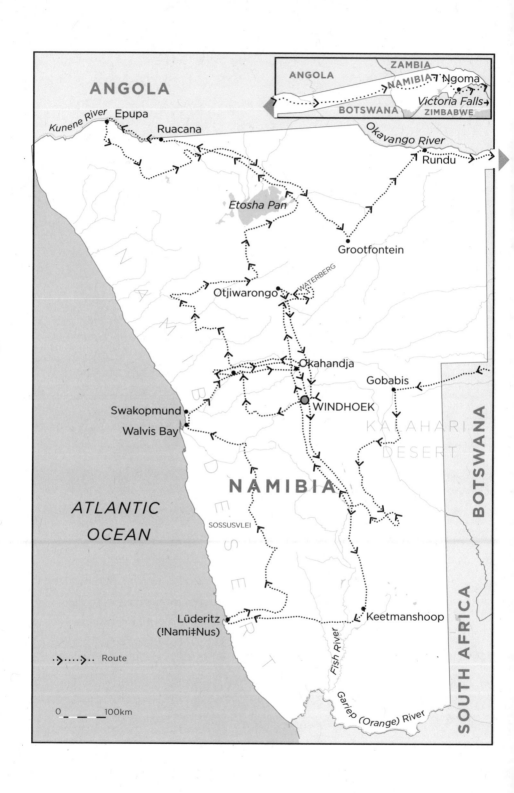

PROLOGUE

1990

"So Whitey, what can you tell us about revolutions?"

The past few days were a blur. Four days earlier, on Thursday, I had been walking along High Street in Grahamstown, a small South African university town. A single thought occupied my mind as I made my way toward the university: the government had refused to grant me further exemption from conscription, and I was due to report for military service in three days' time. In front of the Drostdy Arch, which divides the campus from the city, Andrew Roos stopped me to ask whether I'd heard about the job in Windhoek. I hadn't. From the Drostdy Arch, I walked straight to my department and faxed in a resume. That afternoon, I had my interview by phone.

On Friday, I packed. On Saturday morning, the day I was meant to report to base, I said my goodbyes to Julie and our daughter, Andreya, and boarded an airplane to Windhoek to lecture Afrikaans at the University of Namibia. It was well after midnight when I fell into bed.

Although I was barely five years old when our family had left Namibia — Dad, a bank manager, had been transferred back to South Africa — the country remained an integral part of my life. It was the fabric that enveloped our family; it was a place of imagination. In our home, any mention of Namibia was filled with love and longing. We returned there for holidays and we welcomed friends and family who still lived there. Always, there were stories: the ones Ma shared and the ones visitors brought with them. The art and artifacts that filled our house came from there. Every photo album was filled with pictures of our time in Namibia. In the narrow alley between the house and the garage, a set of kudu horns grinned at me every time I went to get the lawnmower. Over the years, the teeth and horns had been loosened by decay, yet it remained there in the alley — a reminder of a trip to Namibia. When other children at school chose to do school projects about faraway places like Japan, I had chosen Namibia.

I woke early on Sunday morning, still exhausted from travel, but I couldn't sleep any longer. I opened the curtains and watched the sun rise over the Auas Valley on my first day back in Windhoek in almost twenty years.

I was home.

Later that morning, I had lunch with my new colleagues. I returned with a pile of books and began to prepare for my first classes. At nine o'clock on Monday morning, I introduced myself to the students taking a course called Literature and Revolution.

I am no longer sure who asked the question. The more I think about it, the more convinced I am that it was Freddie Philander, a large, imposing man with a deep voice and greying temples. If I close my eyes, I can still see him about two-thirds of the way up the lecture theatre, near the centre of the row, leaning forward with an air of confidence that unsettled me. Memory can play tricks on one's mind, so I could be wrong about Freddie. In the end, it doesn't really matter. What matters is how a question like that sears itself into your mind. That, and how you respond. I froze.

A handful of students chuckled at the sight of an inexperienced young lecturer standing there *met 'n bek vol tande*, as the Afrikaans expression goes — with a mouthful of teeth. Lost for words. It was the first class I had ever taught and two minutes into it, I was floundering. I searched desperately for something to say, but all I could see in my mind's eye was the grins on their faces and I knew with absolute certainty that the rows of teeth were multiplying as they prepared to devour me. And yet it seemed appropriate, for teeth and Namibia had always gone hand-in-hand for me. Well, if truth be told, it was more like teeth-in-hand that went with Namibia. I had lost my front teeth falling down the stairs as a toddler in Okahandja and they didn't return for many years. While my teeth went AWOL, my mother could remove hers at will, although she always assured me it happened by accident. Ma was sitting in the corner chair, crocheting and talking. I sat on the floor beside her taking in the adult conversation. "*Uit!*" Ma said after a while. "*Jy't genoeg tande getel. Loop speel.*" Out. You've counted enough teeth now. Go play.

I scurried out, but soon snuck back inside and hid behind the couch that divided the lounge and the dining room. From there, I could take in the conversation undetected through the latticed stump of the Owambo stool. Inevitably, conversation turned to Namibia, the land of milk and stories you could chew on for hours as if they were a nice piece of biltong. Ma's story meandered and just at the moment where things became interesting, she reached forward to get a chocolate from the bowl on the coffee table.

While we all waited for her to pick up her narrative, Ma closed her eyes, put the chocolate into her mouth and bit down. The whip-crack echoed across the lounge and the story ended abruptly. Slowly, Ma pulled the chocolate, and her front teeth, from her mouth. Four perfect incisors astride a chunk of chocolate-coated crème caramel. Dad was at her side within seconds, brandishing a tube of Bostik.

"As good as new!" he announced proudly as he pulled the set of uppers from the vice half an hour later. Ma just glowered at him and waited for the dentist to call her back. But I did notice that she slid the old set that Dad had repaired into the drawer by her bedside. She had lived through the Second World War and had learned not to throw away anything that might still be useful.

I dusted off the memory and put it aside. Slowly, I removed the proverbial teeth from my mouth so that I could speak. I was formulating a response to Freddie's question on the fly, but as I spoke, I knew that, once more, I was counting teeth — listening in on a conversation that was way beyond my comprehension, searching for some Bostik to mend the crack that had opened between us. No matter how hard I tried, my theoretical knowledge would never match the practical reality of these students, several of whom were demobbed soldiers who had only recently returned from exile after the twenty-five-year War of Independence.

"I doubt I can teach you anything about revolutions," I said, "but I may have something to say about literature."

At the end of that class, one of the students, Mr. Huiseb, came to the front to talk to me. He leaned against the lectern and ran his fingers through the thick mat of his beard as I collected my notes. Then, just as I slipped everything into my briefcase, he asked, "Do you have a passport?"

"No," I said, for I knew he meant a *Namibian* passport. Other passports were easy to come by, but very few people had passports for a country that, technically, did not yet exist.

"Every Namibian needs a passport. You are a Namibian, therefore you need a passport. Come." He drove me to the temporary passport offices in Klein Windhoek and waited for me to collect the necessary forms.

"What brought you back?" he asked me on the way home.

"Independence. And the South African Army."

"Ah, yes, the army. Well, the passport will help."

I understood. As a documented citizen of a foreign country, I could no longer be conscripted. But it went deeper than that. A Namibian passport meant I belonged here. It was the first step toward becoming part of a nation.

Independence Day came and went in a flurry of flags and festivities. My Namibian identity documents arrived in the midst of the festivities, but I barely noticed, for there were more important things to celebrate. After a week of feasting, we went back to work and life returned to normal. The following week, at the end of March, Julie and Andreya joined me in Windhoek and we got married. The euphoria of independence dragged on throughout the year. By day, we worked hard at making our new democracy work. Sometimes it did and sometimes it didn't, but always we tried. In the evening and over weekends, we found reasons to celebrate the return of friends from exile, or toasted achievements like a successful play or a new book by a Namibian author. Too soon, the year was over and my contract had expired. It was time to move again, back to South Africa, which by then was also tottering toward freedom.

1

August 2011

From the minute I step out of the plane and walk onto the tarmac toward the customs building with my daughter, I know I love this place. We cross the tarmac and enter the shade of the terminal building. The woman at customs examines my papers carefully. "Why do you have this passport?"

"Because I am a South African citizen?"

"Yes, but it says you were born in Okahandja. Why don't you have a Namibian passport?"

There are people queueing up behind us and I try to keep my response simple. "It was stolen."

It's the truth. Shortly after Julie, Andreya and I had returned to South Africa, someone broke into our car and stole my briefcase, which had my passport in it. I tried to get a replacement right away, but the Namibian officials were adamant that I had to apply in person in Windhoek. With each passing year, the chances of getting a new passport seemed more remote. By the time we moved to Canada, I had given up on my Namibian passport, but Namibia followed me across the ocean, just as it had followed me on road trips throughout my childhood. The road to Port St. Johns was filled with stories of the time we travelled to Swakopmund; the trip down to East London was about the time we drove through the Namib Desert. Any dirt road on the way to a farm would remind Ma and Dad of something Namibian. And yet, although these stories filled my life, I knew many of them only as words that accompanied photographs and from a collective family memory, for at the time I was still too young to recall more than fragments on my own and I longed for my own Namibian experiences and for something tangible to tie me to the country I'd always considered home.

Try as I might, I cannot recall Ma and Dad ever looking at a map because the names of places were so ingrained in their minds. Somehow, they just seemed to know which road to take. And they remembered where they'd been. They knew each place and in each town, behind every Karoo bush and every camelthorn tree, they had a connection. And always, Ma had a story to tell. Every tale she told meandered until it returned, safe and complete, to where we had started: in Namibia. Ma could make a story loop out across the veld like an ox whip before she tugged at the handle and let the tale double back and crack to a conclusion. But until then, her stories would bend and twist and prod us toward our destination until we fell asleep, exhausted, and dreamed of Namibia.

After we had returned home from holidays at the beach, we would unpack the driftwood of our days at the florist shop, where Ma could give these gifts of the sea new life in her arrangements. Then we would manoeuvre the caravan into a corner in the backyard, where it rested until it was called to duty again. When the memory of the trip had receded somewhat, I would take the key, the one with the clover-leaf head and the faded woven leather tassel attached to it, and walk to the caravan to pry open those memories once more and give them a new life too. Opening that door to the caravan was to find solace in the imagined roads and stories of past journeys as they retold themselves over and over on the lines of the map that covered the fold-out table. In a world still without television, all we had to divert our attention on rainy holidays were books, board games and maps.

The table map stretched as far north as Zimbabwe and the lower half of Zambia, showing me the location of places with magical names like Kitwe and Kariba and Cahora Bassa. From Mozambique, the map stretched west until it hit the Atlantic Ocean somewhere north of Luanda and Moçâmedes. At the end of 1975, after Angolan independence, Moçâmedes became Namibe, and the thud of land mines and soldiers' footsteps would ring in the ears of a generation of children as they were maimed into adulthood. But in the caravan in the backyard, I was unaware of such changes. The names on that map were simply places beyond my back garden, places I knew from reciting them over and over again as the storm clouds passed, places I knew I wanted to visit one day. And squashed in the middle between these far-off places and the dot that marked our hometown with the caravan in our backyard, off along the west coast of Africa, lay Namibia.

Even in Canada, Namibia kept inserting itself into my life, reminding me of that year I spent there in 1990, the year of independence. One evening during dinner, I mentioned that I would love to go back.

Between mouthfuls of food, our youngest daughter, Sinead, planned the trip.

"There's an awful lot of 'we' in your plans for me," I said to the head of red hair that was stretching across the table for more roasted potatoes. "And don't stretch across the table."

"By the time you leave, I'll be done high school. I'm coming with you." It was more a point of information than a request or a suggestion. She stuffed another roast potato into her mouth.

And so here we were, Sinead and I, waiting to get our passports stamped.

"Well, you're back now, so you have to apply for one, nè?" The customs official's voice startles me out of my reverie. "And who's this?" She looks at Sinead's passport. "You were not born here, I see. That's okay. Your dad's Namibian. You're one of us. Welcome home." She stamps our passports and waves us through.

We wait almost forty minutes for our luggage. Sinead gets bored and wanders off to find a bank machine where she can draw some money. Eventually, our luggage arrives and Sinead leads us toward the car rental desk she'd discovered during her forty-minute walkabout.

As we walk out of the building, two men squatting on the ground look up from their game. Owela, a favoured pastime of many Namibians, is one of the oldest forms of mancala and the two men move the stones about with enthralling dexterity. I watch them play as I soak in the dusty green of the camelthorns and the glorious abundance of black skin that surrounds me. The pulsating heat of stone and sand melts into my head alongside long-forgotten memories. I am breathing *home* after two decades away. The dust of the Khomas Hochland covers my sandals. One of the owela players catches my eye and smiles as he leaps up to offer me a copy of *The Namibian*. By the time he has pocketed my change, I am forgotten and his mind is already focused on the important matter of winning his game.

We leave the two men to continue their battle of wits and begin the search for the pickup truck we've rented. We pack our bags in the back and get in. Before I start the bakkie, I do the unimaginable: I put a map in my daughter's hands and instruct her to navigate.

Sinead grunts. "You're kidding me, right?" The map remains unopened in her lap.

Travel, like Africa, is in Sinead's blood. She grew up between continents on trips back to South Africa to visit family. At eighteen, she knows the best places to snooze in an airport lounge and can navigate her way through customs with her eyes closed. Yet despite her ease with international travel, my directionally challenged daughter cannot find her seat on a plane without the aid of a GPS. Fortunately for her, there is only one road to take from the airport to Windhoek. We enter the city as the sun is setting and head straight for our bed and breakfast. The map of the city unfolds itself from my memory as I round the circle at the Christuskirche, turn onto Independence Avenue and up John Meinert Street.

Sinead had spent the summer before our trip volunteering at a camp in British Columbia where she had picked up a cold. Between the effort of fighting a cold and an eternity in airplanes and transit lounges, she can barely manage to stay awake. We decide to order in. While we wait for our pizza to arrive, Sinead crosses her legs and spreads the map of Namibia out in front of her on the bed. She stares at it for a while before turning to me. "If Namibia has two deserts, where do people find water for farming?"

Namibia's rivers are not the mighty Yangtze River, nor are they the Nile or some other famous waterway about which numerous books are written. In fact, for much of the year, Namibians complain about the sheer lack of water and the majority of its riverbeds are oversized sandpits. "They use underground water where they can, or they rely on water from the dams they've built. The Kunene and the Okavango rivers flow all year round. There's enough water if people are careful."

Sinead looks at the map again. "So, that's desert and that's desert and that's dry and that's wet." Her fingers drift across the map and settle along the Caprivi Strip in the tropical north. "That's why most of the people live in the north, I suppose?" I nod, but already she's off on another tangent. She changes tack sharply, this child of mine. For someone who's suffering from a cold, jet lag and lack of sleep, she's pretty chatty. I keep being drawn from my book, Marion Wallace's A History of Namibia: From the Beginning to 1990, by a barrage of questions. And each time I've answered one of her questions, I return to the first chapter, the one that tells the many tales of migration. If there is one thing Namibians do well, it is move. Throughout its turbulent history, the people of Namibia have trekked. People came from the north, from central Africa, to settle around the Kunene and Okavango Rivers. Later, centuries later, some of these people, like the Ovaherero, packed their belongings and headed further south to the central plains, where they came into contact with the various groups of people who had steadily been moving up from the south.

These southerners were *moerig*, a cantankerous lot. Mostly refugees from south of the Gariep River, bandits and escaped slaves who had fled the Cape Colony, they brought with them firearms and a zealous desire to retain their freedom and independence.

I'm trying to make sense of centuries' worth of convoluted migrations when Sinead pokes me in the ribs for the umpteenth time. "Okay, so we're going to be looking at graves and things. If the war took place in the north, why are we looking at graves in the south?"

"It's complicated," I reply as I go down on my knees and lean over the side of the bed to see the map up close. "It would take a book to explain that." Sinead rolls her eyes, but I am not really joking. Namibia is complicated. Besides stories of endless treks, there are numerous stories of conflict. This is a country steeped in war. For Namibians, the twentieth century is bookended by two major wars, and packed with enough tales of battle to fill up the spaces in between and spill onto the adjoining shelves. By the time the Germans laid claim to the country in 1884, the local people were already well armed and bellicose. They fought the colonists in the protracted Wars of Resistance that ended only after the first genocide of the twentieth century had wreaked havoc among them. When Germany lost its colonial possessions after the First World War, German South West Africa became a mandated territory under Britain's care. Britain, in turn, handed over that responsibility to their ex-colony in the region, South Africa. The South African government was to lead Namibia to independence, but they had other intentions. They set about recolonizing the country and incorporating it as a part of South Africa.

By the mid 1960s, Namibians had tired of sending pleas and protests and petitions to the United Nations. In desperation, they turned once more to war. This time, the war took place mostly in the north. For more than two decades, Namibian soldiers moved back and forth across the border, pursued by South African troops who left behind them yet another trail of broken and displaced communities. The Namibian War of Independence lasted until 1989, when a peace accord was signed at Mount Etjo, just north of the capital city, Windhoek. It was a delicate truce that would reveal its fault lines more than once in the lead-up to independence, but it was a truce nonetheless, and that is what mattered most.

"How big is Namibia?" Sinead asks as reception finally calls to let us know that our pizza has arrived. I've been asked this question so many times that my answer is rehearsed. "It is more than double the size of Germany, or as big as Alberta and just under half of Saskatchewan put together, or larger than Texas by a quarter."

Sinead's questions dry up while she eats. Halfway through dinner, she pulls the blanket over herself and goes to sleep.

◆   ◆   ◆

After stocking up on groceries at the nearest supermarket early in the morning, we head toward the industrial area to pick up our camping supplies. Sinead turns the map around in an effort to determine which way we're travelling. She tries to give me directions, but the street names change faster than she can pronounce them. As we stop at the suppliers, she extricates herself from the maps and announces, "We need a GPS."

"Why? We've got maps. Two of them. The dinky one from the car rental people and the proper one we bought."

"Didn't you see me trying to read the maps? You know I can't read maps."

"Then you're going to learn how to on this trip, aren't you?" Sinead stomps ahead. By the time I get to the counter, she's already ticked off a GPS on the rental form. I leave the details to my daughter. She may not be able to find her shoelaces to tie them, but when it comes to organizing an excursion, I know I'm in good hands. Twelve years of organizing Girl Guide camps means she's got it nailed. Sinead whips through the form and hands it over to me to sign and pay. I hand over my credit card, but the woman just shakes her head: "Cash only."

Sinead and I return to the city to draw some money. We move from cash machine to cash machine, drawing the daily limit at each bank machine we can find until we have collected what we can legitimately lay our hands on at such short notice. We're still several thousand Namibian dollars short, but we've drawn all we can for the day.

"How are we going to get our things?" Sinead asks. "Where are we going to sleep? We only booked a room for one night. We've booked a campsite in the backyard of the hostel for tonight. We need a tent."

"Have some faith," I tell her as we head back to tell the owner of the camping store that we will return in the morning when we're able to draw the balance and collect our equipment.

The owner reaches across the counter for the money as I begin to tell her about our predicament. Her face wrinkles into a laugh and she throws the weight of her head back as she chuckles. "Yes, these machines never give me enough money, either. But that's because I don't have any. You can pay the balance when you get back." She sends us on our way with a flourish that sets the wattles under her arms jiggling. "Enjoy yourselves." A man with oiled black hair standing behind her turns around and shouts into the back room, "*Laai die bakkie!*"

Back in the city, we park the car in a lot just off John Meinert Street. It's almost noon and the throb of approaching midday heat makes me squint. A woman stops us at the corner and says, "Don't ever walk with a backpack in this city! It's Windhoek, you know! You'll be mugged!"

I wish I could turn around to tell her, "You are wrong," but I know she isn't. We could be. We could be mugged or robbed in New York or Amsterdam too. Such is the way of cities all around the world. I tighten my grip on the backpack and continue walking when the lights change. We dodge taxis as we cross the road, the softened tar squelching under our feet. Sinead's eyes dart around, trying to absorb everything.

I could describe how the streets have frayed at the edges, as they inevitably do in almost every African city. I could talk of the cracked plaster and the litter gathering in the street, or the taxis that circle the blocks in search of fares or the intricate array of hand signals that flag them down with explicit instructions on where to go. I could do these things, but that would detract from the new glass and brick monoliths that are steadily elbowing out the old German colonial buildings along the verges of Independence Avenue. Besides, I no longer speak the language of taxis. So much has changed in my absence that I am a familiar stranger in this city.

We stroll up Independence Avenue, past the kudu monument at the intersection with John Meinert Street, toward Restaurant Gathemann. At Gathemann's, we cross the road. At the Ministry of Home Affairs and Immigration, I run in and collect a passport application. Back outside, swathes of new postmodern corporate high-rises jostle for position among the remaining low buildings of the colonial era. The names of colonial administrators and revolutionaries hang side by side on the street corners in an uneasy truce: Lindequist Street, Sam Nujoma Avenue, Dr. Frans Indongo Street, Robert Mugabe Avenue and Mandume Ndemufayo Avenue all leave traces of the town's history at the intersections.

We stop briefly at the warrior memorial in Zoo Park. It is unusual for a colonial-era statue to acknowledge the deaths of indigenous peoples, but the *Kriegerdenkmal* does, which is why it is worth pausing at as you hurry up and down Independence Avenue. An obelisk supports the *Kriegerdenkmal* with the *Reichsadler*, the imperial eagle, perched on top of an iron orb. On the side of the monument, we find the names of the five members of the Rehoboth Baster community who died fighting with the Germans against the Witbooi during the Wars of Resistance.

At Fidel Castro Street, we turn and start walking up the hill toward the Christuskirche. The traders on the other side of the road spot us and call us over. The disarrayed ranks of men's heads jostle for space on the cloth that covers the pavement. Animals migrate to nowhere around them. Phalanxes of carved elephants and baboons and rhinos

march into the void of travellers' suitcases. Among them, the elon-
gated bodies of pitcher-bearing women lie in piles. Yard upon yard
of cluttered tourist kitsch that has become the lifeblood of the informal economy. Two Ovahimba women start showing Sinead their
wares, bartering and calling out competing prices. Within minutes,
they are joined by four more. I watch her struggle to keep track of
the wares that have appeared in her hands without her bidding. She
looks at me, but I leave her to struggle on her own. She has to learn
to barter. They too recognize her discomfort. "She's never had to
barter," I say to them.

"This is how we shop here," one of them says. The others laugh
and together they coach her through the basics.

"Listen to me, my price is better!" says one of the traders.

"No, buy from me!"

"My goods are better quality," another woman remarks, pulling up
her nose at the handiwork of the bracelets Sinead has in her hands. She
stuffs a handful more trinkets into Sinead's palm. I counter their price.

"I'm happy to pay what she asked originally," Sinead whispers to me.

"That's not the point," I say. "They don't expect that at the open
markets. Just imagine you're arguing with me."

Sinead turns to the women and begins to haggle tentatively. They
laugh at her and help her along. Eventually they reach an agreement.

"A very good price," the woman assures her.

While Sinead is haggling, I look around. A short way back from
the women, a man is taking care of two children. The little girl has
settled herself on a blanket and plays quietly with some of the wood-
carvings, but her older brother, who can already walk on his own,
darts off and returns with more toys for her. One of the neighbouring
hawkers calls to the man and he sends the boy back with her wares.
Dad has barely blinked when he makes a dash for his mother.

"I can sell you my child!" the father shouts.

"I already have two," I reply. "I don't need another one." He laughs
and runs after his son again.

"He's healthy," he says as he catches hold of the boy and returns him to a spot beside his little sister, "no AIDS."

I know our banter is in jest, but the lines hit home. Namibia has one of the highest infection rates in the world and AIDS is the leading cause of death in the country. I reject his offer more firmly and move on.

We cross back over Fidel Castro Street and head to the Christus-kirche at the top of the hill. While Fidel Castro needs no introduction, my eye catches the name on the side street as we dodge the traffic. It is named in honour of Reverend Michael Scott. It was he who presented a petition to the United Nations on behalf of Namibia's people, asking the international community to force South Africa to commit to the obligations of their mandate. A simple action, perhaps, but one that planted the seeds of revolution that would flower into independence. After the cold numbered streets and avenues of North America, it is fun to play a gentle game of Know Your Revolutionaries as you walk past Robert Mugabe Avenue or Fidel Castro Street. At the traffic circle, we cross the road onto the island on which the Christuskirche stands.

Rock agamas peek at us from their perches along the sandstone walls of the church. Their yellow and black heads dart this way and that, this way and that as they scout out intruders into their reptilian world. The white accents on the windows shimmer in the sunlight and it is a relief to enter the coolness of the church. Inside, just past the marble portal, a man reclines as best he can in his straight-backed chair. His entire outfit is khaki — from the shorts and socks to the billowing safari shirt. He says little, but the imperial wave of his hand indicates that he may be a guide. After fielding the first questions from the group of German tourists ahead of us, he moves his chair into the back corner. From this new position, he returns to riding the chair, pushing himself onto tiptoe to tilt back with the rhythmical precision of one who has practised this move over many years. Each time his ankles rise, the buttons on his shirt strain in protest. Back and forth he rocks, back and forth, breathing heavily as he tosses fragments of

German at no one in particular. At the conclusion of each utterance, there is a muffled whiplash as his rocking-horse chair hits the back wall of the church. Back and forth, back and forth the *Reiter* rocks as we admire the stained glass windows and the clean lines of the Italian marble altar in the art nouveau interior of the building.

The Christuskirche was built in 1910 to honour the peace that ensued after the Wars of Resistance. Along the wall of the church eight panels list the names of the Germans and Europeans who died in the war. The bleak silence of war beats body and mind into re-recognition of the horrors we bring on ourselves. We look for names we might recognize — a friend, a family member, a fabled hero. Yet as I stand before the *Schutztruppe Denkplatz*, the plaque against the wall throws back only the silenced whispers that once belonged to the Nama or Ovaherero who died in the futile bloodshed.

Back outside, we walk around the church and then cross over to the *Tintenpalast*, the Ink Palace. The gardens stretch up endlessly and here and there, I spot statues of heroes of the Struggle. We try to get in, but the main entrance gates are closed and neither of us feels much like walking around or climbing fences. It's a lazy do-as-tourists-do afternoon and we take more photos before heading down Robert Mugabe Avenue on our way back to the bakkie.

For the most part, Windhoek is a pretty but nondescript city. A few buildings, like the Gathemann House, stand out. The Alte Feste is a fort: its austere white walls have changed little over the past century-and-a-bit since it was built. A few blocks north, the imposing sandstone of the Tintenpalast lies far back in the expansive Parliament Gardens. The Old State House lies halfway down the hill from the Parliament Gardens, hidden behind a wall that only the privileged get to see behind. When this building was deemed insufficient for affairs of state, the government commissioned a new State House, a North Korean design of extraordinary brutality.

Right beside the Old State House lies Daniel Munavama Street, a short side road that is barely a hop and a skip from one end to the

other. An air of disquiet envelops me. I recognize the landmark buildings that surround it, the hues of light and the ramp that leads to the
car park behind Zoo Park. Slowly the change dawns on me. "This
used to be called Göring Strasse," I tell Sinead. One does not forget
a name like that. For many visitors to pre-Independence Windhoek,
encountering this street name remains the lasting memory of the city.
"It was named after Heinrich Göring, the first Imperial Commissioner
of German South West Africa. And yes," I add, "he was Hermann
Göring's father."

We cross over John Meinert Street and walk in a loop down Bahnhof
Street, past the Turnhalle building and the old station building. It was
here, in this old gymnasium in the Turnhalle, between 1975 and 1977,
that the first attempt was made to create a Namibian constitution.
Despite the fact that the United Nations did not recognize South
African rule in Namibia, the South Africans attempted to create a
constitution that would give Namibia self-rule while remaining
under South African control. Understandably, the South West Africa
People's Organization (SWAPO) refused to participate and the conference failed. On the corner, the imposing facade of the Bahnhof
impresses visitors, as it was meant to do. Outside the building, Poor
Old Joe, the narrow gauge train that was reassembled in Swakopmund
for the run to Windhoek, has place of pride.

At the backpackers' lodge where we're staying, I find the receptionist outside planting bulbs by the front gate. "Sword lilies," she
announces proudly. "You need sturdy things to survive in this climate."
In the bar, they're playing a song by Zimbabwe Dread. A group of
twentysomethings wander in and out with their plates of food. They
all have a look of well-travelled dirt about them that suggests the
carefree attitude that comes with plenty of free time. They chat effortlessly, and I eavesdrop on their conversation while I have my beer.
The majority of this group have been drifting from lodge to lodge on
their way south from Cairo; the twenty-first century grand tour.

Places are rated by their party value. Windhoek scores low on their scale. There is little awareness of the weight of the history that surrounds them.

◆　◆　◆

We sleep cold that first night in our tent: in the early days of spring, the night air is colder than I remembered or expected and the canvas walls of the tent offer scant protection. In the morning, we gather in the breakfast lineup at the bar: a cup of coffee and crepes doused in cinnamon sugar and butter. Our plan is to spend a few days in Okahandja and surroundings so that we can attend the annual Herero Day festivities. Before heading out to buy warmer sleeping bags, we stop by reception.

"Yes," the receptionist confirms, "it says in our handbook 'The festival is held on the third Sunday closest to August 23.' That's this coming Sunday."

With that information in hand, we set out for the day. Our first stop is the camping store to find warmer sleeping bags. From the camping store, we make our way to the Alte Feste, the oldest surviving building in town. As soon as the Germans arrived on the eighteenth of October 1890, they laid the foundations for a fort to protect their troops. Windhoek changed hands regularly during territorial disputes, and each time it changed hands, it also changed names. Jonker Afrikaner, Captain of the Oorlam, settled here in 1840 and named the place Windhoek. The Ovaherero settled there for a while, calling it Otjomuise, Place of Steam, after the hot springs that bubble out of the mountains. Likewise, when the Nama occupied it, they referred to it as |Ai||gams, Fire Water. Through all these wars, the buildings of the once prosperous town disintegrated and by 1885, little more than a handful of neglected fruit trees and its original name, Windhoek, remained. When the Germans arrived, they changed the spelling rather than the

name of the town: Windhoek became Windhuk. Later, when the
South Africans took over the administration of the territory in
1920, the name changed once more — back to Windhoek, which
has remained its name ever since.

General Curt von François had his *Schutztruppe* build the fort on
the top of a hill, from where they could command a good view of their
surroundings. And indeed, the view is breathtaking. Windhoek and
the Auas Valley stretch endlessly before us, but a niggling thought
from the previous day has resurfaced and I cannot appreciate the
view. Slowly, it dawns on me: Where Parisian *flâneurs* provide direction simply by conjuring up the name of a *rue*, Namibians use their
monuments as points of reference. There are statues at the one end
of Independence Avenue and statues at the other end. And in between
there are monuments and statues in Zoo Park and other places.
Namibia has more statues and monuments per capita than any other
place in the world. There are South African colonial statues, German
colonial statues and memorials and, since independence, an increas-
ing number of new statues to honour the heroes of the Struggle. "At
the kudu statue, turn left," the people of Windhoek say. "Head along
Independence Avenue until you see Curt von François in front of the
town hall . . ." And so on. Heaven forbid that a landmark should move.
What chaos could ensue! And there you have it: The *Reiterdenkmal*,
the statue that commemorates the courage and valour of the German
Colonial equestrian soldiers, no longer stands at the top of the hill
commanding the gaze of motorists as they round the circle. That is
where it still belongs in my memory; now it guards the entrance to
the Alte Feste museum. Where it once stood, an imposing concrete
structure, still veiled in plastic drop cloth and scaffolding, is taking
shape. The relocated Reiter stares resolutely, daring intruders to
move him again.

We pass by the shadow the Reiter casts and ascend the steps that
lead to the museum. The front porch houses an array of old machinery:
a fire engine and a tractor, a wagon or two and a cannon. In the corner,

off to the right as you approach the door, stands a huge woven Oshiwambo grain basket. We examine these artifacts before entering the extraordinary, delicate creature that is the museum. Over time, museums develop lives of their own, become tiny microcosms that reflect and often oppose the world outside. The Alte Feste houses the State Museum and Sinead and I spend a few hours wandering through the exhibits. If the imposing colonial statues outside lull your mind into some false cultural amnesia, you come here to forget that legacy and focus instead on the path to liberation and independence. I linger at the independence exhibit, remembering old friends in photographs and becoming reacquainted with the sounds and smells of that year.

Back in the courtyard, Sinead turns to me. "This place reminds me of Robben Island. Both were designed as prison yards and both housed political prisoners."

Outside the Alte Feste, we take in the view of the city stretching along the valley. I put my arm around Sinead. "Take a good look at what you see around you," I tell her. "Now close your eyes. Imagine guards in the turrets of the Alte Feste looking out over the five thousand prisoners in the largest concentration camp of the Wars of Resistance."

2

Namibians talk about roads the way Canadians talk about the weather. Everyone we ask, including our rented GPS, tells us that the best way to get to the Spitzkoppe is to head north to Okahandja and then take the tarred road to the coast. Naturally, we therefore choose the scenic route through the Khomas Hochland. We are barely out of town when the tar is replaced by a stony road that is badly in need of scraping. Namibian roads are generally in very good shape, but in that interim between the first rains and the arrival of the graders, potholes flourish. Some partridges scuttle across the road toward the water that has dammed in a one of the potholes. As we approach, they rush off into the grass, yellowed from the winter, but already tinged with the green of spring.

About eighty kilometres from Windhoek, we stumble across the dilapidated stone ruins of the Von François Feste, the fort General Curt von François built as a halfway post when he moved his head-quarters from Tsaobis to Windhoek in 1890. The sign at the entrance gate on the way up to the fort is pocked with several new bullet holes. Drive-by target practice is the sport of young farmers everywhere, but in Namibia, the neat 9mm holes are a reminder that despite the peacefulness of the surroundings, this has always been a country filled with weapons and warfare.

The footpath up to the fort is lined with pyrite — fool's gold. When I came to Windhoek to teach in 1990, the streets of the city seemed to be paved with gold too. There was a shimmer of optimism in the streets of Windhoek, and a real desire to leave the past behind. This was a nation weary of war and as Independence Day approached, we celebrated each step toward the withdrawal of the United Nations Transition Assistance Group (UNTAG) and South African Defence Force (SADF) troops from our country. On my early morning walk to work every day, I would marvel at the specks of gold that flecked the pavement ahead of the rising sun. Optimism, when so many doomsayers were predicting the end days.

Here at the Von François Feste, the pyrite reflects the folly of the early settlers who came to find the fabled mineral riches of this desert El Dorado. Most left clutching little more than their memories. It is the silence of this place that overwhelms you. The immense, almost oppressive silence of the Von François Feste and the Khomas Hochland. Like elsewhere in this country, there are things these stones and this veld remain silent about. Stories that remain untold. The tightly packed stones wait for the alert eavesdropper to uncover their story. Their's is a story of an arduous journey from Tsaobis, the hurried movement of cattle and troops and horses being rushed through the treacherous Bosua Pass and up the Khomas Hochland. The original fort was built in haste during the flight from Tsaobis to Windhoek. After the troops had settled in Windhoek permanently, it became a cattle outpost and a *trockenposten* — a place where alcoholic soldiers were sent to dry out.

There could be worse punishments. The view over the Khomas Hochland is endless and even after winter the stream in the valley runs strong. The strategic value of the post is evident from the view, the easy access to water and the lushness of the grass. The stones are packed tightly in their serried rows, each one carefully hewn and placed. As I bend in close to admire the seamless stonework, a large cattle truck roars past. Each of the densely packed two-foot-wide walls is squared beautifully, held together without any mortar. Only water and lizards wriggle through this rock now. The warmth of the stone comforts me. Swallows circle in thermal currents above us. A hawk hovers briefly over the fort like an aerial sentinel, then catches a ride across the valley on the whorls of air that surround us. It returns at intervals to observe our movements. Here, as in the city, the remnants of the Kaiser's Reich are everywhere: in the farm names, in the buildings, in the monuments. Tiny snippets of information scattered across the stones. It takes patience to draw stories out of such silence.

After a while, the silence of the fort becomes overwhelming. The rattle of a convoy of bakkies intrudes briefly, but in the end, the silence wins out. You become aware of the blood pulsing through your veins and gradually you are filled with the first racking sensation of loneliness that comes from being in open spaces. This is inhospitable, dry territory and life among the rolling hills is deceptive and tough.

We catch up with the bakkies a short way down the road: they're all parked at the upper end of a huge parking lot. Off to one side, a lone cattle truck. As we drive past, we see men mingle and twist around the open spaces, lizards trying to pry a way through the rock walls. Two men in the watchtower by the cattle pens give the proceedings a purpose: today is *vendusiedag*. Auction day. The first spring auction in the Khomas Hochland is a celebration. Farmers from all around gather early in the morning, vying for the prime spot at the auction lot. The cattle milling in the pens glisten with fat. Soon, the auctioneer will begin the bidding war and farmers will trade their cattle, measuring the success of the season by the condition of their beasts and the size of their cheques. In the background, I see the fires starting up — after the auction, they will gather and feast.

I would love to stop, but I want to get to the Spitzkoppe before dark. Too soon, the familiar childhood smell of cattle and dust fades. As the Von François Feste recedes into the background, I open up to the spectacular views of the countryside. A small herd of kudu ewes peeks at us through the bushes. A flock of African hornbills clusters at the side of the road like inquisitive beggars. Yet the sheer drops and the loose sand in the Boschau Pass make driving treacherous. It is easy to forget that this fertile stretch has for centuries been a battleground and that, even today, the land remains contested. Above us, the vultures circle, endlessly rising on the air currents and disappearing from sight, only to reappear low above the valley and circle us again.

The pass folds between mountain ranges and it is hard to know where one range ends and another begins. Once we're through the pass, the hills begin to flatten and soon we reach the turnoff to Karibib. Gone are the folds and precipitous drops of the Khomas Mountains. In their stead, the valley opens before us and the closer we get to Karibib, the more the copses of camelthorn trees thin out and make way for grasslands. We are approaching the desert. In the distance, we can see the rusty outcrops of the Witwatersberge and the copper glow of the Otjipatera Mountains. Somewhere in those hills lies Tsaobis, where Captain Curt von François established his first fort. Von François was belligerent by nature, and felt that the native population had to be treated with a firm hand. To make his point, he established the fort at Tsaobis directly on the trade route between Walvis Bay and Otjimbingwe, where many Ovatjimba — Ovaherero who had no cattle — had settled at the Rhenish mission station. It was a poor choice, bred out of inexperience and a lack of familiarity with the land. Squeezed between Otjimbingwe and Kaptein Hendrik Witbooi's people, the small contingent at Tsaobis was constantly under threat. In 1890, Witbooi demanded permission to water his cattle at Tsaobis. When von François refused, Witbooi attacked. The woefully outnumbered German Schutztruppe retreated to Windhoek in a great hurry, erecting the Von François Feste as a temporary shelter along the way.

The closer we get to Karibib, where we will leave our scenic route through the Khomas Hochland and join the main road to the coast, the more prominent the veins of calcite along the mountain ridges become. In Usakos, I realize I've driven through towns like this countless times before: a stretch of tar that runs from the edge of town to the edge of town. A bank, a grocer, a church and a recently painted town hall. Everything looks clean because there is bugger all else to do but sweep the streets. Even from the moving car, the marks left by the straw broom on the compacted sand of the pavement are visible. Only the garage at the entrance into town shows signs of life. Beside the garage, a lone man leans on the crowbar he uses to dislodge punctured tires from their rims.

We drive past the garage and round the corner to where the road out of town should be. Somehow, we find ourselves in a maze of streets, so we stop to ask for directions at the local café. Sinead decides to wait in the car while I run in to ask for directions. A bulwark of glass counters separates the merchandise from the customers. Glass jars brimming with sweets line the top of the counters, and behind them sits a woman of indeterminate age. Her carefully curled hair has begun to sag as the day wears on, yet when a group of tweens on their way home from school shove their way past me and into the small space between the door and the counter, she extends herself with the wariness of a cobra preparing to strike. They push and shove their way to the counter, demanding her attention.

I see the woman's eyes flit from one youth to the next as she watches their movements. Her hand descends with unerring accuracy onto the fingers that reach for some sweets on the counter. "Don't touch! I'll give it to you. Show me the money first!" In their rush to get past me, the cluster of youths have pushed aside an old lady and her assistant who entered before me. They are still setting down their bags and untying the blankets the younger woman uses as an *abbavel* for her child. The youths crane their necks and wiggle like meerkats fighting over grubs. The woman behind the counter takes their money and shoos them out. As the youths head out of the café, the old lady draws back behind the glass door. The woman behind the counter turns her attention to me. I hold back and wave the old lady through.

She smiles and rattles off in Damara. Her assistant, the younger one, turns to me with an equally big smile. *"Dankie,"* she says. *"Die kinders vandag respekteer nie meer hulle ouers nie. Die Bybel sê mos jy moet jou vader en moeder eer."* Thank you. Today's children don't respect their elders. The Bible tells us to respect our fathers and mothers.

As the woman shuffles back into the street with her package of goods, I ask the woman behind the counter for directions to the Spitzkoppe.

"Ag no," she says, "I'm not the best person to ask. I have seldom left Usakos in my lifetime. Ask Banie at the hardware store next door."

Outside, two men enjoy their coffee and a cigarette on the small porch. One of them must be Banie, I decide and walk over. "The *tannie* next door at the café said I should ask Banie at the hardware store for directions," I say to the man seated at the door. His head barely moves as his eyes scan my body. His disdain for out-of-towners is apparent, but at least I can speak Afrikaans. With an almost imperceptible gesture, he tilts his glowing cigarette toward the road.

"I'm Banie," says the man with impressive lamb chops leaning against the pillar. As I turn toward Banie, the man at the door inhales deeply and blows out the smoke with practised leisure.

"They tell me you know this area well."

Banie shrugs. "Born and bred here," he grumbles. "I know a thing or two."

"How do I get to Spitzkoppe?" I ask, hauling out my map.

"Nee, donner, los daai uitlanders se papiere!" he exclaims with an excited flourish of hands and shoots his cigarette butt into the road. "Dammit, no. Leave those foreigners' papers! Follow me and I'll show you." Like so many locals, Banie neither trusts maps nor understands them. The only way to know a country, to *really* know it, he tells me on the way in, is to live it and to walk the countryside. I follow Banie into the hardware store and to his office in the back. All the while, he's fishing for stories and information. He lights another cigarette. In his office, he scratches about for a piece of paper, stubs his cigarette in

the ashtray. It continues to smoulder as he gathers his writing utensils together from around the room. When he's done, he leans over and kills the smouldering cigarette.

He starts to draw and talk. "You drive out along this road — the one just to the left of where we are now, down there by the end of the block. About sixteen kilometres down that road, you'll come to the spot where they sell stones. You can't miss it. Take the turnoff — it's the road to Uis. Right there, you'll hit a dogleg and then you're on the road to Henties Bay. Keep going toward Henties. Drive till you hit Black Rock and then turn off the road. There's a camp spot with *braai* places and showers. Now where did you say you were from again? How long are you in town?"

I grew up with a town full of Banies and I know he won't let go until he's run through my entire family history. "I'm spending the night at the Spitzkoppe. Just passing through on my way to the Herero Day parade and festivities," I tell him.

"Do you think it is worth it?" he asks. "It's just a bunch of blacks walking down the street. You can see that anywhere."

I ignore the barb. "I was born there. I'm taking my daughter to see where her father's from."

Banie's demeanour changes. "Well, that's different, then. That's *bloedsake* — blood matters. It's in your blood. You have to go. Actually, it's quite nice to see them march all dressed up in their finery. *Ja*, just there by the swimming pool there's a bunch of old Herero graves. They're probably headed for them. You know, those people and their ancestors."

"Ja, it's Maharero's grave, isn't it?" I gently hint at the fact that the march commemorates the death of Samuel Maharero, the leader of the Ovaherero at the time of the genocide.

"Ja-nee," Banie reaffirms, "*Dis bloedsake vir hulle*. It's about blood for them. People have to follow their blood. Now, where did you say you lived now?"

"In Canada."

"Bloody awful place," he says. "Cold and dark. We have a geologist from Canada here and he went back for a week before he came back to Usakos. Couldn't stand the place. Where in Canada do you stay?"

"Edmonton."

"Is that near the Lakes?" He doesn't wait for me to respond. "I know the geology of the land. There's stones there." And he starts to talk stone. It's a language the people here understand.

I leave Banie and Co. to have another cigarette and discuss the directionless strangers who had just wandered into town. Sinead and I head out to the Spitzkoppe and as we near the campsite, two attendants stop us.

"We heard you coming. Flat tire," they tell me and promptly start looking for my cross wrench. Jannie and Elvis introduce themselves and begin to change the tire for me. I am happy to do it myself, but they insist. "The most exciting thing that's happened here today."

As they busy themselves with my tire, I take in the surroundings. "‡Gâingu Conservancy," the sign behind me says. I ask Jannie how to pronounce it, and lesson one in basic Damara ensues. It lasts almost half an hour. Damara has four clicks. We start with those. I have three down pat from having grown up in an isiXhosa-speaking environment, but I work on the fourth, a variation of the palatal click. After the lesson and the tire change, we say our goodbyes and head off to the camping area.

Ahead of us, the Spitzkoppe bleed into the late afternoon shadows. A scab of boulders covers the earth below the sheer ironstone cliffs. We find an open space under a large camelthorn tree at the edge of the cliffs where two boulders shelter us from the wind. We are invisible in the folds of these gigantic boulders. While Sinead scrambles through the rocks to the long-drop outhouse we noticed as we approached, I pitch the tent. In the distance, two specks have appeared at the top of a rocky outcrop. Sinead rejoins me and we build a small campfire to keep the chill of the evening at bay. It is dark when the couple we had seen on the rocks walk past us.

"Darkness comes so quickly and so completely here," says my city-raised daughter.

There is no time to linger and climb to the top of the Spitzkoppe in the morning, for we have to head back to Okahandja for the Herero Day parade. After breakfast, we scramble to the top of a large rock before it is time to leave. On the way back to Uis, we pass a group of children sitting at a roadside stall with their mother. The oldest should be in school, but the rest of the gang is still too young. One, barely out of diapers, runs toward us as we stop, asking for sweets. Instead, I offer apples. We look at the beadwork on display, but what catches my eye is the large tub of water in the shade: a sign attached to the tub lists the cost as twenty-five cents for a mug. In a desert country, water is precious, so it comes as little surprise that it becomes a commodity out here where access to water is limited. On our way to the mountains the previous evening, Sinead had promised one of the young girls that she would buy something from them in the morning. While she looks for some souvenirs, I ask for a cupful of water. It tastes brackish.

Back in Usakos, I find a place to fix my tire. Wherever you turn people sell stones. The guy fixing my tire mumbles something. I nod absent-mindedly and a bucket full of semi-precious stones appears from nowhere. The locals live among stones and it is the crop that is most desired by tourists.

3

Two towns exist alongside each other. They bear the same name, but one lingers amidst the markets of time where old memories are traded for new; the other shifts and pushes against the banks of two converging rivers, the Okakango and Okamita. Okahandja is larger than memory. The town that rises before me in the glaring light of a late spring afternoon sprawls around Moordkoppie. It catches me by surprise, for the town I expected to find ends at the railway line. This town before me is not the town of memory and story. That town is isolated and sparse. It lingers in the bazaar of memories and changes as the light catches each aspect of it. In that town of memories, Moordkoppie is a short trek out of town. There are no houses crowding it as they do now. We lived "just down from the Standard Bank, over the railway line and down a block on the road to Walvis Bay," as my mother recalls before she glances at her handiwork to pick up the count on the chain she is crocheting. "Street names? *Ag nee, my kind.* They just sent the mail addressed to us in Okahandja. The people at the post office knew where we lived."

The twin town, the town of the present, squats uncomfortably in places where memory roamed freely. There is a new road to Walvis Bay now, one that bypasses the town, and the smattering of houses that lay beyond the railway line are now part of the central business district. In an old photograph, my sister and I sit at a small rock garden in front of one of these houses. My sister is playing with her dolls in German, for that was what she was taught to do at the kindergarten where Tante Elizabeth cared for her while Ma taught at the Augustineum. Tante Elizabeth, who also looked after the elderly Oupa Vedder in his dotage. In the town of memories, Oupa Vedder's powerful voice still booms from his frail body.

In the town of memory and illusion, Bishop Mize drives through from Windhoek once a month to come and minister to the Anglican community in Okahandja. On these occasions, our living room is transformed into a small chapel. Joseph, the Owambo contract labourer who worked in our kitchen, emerges to help rearrange the furniture and as he prepares to return to the kitchen, Bishop Mize turns to Ma and says, "Let him sit with us for the service. He, most of all here, needs to hear the Word of the Lord." On such occasions, Ma retreats to the kitchen with me in her arms to make lunch while Joseph sits on an upright chair in the living room. After the service and after lunch, I follow Joseph to the edges of the garden and to the borders of my world. Beyond those borders, things happened of which I was unaware. Things that I have come to discover and, hopefully, understand.

Sinead and I squeeze our way through these adjacent towns that compete for space in our lives. The town of my childhood memory is invisible to her and she relies solely on my fading memories to recreate it. What she sees is the town that implants itself in her own memory; a town she is about to discover is already forgetting itself. This town she sees, the one caught in the stupor of a Friday afternoon, is filled with generic buildings. Occasionally we see a date on the gable that suggests this building once belonged to the town of my memory, but the fading paint on the facade has rendered it indistinguishable from the newer buildings that surround it. I try hard to dredge up some memory that will help us locate the house in the photograph, but the only common ground I find in these twin towns is the heat.

It was hot, almost unbearably hot, in Okahandja and in the reed shelters that functioned as outside classrooms at the Augustineum, the school started by the old Rhenish missionaries. During the summer months, the Ovaherero men attending the school would rise from their desks and stand to prevent themselves from falling asleep in class, according to Ma's stories. Ma no longer remembers the names of her students, but I know that among them were several young men who were busy making plans for their future, plans that would take them beyond the borders of their country to take up arms to fight for independence. Men like Peter Katjavivi.

One day, I too would be called upon to take up arms. Only, I would be required to wage a war against these men and the many women who had crossed the border after them. Just as I was learning to walk on my own in the streets of Okahandja, six men had crept back across the border into Namibia and were hiding in Meme Priskila Tuhadeleni's house at Endola. In 1966, the first shots of the war were fired at a small village called Omugulugwombashe in northern Namibia. The war soon escalated and from 1968 on all white South African males had to register for compulsory military training when they turned sixteen. At the start of our grade eight year, the teachers set aside time for us to complete our initial enrolment forms — lists of hobbies and interests, skills, history, special posting requests and so on. Every year, I would receive the one-page letter stating my duration of service and my training base. Every year, I would have to present proof that I was still at school, or registered at university, in order to defer my enlistment. I would tear off the perforated edges that had guided the form through a dot matrix printer in some military office and file it in a folder I eventually destroyed after Namibian independence.

Sharing the location of our call-ups after a Christmas holiday was part of hostel life at school. We would envy those with the plum call-ups and commiserate those who received call-ups to what was rumoured to be less desirable camps, like Walvis Bay. We performed the ritual even though we all knew that we would not be required to report for a few more years. Since I was born in Namibia, my call-up papers were often to training bases in Namibia, including Walvis Bay and Okahandja.

Even though we only received our call-up papers at sixteen, the military had been part of our lives from the day we started high school at thirteen. Within the first week of the school year, we lined up to collect our cadet uniforms, and twice a week after that, we practised drills and learned to shoot at the school firing range. Well, not everyone. A handful of students were exempt, for they were Seventh-day Adventists, and their beliefs forbid participation in war. But they were all day boys and we hostel kids knew of them only as the oddballs who entered the library as our junior drill sergeants marched us around the school grounds. I envied them the privilege of not having to obey orders from overly eager cadet officers. I drowned out the endless barrage of commands by focusing on finding places where I could hide in future if I chose to skip cadets. The opportunity arose when they changed cadets to first period to avoid unnecessary disruptions to the school day. Then I was able to sneak off to the hostel boiler room, only to rejoin my classmates as they returned to school at the end of cadets, or Moral Education as it was called at one point, for our military education was rounded off by a thorough grounding in Christianity.

In the dusk of the boiler room, I had about an hour in which to entertain myself by reading, or simply poking into nooks and crannies behind and under the boilers. In those nooks, I discovered the first faded copies of Stephen Bantu Biko's magazine, *Frank Talk*, and *Sechaba*, the African National Congress' magazine. I knew that I should report these magazines to the hostel master or someone else, but I didn't. There was something exciting about this subversive world that drew me toward it. These magazines opened a new world to me, one in which I even learned things about my own school that were not common knowledge among the students, like that Bram Fischer, who had defended Nelson Mandela at the Rivonia Trial, was an old boy.

Armed with such knowledge, I asked for Namibian call-ups in my questionnaire. The idea was that if I got posted to a Namibian base, I would desert at the first opportunity and join SWAPO. In reality, my aversion to the military and war trumped the idealistic desire to join the revolutionary forces. And while I waited, I played the game of sharing my postings with my friends at school.

4

I had expected Okahandja to be busier in the days leading up to the annual pilgrimage to Maharero's grave, but everything seems to have been baked to silence in the late afternoon sun. Sinead and I leave the main street and head down a side street where two guards in military fatigues lounge against the gates of a compound of sorts. Through the gates, I can see a row of military vehicles and a sign advertising this as the site of a military museum. It seems appropriate for a town that started off as a military command post and subsequently housed a South African Forces Training Base and also became the training ground for young revolutionaries. Okahandja was founded by the colonial administrator, Theodor Leutwein. His insatiable demand for more and more land for European settlement necessitated a strong military presence among the people whose land he desired.

A story from the oral tradition goes that when Leutwein asked for land, Chief kaMaharero told him to bring baskets and buckets and he would give him land. When Leutwein returned, kaMaharero filled the containers with sand and returned them to the governor. "There is your land," he said. KaMaharero's response did not please the governor and so he took the land he wanted by force. KaMaharero died in these battles over the land. His son, Samuel, was more accommodating and obliged Leutwein by selling off sections of Ovaherero land to him. By 1903, however, Leutwein had begun to put into motion plans to settle the Ovaherero in reserves, forcing them out of their traditional territory. In January 1904, the Ovaherero took up arms against the Germans in an effort to avoid losing more land. The two sides moved around central Namibia, engaging in regular skirmishes. After months of trekking up and down the region, Leutwein was forced to withdraw his troops to the safety of the garrison at Okahandja. At about the same time, Samuel Maharero moved his troops north to the plateau at Ohamakari, where the grazing was better and where his people could regroup after the prolonged campaign. There, they would wait until Leutwein came to negotiate for peace, as he had on previous occasions.

The Germans had other plans. Frustrated by Leutwein's inability to gain a decisive victory, the kaiser removed him from his command and appointed General Lothar von Trotha. Immediately after his arrival, von Trotha demanded, and got, more troops from Germany. The German contingent in Namibia grew from five thousand to twenty thousand in the space of a few months. As the new troops arrived, he moved them up to Ohamakari, cornering Samuel Maharero and his people. On the eleventh of August 1904, he attacked the Ovaherero.

Throughout the day, the women stood behind the soldiers, singing *omatandu*, praise songs of encouragement, and providing spiritual sustenance. "*Ehi rovaherero*," they sang in defiance of the slaughter that was happening before their eyes. The battle continued deep into the night, and shortly before dawn the desperate Ovaherero fled into the *Omaheke*, the western edge of the Kalahari Desert. It was early spring and the wells were dry after the winter. Eyewitnesses say wells were filled with the bodies of cattle and humans. The words of the omatandu paint a dire picture of Maharero's plight:

He had horses of hunger
He was riding with horses of hunger
He was riding, he was riding
And still he had horses of hunger.

The Ovaherero fled east toward Botswana. The Germans pushed ahead of them, occupying the watering holes, poisoning some of them and forcing the Ovaherero back into the desert to starve and die of thirst. On the second of October 1904, General von Trotha issued a now-historic proclamation:

> I, the Great General of the German soldiers address this letter to the Herero people. The Herero people will have to leave the country. Otherwise I will force them to do so by means of guns. Within the German boundaries, every Herero, whether found armed or unarmed, with or without cattle, will be shot. I shall not accept any more women and children. I shall drive them back to their people — otherwise I shall order shots be fired at them.

Thus began the ruthless extermination of the Ovaherero. Von Trotha's proclamation caused uproar in Germany and by December he was forced to rescind it, but he did not end the brutality of his campaign. Instead, the Ovaherero were rounded up and taken to concentration camps, where they died from exposure and hard labour. Samuel Maharero died in exile in Botswana in March 1923. Later that year, on the twenty-third of August, his remains were returned to Okahandja and since then, the Ovaherero have gathered here annually on the Sunday closest to this date to pay homage to their ancestors, to the leaders and to the people who fell during the carnage. Over a period of four years, up to ninety thousand Ovaherero died — about two-thirds of the total population. During the Wars of Resistance, many of the survivors had converted to Christianity out of convenience in the concentration camps, but after the war they began to relight their eternal fires and return to old customs. In the future, the omatandu would talk of the great sadness.

Sinead and I do not stop at the museum, for our main goal is to find Maharero's grave and to establish where the weekend's festivities will start. No one, it seems, can help us. "Maharero's grave?" I ask every person we pass. Not a clue. "Herero Day celebrations?" Never heard of them. The young girl at the tourist information bureau reluctantly ends her conversation on her cell phone when she realizes we're not going to go away or look at the tourist kitsch on sale. She saunters over and insists on addressing me in English even though she has spent the last five minutes speaking Afrikaans on the phone. I respond in English, but it is clear she does not understand, so I swap back to Afrikaans. The light of comprehension on her face is visible. Yet she still tries to explain in English. The graves, we gather, are beside the old swimming pool.

"And where might that be?" I ask. She doesn't know. But she does start closing up shop to indicate that the conversation is over. The swimming pool doesn't show up on the maps, or on the GPS, so we decide to ask at the place where we will be staying for the night. We drive past the craft market that has arisen on a stretch of land on the outskirts of town, right beside the main road that links Windhoek and the north, and cross the intersection to get to the King's Highway Rest Camp. Things do not improve there. The woman at the reception desk has a baby in her arms and she juggles the telephone and the bookings with practised ease. Her husband is from Okahandja, she says, but she only moved up from the Cape two years ago. She's still not sure about much around these parts. She's never heard of Maharero or his grave, but she knows there is a cemetery. "Mind you," she hastens to add, "I've never had a reason to visit it myself."

Another woman appears from the back office. "I've only been here a few days myself," she informs me, "but I know there's a monument of sorts just up the road in Nau-Aib. I walk past it on my way to work every day. Maybe those are the graves?" She gives me directions.

I ask whether either of them knows where the old Augustineum buildings are. "In Windhoek," comes the instant reply from the woman with the baby.

"I know the Augustineum in Windhoek," I assure her, "but for the longest time the school was here in Okahandja. I want to know where the buildings are here. You see, my mother taught there and I'd like to get a picture for her." I persist, and the woman with the baby shakes her head and disappears into the back office. "Maybe the new school is in the old school building," the woman from Nau-Aib suggests and begins to explain where the school is. She stops in mid-sentence. "You know, a Herero woman did come in here yesterday to make a large booking for *next* weekend. Maybe that's when the festival is. It's Heroes' Day next week. Perhaps they will celebrate Herero Day then too."

She looks through her booking register and makes a quick phone call. "Next weekend," she confirms as she hangs up. Sinead and I have no intention of sticking around Okahandja for a week, so instead we decide to head to Lüderitz, a coastal town in the south of the country. On the way out, we take a short detour past Nau-Aib: it's not Maharero's grave, but a memorial to Ovaherero heroes. That, at least, is a step in the right direction.

5

There is really only one way into Lüderitz: south along the B1 until you hit Keetmanshoop. For much of the journey, the Brukkaros Mountains lie to the left of the road like a raised spine. Behind those mountains lies the Auob River. For four years during the Wars of Resistance, Jakob Morenga and Hendrik Witbooi trekked their people up and down the valleys of the Auob, ambushing German patrols and attacking local farms. There too lies Aranos, from where Sam Nujoma and other leaders crossed the border into Botswana on their way to London at the start of the War of Independence. Just beyond Keetmanshoop, you descend into the Fish River Canyon. On either side of the road, elaborate canyons unfold into the second-largest canyon formation in the world.

Beyond the Fish River, the vegetation becomes more stunted and the shrubbery disappears. A lone quiver tree graces the horizon; then more appear. As we drive out of the Fish River Canyon, I see a small pile of stones: *Boesmangrafte*, we called them as children. Bushman graves. Some hug the roadside; others dot the veld beyond the fences. These are *ombindi*, cairns built to honour those who have departed. As we drive past, I spot the occasional footpath joining some of these ombindi. When travellers along these footpaths encounter ombindi, they add a stone and mutter a supplication. Then they continue with their respective journeys. The supplication is a request for help, for a blessing to be bestowed on both the decision that initiated the journey and the eventual outcome of that decision. Some people attach no particular significance to these ombindi, but others see the cairns as informal places of worship, where travellers can unburden their souls by telling their secrets to the shades of the ancestors. For an instant while the ritual of placing a stone on the cairn is performed, the traveller is suspended: the point of origin becomes one with the destination; in the present, the past merges with the future. In this moment, itinerant souls become grounded. The travellers move on, but the ombindi remain as part of the landscape: testimonies to those individual moments of participation in a ritual that, if only for one moment, binds the travellers, with their diverse pasts and futures, together.

Around midday, we reach the edge of the desert. Nestled in the folds of the surrounding mountains lies a little town called Aus. *Aus* happens to be the German word for "out" — an appropriate name for a town that became the first inland refuge for the German colonizers once they'd found a way through the desert. However, a more likely etymology for the name is the Khoekhoegowab word meaning "Place of the Snakes." Just east of Aus, there is a sign by the side of the road: "Commonwealth Graves." We veer off the road to search for the graves. As we pass the roadside fence, we encounter a fork in the road. I turn left and head toward the settlement I spot about a kilometre and a half away. We find ourselves in a dusty street lined by shacks and several stores that sell minutes for pay-as-you-go phone plans. I spot a young woman outside one of the stores and ask her for directions to what is clearly a major tourist site in this area, if the size of the sign on the main road was anything to go by. She shakes her head and points me to someone walking down the road. He stares at me blankly from half-stoned eyes.

I drive slowly down the streets of what I now realize was the old black township of Aus. Now, it butts up against the highway and spills over into the old white town. It takes decades for the stark divisions of the past to disappear; even longer, it seems, for the festering disparities in living conditions to heal. There's a little open space just across from the barbershop and I begin to make a U-turn to head back to the highway. A man watches me manoeuvre between the young children who push against the bakkie. He chases them away and waits for me to approach.

He sticks out his hand as I stop beside him. "Willem Goliat!" he announces without my asking, and then, in response to my questions, he continues. "*Ja, ek weet waar die grafte lê.*" Yes, I know where the graves are. His English, like that of many older rural Namibians, is limited. I try to get directions from him, but he insists it will be easier if he simply shows me.

I open the door and start making space for him beside our suitcases, which we have put on the back seat to avoid some of the dust from the roads, but Willem Goliat insists he'll just hop into the back of the bakkie and direct me. He opens up the back flap and jumps in with the seasoned grace of someone who has been doing this for almost sixty-two years. Willem Goliat points straight ahead and we bash our way up another township street and into the dusty yonder. I try to follow Willem's directions through the rear-view mirror. He waves with his left hand and dangles his right toward what could be the left, but having taken my eyes off the road to follow directions from the back, we hit a bump. Willem's hands become a flurry and I know for certain that he's not giving directions — he's hanging on for dear life. Having made the wrong turn once this morning, this time I veer right. Wrong again. We end up in a dry riverbed and the bakkie sinks up to the chassis in the loose sand. I manage to keep the bakkie moving, engage the diff lock to fool the bakkie into thinking it's a four-wheel drive and chug my way through the riverbed at an even pace. When we hit solid ground, the bakkie lurches forward. And so does Willem Goliat.

As soon as I get a chance, I stop. Sinead gets into the back and Willem joins me in the front. "It's not right," he insists. "Will the young lady be okay?"

"She's got young bones," I tell him. "The experience will toughen her up."

Now that he can talk his way through directions, things go better. He spends the first five minutes apologizing for his bad directions that forced Sinead into the back. I tell him again that she's a youngster. He laughs. *"Ma' jy's nog self nat agter die ore!"* But you're still wet behind the ears yourself. Willem points to two parallel tracks in the sand and I head down the road. He warms up to me and chats incessantly. Aus is a good place to live, he says. No crime, no murders. He's a farmhand who's come into town to spend the afternoon in the hotel in Aus. Lived here all his life. He's travelled to Keetmanshoop and Lüderitz on farm business, but that's it. Willem directs me back to the main road and we head back toward Goageb, away from the sign that led us to Willem in the first instance. I quiz Willem Goliat about the graves. "Oh," he says, "you want the soldiers' graves! I thought you were looking for the Aus graveyard, the white cemetery. Bloedsake, you know. Most white people who come here want to find deceased family."

I assure him this is no family matter. "Then turn around," he instructs.

Back at the turnoff to Aus, we take the right-hand fork and head into the open veld. We go through another riverbed and take a left at a lone camelthorn. A few bumps later, we arrive at our destination: a dilapidated fence encircles a neat little cemetery. This is all that remains of the prisoner of war camp here at Aus. At the start of the First World War, South Africa invaded what was then the German colony of South West Africa. On the ninth of September 1914, one part of the invading force landed at Lüderitz; the other landed at Walvis Bay on Christmas Day of that year. The Germans simply withdrew from the harbour and retreated inland, trekking north, north, ever north along the railway line that runs like a backbone along the centre of the country until they surrendered on the ninth of July 1915 at Mile 500, just north of Otavi. The Treaty of Khorab required that all German troops be interned until the end of the war. And so back they trekked, the Schutztruppe and their guards, back to Aus, where they built a ramshackle camp to house the 1,438 prisoners and their six hundred guards.

The camp is situated on a bleak outcrop of land east of the settlement of Aus. From where we stand, the only evidence of life is the peregrine falcon on a telephone pole. For the first part of their internment, the POWs lived in army bell tents that offered little protection from the unpredictable weather of the area, which in the space of a single week in September 1915 offered up a heat wave, followed by a snowstorm and hot sandstorms.

Willem Goliat knows little beyond the location of these graves. "Graves creep me out," Sinead says as I climb through the dilapidated fence.

"We'll be looking at a lot of graves in the coming weeks," I remind her.

"I know. But they still creep me out. As long as we get to do some fun things too."

I wander the area on my own while Sinead and Willem Goliat lean against the fence and communicate as best they can without me acting as interpreter. The Kaiser Monument that paid homage to the prisoners who died has been destroyed and the plaque on the stone near the ruins of the camp has been torn off. A solitary obelisk is all that remains. The only knowledge we gain about life in the camp is found in the archives in Windhoek: shortly after their arrival at Aus, the prisoners built themselves mud-brick homes and camp life eased after those first few months of unpredictable weather. By 1916, the camp had a vegetable garden and the prisoners had put together a sports league of their own. In terms of POW camps, life was good. There were few casualties until the influenza epidemic of 1918–19 intruded, claiming the lives of sixty-five POWs and sixty guards. It is these graves that remain in the cemetery.

We mark our dead and protect their resting places, turn them into sites where we can commemorate their actions and, more often than not, inadvertently perpetuate our prejudices by doing so. The cemetery at Aus is the only war cemetery in the world where German and Allied soldiers lie side by side in the same cemetery. Their strife ended when they lost the battle to a common enemy and their shared resting place is a testimony to reconciliation. Yet, the upkeep of the graves is divided: the Volksbund Deutsche Kriegsgräberfürsorge (German War Graves Commission) tends to the German graves, while the Commonwealth War Graves Commission maintains the Allied graves.

On the way back to Aus, Willem Goliat insists that he should sit in the back. I head straight for the open plain where we first met our guide. As we pass a shack with a green shade cloth, he bangs on the canopy. I stop. Willem leaps out and shakes my hand enthusiastically. This is the hotel, he assures me.

"Drive safely, and drive sober. May God bless you!" he shouts as we drive off toward the main road.

"*Kai-aios*," I shout the only Khoekhoegowab phrase I know in return. A big thank you.

About halfway between Lüderitz and Aus, there is a turnoff to the Garub Horse Project. German soldiers on the retreat from the advancing South African troops abandoned a handful of horses as they moved inland and up toward Windhoek. The horses did not die as the soldiers had expected them to, but managed to survive and multiply. As Zirkie Kloppers, the owner of the hotel at Seeheim had told us earlier in the day, "Here people, like the animals, adapt. You get used to this country, then you learn to love it. It becomes home." For these feral horses, this is home. After a particularly severe drought in 1993, the government decided that the horses were a moving monument to the past and that despite their alien presence in a fragile ecosystem, they belonged and should be protected. I feel a kinship with these horses, for I too am an alien taken root among these African stones. Namibia is very accommodating.

As we head deeper into the desert, the shrubs and quiver trees beyond the Fish River Canyon gradually give way to grass; eventually, the grass gives way to stone. Along the verges of the main road, magenta shrubs and rusted vygies bleed onto the sand. The blood of the earth lies close to the surface here and you can feel the pulse of the desert with every breath you take. I stop the bakkie at the top of a hill and we get out to watch the clouds push their way into the bay, forcing the sea air inland, where it mingles with the scent of the sand to form the fine mist that clings to the desert coastline.

At the bottom of the hill lies Lüderitz — a quaint, lazy, windswept seaside harbour with rocky outcrops that hide a handful of delightful little beaches. As we drive into town, I wonder briefly whether anything has changed since Bartolomeu Dias put a woman ashore here late in the fifteenth century at the place he called Angra Pequeña. It was the Germans who gave it the name Lüderitzbucht when they arrived at the end of the nineteenth century. But it was Dias who allegedly dropped the woman along these shores as he made his way down the coast of Africa. Capturing natives and taking them to Europe to learn Portuguese or Spanish was fairly common at the time. All that history books have to say about her is that Dias set a Guinea woman ashore at Angra Pequeña. Why? Had he tired of her affections? Was he hoping to use her as an intermediary with the locals? Did she survive in this country, where she was as foreign and unprepared as he? Where do her bones lie buried in the sands of the Namib? Is it anywhere near those of the thousands of Ovaherero and Nama who died at the hands of the Schutztruppe between 1904 and 1908? Those bones lie in unmarked mass graves in the desert, exposed by the desert sand, but where are the bones of Dias's woman? What stories do they tell of her suffering?

It's been twenty years since independence, but sections of Lüderitz still cling resolutely to a colonial past. The Germans were latecomers on the colonial scene, and seemed to draw the short straw when it came to divvying up colonies at Berne in 1884. Shortly before the Berne Convention, the British got wind of the kaiser's scheme to lay claim to parts of Africa and promptly annexed Walvis Bay, the only truly viable harbour along the Namib coastline. From there, they monopolized the inland trade and the guano and fishing industries. At about the same time, a German businessman, Adolf Lüderitz, traded ten thousand German mark and two hundred rifles to the Nama chief, Joseph Fredericks, for the land surrounding the bay. But Lüderitz's emissary to these negotiations forgot to mention that he was using German geographic miles in his calculations, not English land miles. Lüderitz's transaction brought him little discernable benefit: no minerals, no water, no arable land and after a while he sold it to the German Colonial Society and placed it under the protection of General Heinrich Ernst Göring, the German colonial administrator. Göring did not linger in the backwater port: he pushed inland toward Windhoek, where he established a threadbare colonial administration. Adolf Lüderitz may have given up too early, for in 1908, a migrant labourer by the name of Zacharias Lewala found the first diamond just east of the town. Things changed after that, but Lüderitz would not have known. He drowned in the Gariep River in 1886 during an exploration trip.

It is late Friday afternoon and Sinead and I head straight for Shark Island, where we will camp for the weekend. Shark Island, now accessible to the mainland by way of a road, forms a bleak promontory in the middle of the bay. It was here, on this island, that the Schutztruppe created a concentration camp during the Wars of Resistance.

After the glorious sunshine of the interior, the coast is dreary and overcast and, aside from a handful of German tourists huddled around a fire at their campsite, we have the place to ourselves. The wind buffets the bakkie as we make our way down the pathway toward the campsites. There are sheltered spots on the northeast side of the rocks, but Sinead insists on finding a spot right on the edge of the Atlantic, where we can feel the full force of the wind on the tent. The spot she selects is the one where, in photographs of the camp, I have seen Nama prisoners huddled together for shelter against the elements. I have deliberately chosen to stay here on the island rather than in one of the quaint German *gasthauses* in town, for I wanted to feel the wind that ripped through the prisoners' meagre protection in this place of horrors. I want to imagine what it was like to have to survive on this bleak piece of stone and sand.

By the time we are done pitching the tent, the wind has picked up and the mist has settled into a steady drizzle. Sinead has wrapped herself in whatever warm clothes she could lay her hands on, but still she is shivering. The cough she brought with her has developed into a full-blown sinus infection. I insist that we look for a pharmacy even though the chances of finding one that's open are slim. Everything is closed and so we decide instead to head toward Agate Beach to watch the sun set. As we drive along Talstrasse, Sinead spots a clinic. The nurse on duty is a bundle of warmth and compassion. While she is busy attending to Sinead, I chat to one of the hospital staff. He talks enthusiastically about local history and the changes that have happened since independence. "The government is corrupt," he states, "but at least they still provide basics, like health care." It's true. Namibia has a very good primary health system that ensures access to basic treatment. It's more than a month away, but already I see posters raising awareness of National HIV Testing Day and on the radio I hear youths from around the country airing their views on the importance of being tested. Even the mobile service provider sends out regular text reminders to its customers.

Our conversation shifts and I ask about local places of interest. "Dias Cross and Agate Beach," he replies without hesitation as Sinead and the nurse emerge from the consulting room. No Shark Island. The nurse has prescribed some antibiotics and painkillers and I hand over the obligatory twenty Namibian dollars for the prescription. As we leave, she tugs at Sinead's collar. "*Los die sexy,*" she reprimands her, "*bly warm!*" She zips Sinead's collar tight and hugs her on her way out.

From the clinic, we head to Dias Point. Once more, the road forks as we leave the main road and the signs dry up. A little further down the road, we reach the first of several signs that read "*Sperrgebiet*." Forbidden Territory. This is land that belongs to the diamond-mining companies and access is strictly controlled. We drive on along the road, past Second Lagoon toward Guano Bay and the lighthouse we see in the distance. A little way beyond the lighthouse lies Dias Point. It is here that Bartolomeu Dias set foot on South African soil and erected a *padrão* to claim the territory in the name of Christ and king. And it is somewhere here too that he allegedly left the Guinea woman before heading off toward Algoa Bay. No one here can tell you what happened to Dias's lady; yet almost anyone in Lüderitz can tell you where Dias left the padrão — over there, right by the lighthouse. Nothing remains of Dias's original cross at Angra Pequeña, but he did erect another — further south, near Alexandria in the Eastern Cape in South Africa.

The wind lashes against our faces as we cross the wooden bridge to the rocky promontory on which the replica cross stands. The original has been lost, most likely worn down by the incessant wind. The desert has a habit of taking back what is stolen from it. No traces remain, except for the cross planted here by descendants. As we leave, I take one last look at the sun setting over the Atlantic. For a brief moment, the bleakness of the day has lifted and I am able to savour the golden lining on the horizon.

On the way back, we have coffee at the Diaz Point Coffee Shop. It is a bare-bones outfit with a menu that offers little variety and a wine list fit for the palate of a stranded sailor: Old Brown Sherry and port. Lighthouse paraphernalia and an obligatory overturned boat round off the shoreside kitsch. The coffee, however, is divine, and so is the nut cake and the slab of chocolate cake that is served with it. If there is one thing *boeretannies* excel at, it is baking. We finish off our coffee and head back to our tent.

We huddle in our sleeping bags until hunger forces us out of the tent in search of something to eat. I rummage for stray cans in the food bin while Sinead runs up to the camp kitchen with the gas stove. We mix a tin of lentils with chakalaka, a spicy blend of tomato and onion. That and some noodles constitute supper. We sit on the cement floor and eat by the heat of the gas stove while the water boils for tea.

Sinead looks a little off-colour and has descended into silence as we wash our dishes and prepare for the dash back to the tent. I ascribe it to the sinus infection, but suddenly she looks at me and says, "It's a little weird being here. Why would they turn the island into a camp-site when they know it was a concentration camp? It's a bit like taking your tent and pitching it in the middle of Auschwitz."

Back in the tent, we settle in for the evening. The wind tears at the tent all night long. Thank heavens for a thick waterproof covering to deflect the sea spray and the rain. Where the wind does manage to find a crack, it's icy. Despite the warm days we've had in the interior, it is bitterly cold here in Lüderitz.

"Would you like to find a more sheltered spot?" I ask Sinead before we settle down for the night.

In response, she pulls a second hoodie over her head and draws the spare summer sleeping bag up over herself as an additional blanket. "No, I want to feel the ocean." I lie awake and listen to her breathing. Only when I am satisfied that she is sleeping peacefully, do I allow myself to fall asleep.

I wake around five-thirty a.m. It is still dark and the seabirds are just beginning to stir. Gusts of wind slam into the tent, punctuated by the drumbeat of waves on the rocks below us. I pull the cowl of my sleeping bag tighter, but the dampness has leached into my bones. Shark Island is a low-lying, rocky promontory that offers no respite from the elements. Living here in makeshift tents and lean-tos, with-out any protection from the elements, as the inmates of the Shark Island Concentration Camp had to do, must have been unbearable. The statistics concur. The mortality rate was more than seventy per cent, some say up to ninety per cent, with most of these deaths occur-ring from exposure and overwork during the construction of the railway line between Lüderitz and Keetmanshoop — the very line that the Germans used to get themselves out of the desert when the South Africans invaded during the First World War.

I crawl out of the tent and look for warmer clothes in the car. Everywhere, there is wind. When it is not coming in from the ocean, it howls in from the desert, or along the fringes of the bay. The only greenery is from the grass planted there by the campsite developers. I watch the day break with a cup of coffee to warm my hands. The first building to burn gold is the guard tower at the eastern tip of the island. In the distance, I can see the lighthouse at Dias Point. A throwaway piece from one of Antjie Krog's poems enters my head:

by die pilaar van Sao Thiago los hy haar
as lyk in die duine by Angra Pequena vergeet hy haar
die donker vrou van Diaz

at the pillar of Sao Thiago he leaves her
as corpse in the dunes at Angra Pequena he forgets her
the dark woman of Diaz

Angra Pequeña is where he allegedly dropped off the woman from Guinea who had been taken to Lisbon and taught Portuguese. An assimilado, she was no longer at home either in her own land or in the highly racialized and stylized courts of Europe, but Dias left her here, on the desert shores of Namibia.

Sinead wakes and we have cereal and coffee before heading off to Kolmanskop, the abandoned mining town a few miles inland from Lüderitz. Here, the mist has dissipated, leaving only a hint of moisture for the sunlight to filter through. From the hills of the ghost town, one can still see the railway line where Zacharias Lewala was cleaning sand off the tracks when he found a diamond lying in the sand. After that, contract labourers built railway lines and crawled on their hands and knees through the desert sand in search of the elusive stones that could grace the necks of European gentry. We have come to marvel at the crumbling buildings of Kolmanskop as they are engulfed by the desert. As we walk through the town, my eye keeps falling on the buildings in the Sperrgebiet across the road from the crumbling opulence of the mining town. These are the remains of a hostel where African contract labourers lived separate from the white miners.

The old music hall has been transformed into a small display area where visitors can see a pictorial history of the town and read more about the development of the diamond industry. A major part of the display is taken up by the various methods used to smuggle diamonds out of the Sperrgebiet, and more importantly, by the methods used to foil would-be thieves. Even I have overheard a bit of family lore that tells of a distant cousin who tried to smuggle diamonds out of Namibia in the shaft of a javelin. Kolmanskop is a symbol of the Reich gone to shreds. In the 1930s, the images show us, the citizens of Kolmanskop gathered to sing patriotic songs in honour of the führer. By then, the bald racism of the Nazi era had gripped the desert sands like lichen on a stone. Hearts and minds were infected. Even as the tide turned against Hitler in Europe, here in the colonies, support remained strong. As the diamonds around Kolmanskop dwindled, the town was abandoned and the patriotic young men headed north to fight for volk and führer.

While we walk around, visiting the sick bay and the residences of the quartermaster and the doctor, the barracks that housed the labourers stand deserted, abandoned and unvisited. The buildings glimmer in the sand and we begin to feel warm in the glare of the sun despite the chill of the breeze that reaches in from the ocean.

Lüderitz comes to a standstill on a Sunday, so after walking around Kolmanskop for the morning, we head back to Shark Island for lunch. A walk along Shark Island's periphery takes us up close to a small colony of seals stretched out on a rocky promontory. We spend some time watching the seals. On the island, the breeze we felt at Kolmanskop is a gusty swirl that encircles the camp. A group of German tourists huddle around their camper van, clinging to their belongings as they scurry to and from the central washrooms and camp kitchen. Sinead is restless as a teenager can be. The antibiotics we got from the clinic have started working and she wants to move. There is no time to waste sitting in a tent when there are places to see. She bends over the tourist map, pressing the bottom edges down with her knees. "There's a ton of little bays and coves. Let's explore them all," she throws the challenge out to me.

We stick to the road on our foray to Grosse Bucht, for every so often we see the signs that remind us that we are in the Sperrgebiet. Sinead uses the GPS to find the turnoffs to the many little bays that grace the coastline. There are markers, but the wind and the sand have eroded the writing and some of them are no longer legible. The beaches are as deserted as the town. It is winter, after all, and the influx of holiday visitors will only come with the summer holidays. On the way to Messemb Bay, I spot a turnoff to Angra Point. The sign is clearly marked 4 × 4 only, so we park in the track and walk up the hill to the point. The sand lies deep here and despite the chilliness of the wind, the heat of the sand becomes evident as I lean down to tie my shoelace. I run my fingers through the abrasive granules and smell the sere, salted beauty of the landscape.

To our right as we climb up the hill lie the remains of the ramparts built by the South African troops during the First World War. Stone upon stone, red against black, the raised trench snakes up the hill toward more stone. Behind the hill, we look out over a rocky bay. There is a sliver of land reaching into the ocean to form a small bay, hence the Portuguese name, Angra Pequeña. The steep pathway leads onto a tiny beach that flanks the promontory. No place, this, for a soldier or for an abandoned woman. Where would Dias's woman have gone, if this were indeed the place where she was set ashore? As we leave, a necklace of ironstone girds the hillside. As Angra Point disappears from sight, we look across Griffith Bay toward Shark Island.

By the time we arrive at Grosse Bucht, our final destination for the day, the mist has settled in and the wind has picked up again.

Gone is the sunshine that kept the chill at bay. The spray flails high over the rocks. The wide bay disappears into the fog. Suddenly, a Damara tern swoops overhead. It is a resilient holdout, that fragile little bird pushing its way out to sea against a headwind. Grosse Bucht is one of the last remaining breeding grounds for this migratory bird: only about two thousand breeding pairs remain. In winter, all but a handful of diehards migrate up the coast to Nigeria; spotting them now, out of breeding season and in the middle of winter, is rare.

To my left, I spot a large ombindi on the rocks beside the beach. An Egyptian goose forages beside it. On our way back to the car, I pick up a stone. It is slippery from the mist and I have to dig my hands into its surface as I reach out and place it on the pile. *"Siph'amandla!"* Give me strength. And into my mind flashes a single name: Josef. I know little more about him than that he seems uncommonly tall in the photograph in which he and I stand together in front of our house — he wearing his cookboy shorts and me wearing diapers. After his contract expired, Josef returned to the reserve and disappeared from my life. But his ghost remains. As do the fragments of *Otjiherero* that surface in my mind occasionally. My prayer on this blistery afternoon is for the souls of this land, but it is in isiXhosa, the only tongue in which I know how to commune with these rocks. *"Thixo, Siph'uxolo!"* I ask. Lord, grant us peace.

◆ ◆ ◆

Back at camp on Shark Island, Sinead and I visit a memorial of a different kind, one built to commemorate the German soldiers who died during the Wars of Resistance. The names of the soldiers, neatly engraved in slabs of white Karibib marble, are embedded in a low stone wall. At the back, nestled against a boulder at the centre of the island, stands a cross commemorating the deaths of the sailors on board the ill-fated *Nautilus*, which sank off the coast of Lüderitz in 1976. As I lean forward to read the faded plaque and my head is sheltered from the bite of the incessant winter wind, I am overwhelmed by the smell of stale urine.

Separated slightly from this cluster of plaques and crosses, a faded marble headstone commemorates Kaptein Cornelius Fredericks, leader of the !Aman people of Bethany. His name is barely legible, washed away by the ocean spray. Soon he will be forgotten, just like the rest of the Nama and Ovaherero prisoners on this island. We can take comfort in the fact that they are not alone in their oblivion. In 1999, workers found a mass grave in the Sperrgebiet just north of the Lüderitz airport. Although no forensic tests were done on the bodies at the time, other evidence suggests that they may have belonged to Shark Island prisoners. Traditional leaders lobbied to have the bodies reburied on Shark Island, but despite assurances that this would happen in 2009, and that visitors would be allowed access to the graves on Shark Island, there is still no sign of a tribute to these fallen heroes of the Namibian Wars of Resistance.

Two young German tourists approach us. They read the names on the marble plaques with great care, shaking their heads as they move along the low wall.

"They say this was a concentration camp," the young woman says to her friend as they pass us.

"Yes, this was an extermination camp," I say deliberately and turn away. I do not tell them how the Schutztruppe harvested the heads of the dead and shipped them off to Germany. I do not tell them about Eugen Fischer and the eugenics experiments he conducted on these skulls. I do not tell them that Fischer's most famous protege was Josef Mengele. I do not tell them that in 2007, Peter Katjavivi, then ambassador to Germany, discovered some of the Shark Island Skulls in the Ethnological Museum in Berlin's Dahlem district and that ever since, he has been fighting for their return to the land of their ancestors. I do not tell them. I simply do not have the heart to do so.

6

The condensation on the inside of the tent is thick when we wake in the morning. I peek outside, but can barely see two feet ahead of me. The rain blew in from the ocean last night and the sunshine of the past few days has been replaced by drizzle. It is Monday, and Lüderitz has reopened for business. We drop off our laundry at a local laundromat and go for a walk around the town. Outside a curio shop, I find an ATM and draw some cash. We go in and browse for a while before buying some books and postcards. I ask the woman behind the till about Dias. She can't help me, but directs me instead to Crispin Clay, the owner of the Grillenberger Bottle Store.

The store is a narrow sleeve of a room squeezed in between other shops in the row. Crispin Clay stands a fiery 5'6" and directs proceedings from behind his counter. He reaches for the bottles of liquor behind him without so much as a glance, punching in the amounts as he does so. If the bottles are more than an arm's length away, he clips instructions to his assistant: "Two bottles of Klipdrift Brandy. Third shelf, next to the Richelieu." He's an expat from Northern Rhodesia (now Zambia) who made his way from Livingstone to Lüderitz some thirty years ago. He meets my enquiry into Bartolomeu Dias with a suspicious "Why do you want to know?"

I tell him it's a small part of one story and a long part of another. He laughs. "Ah, a story on Dias. That's what I came to Lüderitz for in 1973! And here I am still standing behind the counter of my bottle store — no closer to the truth than when I arrived. But why should I share my story with you?"

I tell Crispin about my interest in Dias's woman in particular and my desire to see the crosses. He warms up slowly, helping customers while paying half-hearted attention to me.

"It's all hearsay," he reminds me. "Nothing I can tell you is confirmed. Nothing. All Dias's records were lost at sea when he went down in 1500. You'll only find John Barros's thirty-page Hakluyt Report that tells us something about the journey."

"I heard the records got lost in a fire at São Jorge da Mina," I venture.

"Hearsay. Nothing to prove that." The cagey staccato sentences soon give way to an expansive narrative that meanders deliciously from gossip to snippet to rumour. There was not one woman, but four, taken from West Africa to Portugal, where they became assimilados. "They were trained in contemporary metaphysics and taught to relay the trading needs and desires of Portugal. Venice was collapsing as a trade power, and with the advent of the Spanish pope, Alexander VI, to the papal throne, the time was ripe for expansion.

"The Spanish went west; the Portuguese headed down the coast of Africa. Three of the women were dropped off higher up the coast and charged with interacting with the locals to improve trade and perhaps, just perhaps, to find out more about Prester John.

"The last of the four women was allegedly dropped off here at Lüderitz — Angra Pequeña, as it was known then. What happened to her after that, no one knows. A while back, they discovered some bones in Griffith Bay. The find caused quite a stir as the person was buried in a way that was different to local custom and, intriguingly, the body was surrounded by cowrie shells from East Africa. This led some to believe that the bones may be those of the Dias woman."

Crispin stops to help three men with their order before returning to the story. "As it turns out, she was a he and the DNA was not
Negroid. So much for that."

This is a treacherous coastline filled with little bays and inlets. All
we can know for certain is that Dias left a Negro woman somewhere
along this coastline, possibly here at Angra Pequeña, or at a place he
called Angra das Voltas. "That may or may not be Angra Point across
the bay," Crispin warns. "There are many narrow bays just north and
south of here. We do know for certain that he landed at Dias Point,
where the cross is. I spent a fair deal of time there. My late wife was
the last lighthouse keeper."

The rumour of the woman persists, but to date there has been no
confirmed record that she existed. "We do know that training up
assimilados was a common practice, so that's at least plausible,"
Crispin concludes.

Dias never got a hero's welcome in the way that Vasco da Gama
did when he returned from India after successfully navigating all the
way around the southern tip of Africa. Some rumours have it that he
never was a noble and therefore was not entitled to any recognition;
others hold that he fell into disfavour at the court. There is something
to be said for this theory, as Dias returns in 1489 and is not heard
of again for ten years. His name does not appear on any ships' rolls
and he does not receive another commission until he is appointed
captain on one of Cabral's ships in 1500.

Yet so much of the eventual discovery of a sea passage to India
relied on the work Bartolomeu Dias did on his first voyage south. It
was Dias who discovered the southern trade winds and suggested
that future travellers head out west before looping down the coast.
A slight miscalculation in 1500 led Pedro Álvares Cabral to South
America and Brazil before he got back on course and rounded the
Cape of Storms, or the Cape of Good Hope, as King João II insisted
on calling it. Hugging the coast and tacking against the prevailing
wind, as Dias had done before, was not economical.

"We don't know exactly what happened to Dias's ship," Crispin takes a different tack on his story. "We know from Cabral's records that the ship disappeared in a storm northwest of the Cape of Storms. It could have been tossed about on the ocean for days, drifting with the prevailing current and the winds. That is why there was such excitement about the wreck of the caravel they found near here a few years back. But that didn't pan out, for the ship had coins with Ferdinand and Isabella on them. They came after Dias."

And so both Dias and his woman remain lost in a cloud of fact and fiction. If Dias did indeed drop a woman off along this coast, she stood little chance of survival. Da Gama's account of a landing further south, at Saldanha Bay, records the hostility of the locals and the treachery of the travellers. Colonial encounters are always tricky.

We leave the bottle store shortly after noon and we stop again at the curio shop to get some postcards. The woman suggests we take the scenic route D707 to Sesriem and travel along the edge of the Namib. From there, it is plain sailing to Walvis Bay and Swakopmund. From the curio shop, we head to the Diaz Coffee Shop for lunch. Beside us two women talk about the upcoming Heroes' Day celebrations. As the speaker becomes more animated, I overhear a snippet of their conversation: "*Cuito!*" she says. "Always *blêrrie* Cuito Cuanavale. I'm tired of Cuito! We spent decades in Angola and it's time we left. What are we still doing there? We need to forget about the past. Think about the future." I'd like to agree with her, but I can't. The road to Cuito Cuanavale coils repeatedly through my memory as it works its way slowly northward. It is strange, for since I have been here, I have not heard a thing about Cuito. So unlike when I was here in 1990 and Cuito Cuanavale was on everybody's lips.

Sinead and I finish off a series of postcards and mail them on our way out. We collect our laundry and find the Lüderitz Museum. I had hoped that the bones of the body they found in Griffith Bay were still on display, as Crispin Clay had suggested they might be, but no such luck. It is a small-town museum filled with the usual ephemera and heirlooms from local families. Ghosts from the past and mildewed memories. In the end this is what remains of all those voyages of conquest — muddled memories and the smell of piss on a weathered stone cross.

7

|Kaggen is a man in a hurry: he's trying to find his child, the eland-child born of Coti, his wife. As he passed by the Tiras Mountains during the night, he hucked up streaks of red against the edges of the Namib. The early morning sun attempts to break through the night's clouds and we can see clearly where |Kaggen dragged his white karos across the mountains. Snow! That's a rarity in this world and we take several pictures of seed-cotton fluff that is so unlike the thick layers of Canadian snow that I have become accustomed to.

This is surely the world created by |Kaggen in his stories. It's an ancient world in which sometimes only the stories of those times have survived. Here, I'm convinced, |Kaggen still wanders about searching for his eland-child, the child who was slain by its siblings. Here he is determined to create new life, a whole herd of eland from the nothingness of his sorrow. Here, against the bleeding cheeks of the Namib, in |Kaggen's creation garden, my daughter and I find ourselves on the road to Sossusvlei and Swakopmund.

We left Gunsbewys farm early. We'd slept cold the night before as the temperatures dropped to minus eight and we woke to snow on the Tiras Mountains for the first time in living memory. The sun peeks through the clouds and gradually Sinead wiggles her body from the folds of her sleeping bag. At Betta, we fill our tank. Who knows where the next gas station will be.

Gradually, the road tears itself away from the bleeding hills of the Namib and climbs its way through the Tiras Mountains. Small herds of zebra and springbok graze by the roadside and a stray ostrich kicks its way down the road ahead of us. In the distance, a pack of bat-eared foxes chase each other in play. Then the rolling grasslands give way and the bleeding hills appear once more. Somewhere near the tip of the rib of fertile valley that sticks out into the desert lies our first destination, Sossusvlei.

Just inside the gates of the Sossusvlei Rest Camp, a road leads to a tear in the earth, just like the one through which, we are told, the cries of the children of IKaggen were first heard on earth. "Tomorrow morning, as soon as the sun has risen, you and I will be travelling down that path," I tell Sinead as we drive past. "That road leads to the Sesriem Canyon. It is in such a place that the stories of this earth were born. And that too is where I was born in stories."

"Before we reach for more stories, can we at least unpack and drive to Sossusvlei?" It seems as if the last of the antibiotics coursing through Sinead's veins have done their work well. She's been chatting steadily all morning on the road here and clearly, she has an answer to everything I say. She knows me well, this child of mine. She knows my head gets stuck in stories and then I forget about other things. The Namib is a tangle of stories that have me stuck in the branches of an ancient camelthorn tree and her job is to pull my feet back onto the ground and to keep us on track as we make our way north.

After checking in, pitching our tent and throwing down some lunch, we head into the desert to the *vlei*. The deeper we travel along the artery toward Sossusvlei, the redder the dunes seem to become. We stop briefly at Dune 45 and scramble to the top. From there, the Namib stretches in all directions. In the distance, along the ridges of the dunes to the north, we can see the thin strip of trees that marks the course of the Tsauchab River. To the west, and running along the southern part of the valley, the dry bed of the Aub River contours toward Sossusvlei.

Exhausted from our climb, we drive deeper into the red desert. In the parking lot at the end of the tarred road, we transfer into a 4 × 4. Our guide negotiates the deep sand of the dry riverbed with skill and we inch closer to the heart of this oasis. About halfway down the track to Sossusvlei, he stops and points to his left. "Dead Vlei," he says. "See you in an hour's time. I have to go and rescue someone stuck in the sand. Bloody foreigners who always want to blunder into the sand dunes."

Between the sand dunes we walk, Sinead and I. Through the sand and the shrubbery until we reach Dead Vlei. It's an ancient, dried out pan that leans white against the bleeding red of the sand dunes. And believe me, these dunes bleed, for reports suggest that underneath them lies oil. Fifteen billion barrels full, if the prospectors are telling the truth. Most of this black seed is hidden under the ocean, but there have been some promising finds in the desert too, just beyond this karos of red and white in which we have swathed ourselves. If the oil barons have their way, they will be drawing the black blood from the earth very soon. As if they know what's coming, the blackened trees of Dead Vlei hang their branches like oil derricks caught in mid sway. I can imagine the oil barons of Calgary exporting masses of steel padrões to be planted in the desert like Dias's cross. In this nightmare, the padraõ-derricks proliferate in the Namib: our future is bleak if we continue to rape the earth like this.

I force these dark thoughts aside and help Sinead find a decent tree to climb. A scarab beetle scurries into the knotted trunk of the tree.

The guide is waiting for us by the time we get back to the drop-off point. "The last trip back to the parking lot leaves Sossusvlei in an hour," he announces when he drops us off again.

Sossusvlei has always been a transient place. No one lives here. They all stop here en route to elsewhere. Here, |Kaggen walks side by side with his children and those who chased them from these lands, the Dorsland Trekkers and the Germans who followed after them. Once their calves had been fatted, they departed. Just IKaggen remained and as the greed of his children became overwhelming, he cried in the hollow between the sand dunes. Then the vlei filled with water and the abundance brought the birds and the herds back to Sossusvlei. This has been a year of abundance. Sossusvlei is filled with water and the avocets and ducks play. What will become of them once the oil mines splatter their acid rain over this place?

◆　◆　◆

A gusty wind blasts through the rest camp and tosses about anything that has not been tied down properly. I pull a sweater over my head and stoke the leftover coals from last night. I've caught Sinead's cold and I feel exhausted. Minutes later, she pokes her head out of the tent. By the time she's done folding the sleeping bags and striking the tent, I've got coffee and breakfast waiting. As soon as the sun has dulled the worst of the morning's sharpness, we drive to Sesriem Canyon.

At a first glance, there's little to see: stunted grass stretching out endlessly and, in the distance, the blue of the Naukluft Mountains rising above the plain. In this vast expanse, it is easy to miss what is right under your eyes. The tear IKaggen left when he created the earth is well hidden, but as you approach it, the ground gives way suddenly. The wind pushes hard against us as we descend into the bowels of the earth.

No photo, no idol from an enclosed box of light or panoramic film can capture the heart of Sesriem. Here, only words whirl in the wind, mixing with the hesitant cries of IKaggen's children.

"The stories lie! They lie! There never was a world like this! Look! Look around you. The world mourns at the gaping wounds of our greed. There were never grass stubbles here. You did not see mountains in the distance. Only the wind that howls between your legs has always been here, mourning." ǀKaggen's children wail over their own obduracy and the walls of the canyon groan as we walk past them. This is how the earth mourns.

I know the wind tells the truth. Stories and pictures lie. Here in the upper reaches of the Sesriem Canyon, the years of abundance leave small pools of water like the one we're approaching. Somewhere in the sand beside that pool you might still find a short piece of rib from a fat-tailed sheep buried in the sand. The rib isn't as old as Adam, and not as old as the wind that howls down the canyon, but it is older than I am. There's a story attached to that rib that makes this place part of me. A story from the time when Sesriem Truter still owned the homestead where the rest camp now stands. Old Man Truter wasn't filled with book knowledge, but he knew how to make his karakul herds flourish and he knew who he should count among his friends: the minister and the bank manager. The one to care for his soul and the other to ensure that his earthly belongings were also proliferating. Dad was a religious man, but he was no preacher. Fortunately, he was a bank manager, and so it happened that every now and again, he would be invited to come and spend a day with the Truters on their farm. Early on a Sunday morning, before church (the minister would surely understand), he and Ma would set out from Maltahöhe and head for the edge of the Namib. Then they and the Truters would drive out to the Sesriem Canyon to have a braai in the pool at the upper end of the canyon.

"Right here," I say to Sinead as we settle down on the sand beside the pool to enjoy the water and the coolness, "right here, your Grandpa and Ouma also sat and told stories. I grew up hearing this story. Every once in a while, Dad would take down the old 8-mm projector and film reels, and he and Ouma would give us running commentary on the silent films. That is how we got to know our family. In amongst all those films is a scene that was shot right here beside this pool. Now let me tell you, Sinead, a picture only paints half the story. You have to hear your Ouma tell the whole thing.

"Ouma and Grandpa and the Truters would come and braai here. They chatted while the rack of ribs sizzled on the coals. Just when it was done, Sesriem Truter lopped a nice chunk of the rib off and gave it to Dad.

"'It was mostly fat, with a thin strip of meat buried somewhere underneath,' Ouma would always remind us.

"'And then his wife stuck a piece of *boerbrood* in my hands,' Grandpa would chime in. 'A nice fat slice that had risen to the size of a paving stone.'

"'I could smell from afar that it was sourdough bread.' It was Ouma's turn. 'Listen, I'm not fussy about food, but sourdough bread is disgusting.'

"'So I went and sat next to Ma . . .' Grandpa picks up his side of the story.

"'And he stuffed the entire slice of bread into my hand! "There, Daleen, you love boerbrood, don't you?" So there I sat with a chunk of sourdough bread in my hand. I couldn't be rude and refuse to eat it, so I chewed my way through it bit by bit.'

"By now, a chuckle had started deep in Grandpa's soul. He'd shake like a car on a gravel road and his face would grow redder as the sound welled up inside him. Beside him, Ouma's face would also turn red, but that was from being irritated, fifty years later.

"'Ja, John, you laugh, but you were sitting behind me digging in the sand like a chicken. You'd tear off strips of fat and bury them behind my back. Then when you were done, you waved the rib in the air and buried it too. You buried your deceit. I had to eat your lies.'

"By this time, the laughter would burst out of Grandpa's body and wash over the company. Ouma would pick up her yarn and start crocheting indignantly, but she knew: in the morning there'd be a fresh rose beside her coffee. That's how love works and that's how Grandpa and Ouma always told their stories together. Stories that crept from mouth to mouth until we no longer knew who had been part of it and who hadn't."

There are quite a few Namibia stories where I know I could not possibly have been around, but over the years they have become such a part of the family lore that I may as well have been there. Like the story of the braai at Sesriem. That's how families are made, in those moments when the silence descends after the storm.

Sinead and I sit by the side of the pool and rest a bit before heading back to the car. As we emerge near the parking lot, the icy wind throws itself at us. Sinead cannot wait to see the coast again. "I hope Swakopmund is warmer!" I have to agree. The harshness of the air tears at my infected lungs.

In the car, we pore over our maps. Distances are deceptive: the GPS tells us we are now two hundred forty kilometres from Walvis Bay; the map says three hundred twenty; the odometer says three hundred sixty. All you can do is watch the level of the mercurial gas meter. It sticks at three-quarters and then drops suddenly to below half. It is anyone's guess just how much there is in the tank, and so I tend to fill up whenever and wherever I can. The last thing I'd want is to be stuck here without fuel. At least I have a jerry can full of diesel for an emergency. Through the Polaroid filters of my dark glasses, the Naukluft Mountains glimmer in a golden hue. It's a fool's trick, I know, an illusion, like the gold the Germans sought in these lands and the stories that swirl around us.

"We need to leave," Sinead says. "I don't care how far it is to Swakopmund, but we need to leave. I want to walk on the beach. We have to get there before darkness comes."

As the Portuguese made their way down the coast of Africa in the late fifteenth century, they erected wooden crosses along the shoreline to indicate the arrival of Christianity in these places and to stake their claim to the land. The wooden crosses used by the earliest Portuguese explorers proved to be too fragile for the harsh African climate and were soon replaced with ones made from limestone. The first explorer to use these new padrões was Diogo Cão, who set sail from Lisbon in 1482. Cão soon passed the usual turnaround point at São Jorge da Mina and continued down the African coast. Just south of the Congo River, he erected a stone padrão. From there, Cão and his crew sailed down the coast until their provisions ran low at a place they called Cabo do Lobo — Seal Cape. There, he erected a second padrão before heading back to Lisbon and a hero's welcome. The name Cabo do Lobo has disappeared from maps of Africa and the cape where this second stone padrão was erected is now known as Cabo de Santa Maria, which lies along the present-day Angolan coastline.

On his return, Cão immediately began preparations for a second journey, setting sail in 1485. This time, they passed Cabo de Santa Maria and a little further south, at Cabo Negro, he and his men erected a third padrão before pushing even further south. Early in 1486, the

explorers passed the Kunene River. The desert coastline seemed endless and offered the exhausted sailors no hope of replenishing their
supplies, so they decided to plant their last padrão at a place they
called Cabo do Padrão, Cape Cross, and return home. The words on
that cross read, "In the year 6885 of the creation on the earth and
1485 after the birth of Christ the most excellent and serene king Dom
João of Portugal ordered this land to be discovered and this padrão
to be placed by Diogo Cão, gentleman of his house." Cão died shortly
after landing at Cape Cross and the cross he planted remained alone
on the desert sand for centuries before the entrepreneurial Captain
Becker found it in 1893 and decided to take it to Germany, leaving a
wooden replica on the rocky outcrop to mark the spot.

Little more than a hundred and sixty kilometres south of Cape
Cross lies the holiday town of Swakopmund, the place Cão may have
been referring to when he mentioned Baie de Verde in his journals.
The town owes its existence to the importance of seafaring and has
built a tourist industry out of the wrecks that litter the Skeleton
Coast to the north. For many years, Swakopmund served as the primary port in German South West Africa. The Germans did have a
port at Lüderitzbucht, but it was inconvenient and remote and so,
in 1892, they chose an inlet at a place the Nama call Tsoaxaub-ams.
In Khoekhoegowab, *Tsoa* means "anus," while *xaub* refers to the excre-
ment that emerges from it. The suffix, *-ams* simply means "place of."
This is, quite literally, the arse-end of the world, where the desert
deposits copious amounts of brown sludge from the hinterland into
the Atlantic Ocean when the river floods. In the mouths of the settlers,
however, Tsoaxaub corrupted into Swakopmund, the Mouth of the
Swakop River.

We find a place to stay at the Alte Brücke, a self-catering establishment just back from the beachfront. It is pure indulgence after a
week of winter camping in the desert and several hundred kilometres
of dirt roads. We have dinner at a restaurant on the beachfront. The
entire room is flooded with light from a sunset over the Atlantic.

"I haven't seen any signs in town that show where the concentration camp was," Sinead remarks. "Is it like Shark Island, where all signs of the camp have gone?"

"Pretty much. No one knows exactly where the camp was. Pictures of the prisoners off-loading cargo in the surf suggest it was along the beach somewhere."

"Aren't there any buildings?"

"None that we know about. There is the *kaserne* on the beachfront where the soldiers stayed while they oversaw the building of the railroad to Windhoek. The railroad was built by prisoners from the Swakopmund camp. Maybe the camp was nearby. We also know from missionaries' accounts that most of the structures were built from corrugated iron, and that the prisoners slept in canvas tents — if they had any protection from the elements at all. The desert has claimed what people didn't steal after the war. But they do think they may have discovered some of the prisoners' graves," I note in reference to a recent newspaper article that mentions the discovery of some seven hundred unmarked Ovaherero graves.

"Why are you talking about skulls and graves on such a beautiful Namib evening?" our waitress asks as she puts a glass of wine down beside me.

"I'm trying to find out more about what happened to the bodies of those who died in the concentration camp."

The beads at the end of her extensions click as she shakes her head vehemently. "No, not here. No graves here in Swakopmund. There was a camp at Walvis, I think, but no, no graves here."

The glorious sunset over the Atlantic and the glass of fine South African wine allows me to forget my quest for the graves temporarily and enjoy a dessert of caramelized fruit in a sherry reduction sauce. We leave the restaurant shortly after seven. Sinead flops into bed as soon as we get back to our room. I settle in with the remainder of the port I bought from Crispin Clay in Lüderitz and catch up on my diary and my notes and do some research to find the graves.

Outside, the wind has picked up and bits of sea spray cover the windows of our rooms. If I listen carefully, I can hear the waves pounding into the sand on the beach. I pour myself another glass of port and surf the Internet. The Swakopmund Memorial Park Cemetery, where the unmarked graves lie, is just up the road from the Alte Brücke. The community has removed the divisions between the old European and Native sections and has built a new wall that includes the unmarked graves. The focal point in the new cemetery is the meditation centre: besides an interfaith cross, there is a heritage circle with a monument of stacked cattle horns that mark a traditional gravesite and an ombindi where people can pay their respects to the ancestral spirits who reside here.

I find several photos of the concentration camp at Swakopmund online. There are tantalizing clues to its location, like the missionary Dr. Heinrich Vedder's comment that those prisoners "who did not die in Swakopmund, were brought to Shark Island in Lüderitzbucht, where it was even colder than on the beach in Swakopmund." But no answers. It strikes me that the location of the Alte Brücke — right on the beach just north of the Swakop River, close to the cemetery with unmarked mass graves, the kaserne and the jetty — could have been a likely spot for a camp. Have we chosen to sleep on the whispers of the dead once more? But it is the text that accompanies one of the photos that haunts me through the night: in the photo, Schutztruppe are carefully placing skulls into a shipping crate. The women, the caption notes, were made to scrape the flesh off the skulls before they were packed. As I lie in bed, I hear the echoes of their cries drifting in from the beach: "*Ombepera i koza . . . Ombepera i koza.*" The cold is killing me.

◆　◆　◆

A fitful wind tries to push us back into the room in the morning. Despite the miserable weather, we have decided to go sandboarding. I believe quite strongly that humans were not meant to strap things

to their feet and careen down a hill, but Sinead has convinced me to
at least try. Our guide, Bambo, and his sidekick pick us up at the Alte
Brücke and take us to a set of dunes somewhere on the road toward
Walvis Bay. Daniel, Bambo's nephew, is a strapping sixteen-year-old
who is helping out during the school holidays. He and Bambo are
careful to lead us through the basics of sandboarding and take us
down a few gentle slopes until we get the hang of it. Canadians,
Daniel says, make excellent sandboarders and it is true — Sinead, who
has grown up in Canada, makes the transition from snow to sand
without much effort. Between my successive face plants, I learn from
Daniel that he intends on being a rap artist or a comedian.

"I listen to a lot of American rap," he says, and breaks into some
improvised beatboxing. He raps in a mixture of Damara and English
while I strap a board to my feet. We've progressed to the real dunes and
it's an exhilarating ride down. The sand is more forgiving and stable
than snow, and I find that I am able to get myself downhill with relative
ease. At the bottom, I wait for the others to finish their runs before
heading back up the hill. There are no chairlifts or T-bars in the Namib
and the hardest part is slipping your way up the hill. On the way up,
Daniel explains that he listens to American rap because he finds the
local artists false — they pretend to have bling when they don't. He's
seen them and he knows some of them. They are poor like him.

"How can they sing about wealth in a country where the average
person does not have it?" he demands. "I cannot stand their lies! That
is why I listen to American rap — they're more genuine."

Bambo and Daniel provide a lunch of sandwiches and beer on the
beach. I use some of the beer to wash the grit of the dunes from my
teeth. We don't stay long, for the mist that clung to the sand dunes
all morning has thickened and feels more like a persistent rain.
Sinead and I clean up at the hotel before visiting the museum at the
mole. Sinead stares longingly at the ocean while I marvel silently at
this linguistic remnant that has filtered through the medieval French
and German into colonial Africa. One of the earliest known moles in

Africa is the breakwater built in Algiers by the Turkish pirate Hizir in 1516 to protect his stronghold. More than a century later, when the British gained control of Tangier through the marriage of Catherine of Braganza to Charles II in 1662, they immediately set about building a mole to protect them from the pirates. When Lord Dartmouth, with the assistance of none other than Samuel Pepys, finally abandoned the colony in 1684, the still unfinished mole became a hindrance to their retreat. It took several months to destroy it while the Moors banged at the city gates.

After the British retreat from Tangier, one hears little about moles along the African coast. Until one reaches Swakopmund, that is, where a remnant of early modern seafaring terminology survives to this day. The entrance to the museum at the mole contains a small bookshop. There are a handful of English titles amidst the shelves of German books: Heinrich Vedder's *Das Alte Südwestafrika* and a litany of titles dedicated to the Reich's medals and troops' accounts of the war. I pause for a moment at Oupa Vedder's book. A water-damaged copy of the English translation, *South West Africa in Early Times*, remains in our family. Oupa Vedder's first posting as a missionary was at Swakopmund in 1905, where he tended to the prisoners of war. He eventually settled in Okahandja, where he taught at the Augustineum until his retirement.

Colonial bric-a-brac is bookended by natural history displays on the lichens of the Namib and an assortment of stuffed animals. In between, there's a parade of medals and stories about Swakopmund. Upstairs, a series of dioramas from the 1950s take you through the anthropological and archaeological history of Namibia. Not a word about the political struggle for independence, nor about the black people of Swakopmund, nor about the concentration camp. A single panel on the Nama uprisings focuses almost exclusively on the ethnographic images of the kapteins. The wind along the mole plucks the fronds of a palm tree in despair — Ombepera i koza.

I stop. In the display case in front of me lies a rusted piece of metal, blackened by silt and rust. Among the Portuguese inventions during the Age of Discovery was a new type of sword, the carrack black sword. The long, tapered blade of the traditional battle sword was perfect for stabbing through a knight's armour on land where there was enough open space to wield a long sword, but at sea, the long blade easily got caught in the rigging during boarding. Caravels and their successors, the carracks, necessitated close combat, a task for which the long battle sword was ill suited. Gradually, the blade grew shorter and broader and the cross guard curved forward, ending in two rounded terminal plates that were sharpened and used as extra blades in close combat. It was these round terminal plates that gave the carrack black sword its nickname, *colhona* — big balls. The blade was painted black to prevent it from rusting at sea and also to mask the gleam of the blade in the sun. Between the time of the long sword and that of the colhona came several bastard swords that straddled the past and the future. The development of the carrack black sword, like that of the ship it was named after, was tied closely to Portuguese navigation down the coast of Africa. When Diogo Cão became the first European to sail across the equator, he did so in a caravel; less than a decade later, when Vasco da Gama opened up a sea passage to India, he did so in a carrack, with a black sword at his side.

During a routine dredging of the bay at the mole, someone spotted the old piece of metal that turned out to be the unlikeliest of artifacts for this town: a bastard colhona. Its blade is fairly short and flat, yet even now it appears to be well edged with an acute point. The straight cross guard tapers back toward the hilt ever so slightly in the fashion of a battle sword.

Could Diogo Cão have landed here at Swakopmund before turning his ship around? It is unlikely that he would have found people at Cape Cross, but Swakopmund was a known trading destination for local peoples in pre-colonial times. If indeed Cão or Dias had taken people from the Namib, this would have been the place to find them. The sword provides no answers. Sinead makes her way over to me. "I saw a craft market near the mole last night. Let's go there."

The craft market is right behind the kaserne. In the entrance hall of the kaserne, a poem written by one of the soldiers praises the work of the engineering corps in building the jetty. Beside it, a second plaque lists the names of the eight German soldiers who died. I nudge Sinead. "Let's come back here. I need to go to the library before it closes."

Sinead decides to stay in the car and read while I run into the library. The receptionist directs me to the librarian at the back of the room. I explain to her that I am looking for information on mass graves in Swakopmund. She gives me a pamphlet on the Swakopmund Memorial Park Cemetery. I admire the spirit of reconciliation behind the project and the thoughtfulness with which it has been executed, but it does not provide me with the answers I seek.

"What about the mass graves in the desert?" I ask. I show her the newspaper clipping, which tells of the mass grave found in the desert just across the road from Nonidas — right along the railway line. "Did those graves have anything to do with the concentration camp?"

The librarian denies categorically that there are any mass graves. "Not even in the new area beyond the Native cemetery?" I ask.

"No," she replies, "those are all individual graves of blacks who died here. They didn't know their names, so they just buried them. That's often the case with black people, you know. We don't know their names. That's why the graves are unmarked."

"Can you tell me where the concentration camp was?" I ask as I begin to pack away my notebook.

"There was no concentration camp in Swakopmund," is her swift response.

"But I have seen the photographs of forced labour . . ."

"There were hired labourers brought here during the war of 1904, but no camp."

"Where were these labourers housed?" I try again.

"I don't know where the labourers were housed. Probably in the township."

"These labourers — they were prisoners of war, weren't they?"

"Yes, some of them."

"So they were forced to come here. And the German chancellor asked for concentration camps to be set up in Namibia for the POWs?"

"There were no camps like that here."

It is closing time and I sense that I am going to get little information out of the librarian. As I turn to leave, I ask, "What would you call a place where they keep prisoners of war against their will and force them into labour?"

"Not a concentration camp. Not quite that," she says and her eyes shift along the carpet.

As I walk back to the car, the wind blows a fragment from J. M. Coetzee's *Disgrace* into my head: "Not rape," David Lurie says of his unwanted sexual encounter with one of his students, Melanie Isaacs, "not quite that . . ."

9

Sinead and I both hurt from the morning's sandboarding. We return to our hotel and collapse for the evening. We wake early and head to Walvis Bay to go kayaking. It is Sinead's choice. I would have liked to visit Cape Cross, but it is closed to visitors during the annual seal cull. Namibia is one of three countries, including Canada, that harvests seals commercially. The hunters try to waste as little as possible. The oil is used in cosmetics; the carcasses are ground up and used in pet food; the skin is used in the clothing industry. Even the testicles are sent to Asia as an aphrodisiac. I grew up in a small rural town where people regularly butchered their own meat and where, on slaughtering days, my mother always cautioned: "'n Mens mors nie met vleis nie. As jy klaar is, gooi jy net die skree van die dier weg." One should not waste meat. When you are done, you discard only the scream of the beast. And that dictum holds true for the sealing industry too it seems. All that remains at the end of the day is the bleat of a seal pup as the club descends.

Where Swakopmund has the lazy, windswept feel of a resort town to it, Walvis Bay presents itself with well-groomed military precision. At the Dias Circle, a road sign directs visitors to Dune 7, the most notorious of all the Namib dunes. It was the scourge of every troop stationed at the local Rooikop military base in Walvis Bay. If there was anything that could possibly make a call-up to Rooikop worse than the isolated location in the middle of the desert, it was the horror stories about running up Dune 7.

This morning, however, we are headed in the opposite direction, toward the beachfront and the sheltered bay where Bartolomeu Dias is alleged to have anchored his ships in 1486. Jean Meintjies, who runs an ecotourism company, meets us in the parking lot of a local restaurant. The importance of ecotourism here in Walvis Bay is partly due to the fact that the lagoon, mud flats and shoreline around the town were recognized as a Ramsar Wetlands of International Importance in 1995 — although the struggle to have the Namibian government declare it a protected site continues. Even the salt works we drive past on our way to Pelican Point have, in an ironic twist of events, come to play a central part in protecting the birdlife.

The salt pans glimmer pink with algae, as do the piles of raw salt beside them. The salt pans are a mixed blessing. They provide much-needed work in this desert town, but they have also eaten away at the intertidal habitat that supports the birdlife of the area. But not everything can be blamed on development. The Namib winds deposit large amounts of sand on the mud flats and the natural currents off Pelican Point push sand from the ocean back onto land. The lagoon is a dynamic organism that grows and shifts with the seasons. This has been a particularly wet season and the high rainfall inland has flooded the Kuiseb River basin and the water has flowed strongly to the coast. Normally, the river barges its way across the mud flats, pushing the accumulated silt back toward Pelican Point and the open sea, emptying itself into the ocean after this Herculean effort. Things have been different recently. During the dry years that have preceded this year of plenty, the lagoon silted over more than usual and the barrier has proven too much for the Kuiseb River. Rather than push out into the ocean, the water has flooded the shallow pans along the road to Pelican Point, covering the avocets' breeding ground. In its beneficence, the salt mining company has created new shallow pans to provide a haven for the birds.

"It is such environmental concern that makes the relationship between industry and the environment so important and so special in Walvis Bay," Jean says as we drive through the swath of cubed salt pans and trucks carting the profits away from the community.

There are birds everywhere. We drive through clouds of terns, avocets and plovers. Some pelicans huddle at the edge of the pan and a stray flock of flamingos loll overhead. These are true early birds, leading the spring migration from Etosha Pan back to Walvis Bay for the breeding season. Their plumage is a gentle pink after the winter up north, but over the course of the summer, the colour will deepen as a result of the spirulina and the shrimp they eat here in Walvis Bay. The lighthouse at Pelican Point guards the lagoon and the sandbank that stretches out into the ocean. Jean tells us how the derelict caretaker's building is being restored and that the owners plan on turning it into an eco-friendly guesthouse. One of the local business stipulations is that it has to be completely green: everything that comes in has to go out again.

Like silt in the lagoon.

We off-load the kayaks and set out toward the point, where the dolphins play. A Heaviside's dolphin breaches right beside our kayak and then disappears. We are moving too slowly for it to have any fun.

"Paddle harder," Sinead says, "make it come back." She stops paddling and takes the camera from its waterproof bag while I try to entice the dolphin back. It is chilly and misty, but I can feel the sweat building up under my waterproof jacket. The dolphin returns and races along beside us. After a while, it tires of this game and disappears. We slow down so that I can catch my breath. A petrel, a beautiful black buttonhole of inquisitiveness, swoops in close for a good look at us. Soon, it too loses interest and we turn back to the lagoon and paddle leisurely toward the small group of seals that are lazing in the shallow water just offshore. On the beach, the main herd coughs and grunts its disaffection. The members of the reconnaissance team prod at our oars tentatively, but after a while they ease to our presence and begin to play exuberantly. The heightened activity in the water stirs the mob on the shore. It's a muddle of barks and flippers as they waddle into the water. Soon, they too nip at the oars and tug at the water bottles we hold out for them. One of them even sniffs at Sinead's fingers before diving and resurfacing on the other side of the kayak with a catch-me-if-you-can grin on its face. A little way off, the ferries chug in and the hordes of tourists snap pictures of the playing critters.

Sinead laps up every moment with the seals and it is only after Jean's third call that she and I reluctantly beach our kayak. The thrill of surfing alongside the Heaviside's dolphins is forgotten as Sinead babbles about the seals. She's ready to start the trip all over again.

"Has this colony been here forever?" she asks Jean as she helps us lift the canoe onto the trailer.

"There have always been seals around here. They'd come and visit and then disappear. This permanent colony is fairly new — twenty years or so. We think it's an offshoot of the main colony up at Cape Cross," Jean says as she ties the kayak onto the rails.

"Even the seals at Cape Cross seem relatively recent," I note. "In the contemporary accounts of Diogo Cão's voyages, the only mention of seals is in the name Cabo do Lobo, which is the original name given to Cabo de Santa Maria in Angola."

"Weird. Isn't the colony at Cape Cross one of the biggest in the world?"

"Apparently, but seals really don't feature much at all in seafarers' accounts." I pause, trying to recall what I'd read in the booklet on Cape Cross the night before. "Except for entries in the Dutch East India Company logs from 1610 onward about seal hunts off the Cape of Good Hope. The seals at Cape Cross are first mentioned in 1894, when Walter Matthews, an employee of the *Deutsche Kolonialgesellschaft* mentioned their presence on an exploratory trip. A year later, the seal hunting began."

"Still weird," says Sinead, "but Namibians knew about them. I've seen rock drawings of them."

Robard, our Norwegian kayaking companion, overhears our discussion and over lunch he asks Jean about the seal cull. Her response is rehearsed: "The seals decimate fish stocks and have a negative impact on the fishing industry. They have to be culled."

"But evidence suggests that the seals don't eat the fish that the commercial fishermen hunt," Robard counters.

"Clubbing becomes merciful when you've seen starving pups," Jean says after a short pause. "It's no worse than what happens in nature itself — the moms abort babies when they sense tough times ahead. Human intervention in the oceans has made culling a necessity. It is a cruel kindness. The government has invited opponents of the culls to offer alternatives for controlling the population, but they have not done so. And so, while we wait for them, this is the most humane option."

Robard backs off and we drive back to Walvis Bay in silence. One of the clubbers quoted in the ombudsman's report on clubbing commented that clubbing seals "was not nice, it bothered me a bit, but after the fourth harvest it was like killing a sheep." I begin to wonder whether the same impulses in the brain are triggered by the clubbing of a seal and the clubbing of a human being before you roll the body into a mass grave. At what point does this slaughter become as normal as "killing a sheep"?

It is mid-afternoon by the time Sinead and I leave for Okahandja to attend the Herero Day parade. For a brief moment as we round Dias Circle on the way out of town, I consider visiting Dune 7, even climbing it. I let go of the idea almost immediately. After days of searching for remnants of graves and concentration camps, I am exhausted by the detritus of war.

10

In Okahandja, we manage to book a bungalow at the King's Highway Rest Camp for one night, and secure a camping spot for the next. Everything is quiet and I begin to wonder whether we've missed the festivities. It is a long weekend and the entire town has ground to a halt. Nothing stirs. The woman at reception informs me that she "hardly knows what happens up in the location. We're on the edge of town here, you know, and events pass us by." Sinead and I head into town to investigate.

"Isn't this parade meant to be a cultural highlight of the year?" Sinead asks me. "Why does no one seem to know what is happening in their own town?" I wonder that too.

For the most part, public holidays and festivals have lost their lustre for me. It has something to do with the clogged airways and the barrage of advertising jingles and the radio talk-show hosts asking listeners to tell them what makes the day special. By the time the hallowed day arrives, everyone is too exhausted from the hype to appreciate its significance. Thankfully, shops in Namibia close on public holidays and we have been spared the incessant radio jingles. But while North American holidays have come to reflect consumerism at its worst,

African holidays tend to reflect the sharp political divides that continue to haunt the continent decades after independence.

New holidays were invented and reinvented as fast as governments fell. In South Africa and its mandated colony, South West Africa, Union Day gave way to Republic Day when a defiant South Africa seceded from the Commonwealth in 1961 and declared to the world that they were officially implementing a policy of apartheid. In 1995, a year after the first democratic elections, Republic Day died an ignominious death, along with the policies it had spawned. Some holidays, however, have endured in a changed form. Dingaan's Day morphed into the Day of Reconciliation, but the original intent of the day, which was to recognize a Boer victory over the Zulu Army, remains in the background. Every year, neo-conservative Afrikaner groups gather to lament the perceived loss of their cultural heritage, while the rest of the country stays at home in an effort to maintain the peace. Yet, here we are, driving to Okahandja to see a parade on Heroes' Day.

I pull into an open parking space and Sinead continues her thought, "Like the woman at the rest camp. The Herero festival doesn't seem to matter to her." A woman wearing a gorgeous deep plum *otjikaeva* and matching dress gets out of the car behind us and I ask her about the festival. She calls her husband over.

"It's on Sunday," he confirms. "Preparations will start tomorrow and the parade itself is on Sunday. Events will happen in the township, Nau-Aib."

"Ah, in the plain by the monuments." He seems surprised that I've seen the monuments. The graves, he assures me, are in Okahandja, not outside of town as some rumours have it. Where exactly, he doesn't know, but they're definitely in town. He's never seen them himself. He laughs. "I only come for the party, not the parade. But my uncle's seen them. They're that way." He points east.

We follow his vague directions and just before we leave town, we find Heroes Avenue. A little way up, there is a sign in black and red on white that simply says

HERERO

GRAFTE

GRAVES

GRÄBE.

Afrikaans, English and German. The arrow below the letters points away from the road so deciding which way to go is pure guesswork.

We decide to take the two-rut track that leads down a narrow lane of palm trees. At the end of this lane, a nondescript wall and a slab of concrete appear in the late afternoon sun. It's the fencing that gives it away more than anything else — I recognize it from photos. A headstone contains the names of three chiefs of the Ohorongo clan who lie in this small cemetery: Tjamuaha; his son, kaMaharero; and *his* son, Samuel Maharero. Samuel was the chief who led his people into exile in the dark days of the genocide. His grandfather, Tjamuaha, was an associate of the Nama chief, Jonker Afrikaner, and was required to pay tribute to him. It was a strained relationship, with Tjamuaha constantly attempting to break out from this subservience and with Jonker Afrikaner asserting his dominance by raiding Ovaherero cattle. Tjamuaha eventually settled in Okahandja in 1846, leaving his son, kaMaharero, with his people at Otjimbingwe. In 1852, kaMaharero joined his father in Okahandja. It was kaMaharero who became chief after his father's death and who freed the Ovaherero from the yoke of Jonker Afrikaner in the 1860s.

There is nothing here at the cemetery that illuminates this complex and heroic history in the struggles of the Ovaherero. Only the stark traces of a straw broom and a carelessly hung sign suggest that this is a place of historic significance. Just like at Shark Island, the memory of the genocide has been obliterated.

The next morning, I walk over to the fence that surrounds our campsite and look out toward the bridge over the Okahandja River. A long-buried memory surfaces of me playing in the sand in the riverbed. Later, when we're visiting my mother before returning to

Canada, Ma confirms that this is true: "On weekends, we would go down to the river and you and your sister would play in the sand in the shade of the bridge while Dad and the older boys went on hikes up and down the river."

It's a quiet Saturday morning and I walk back to the picnic table outside our bungalow. There's a slight chill to the air and I feel the residual coolness of the night in the concrete seat as I drink my coffee. A man, resplendent in his colonial German regalia emerges from the bungalow next to ours. We wave a greeting to each other and he begins to pace up and down the area in front of his bungalow, holding his hands behind his back. I walk over to introduce myself.

The man removes one hand from behind his back and gestures toward the gate. "Walk with me," Welcome Kalondungwe says. He is delighted to hear that we have come to see the parade and smiles when he hears that I have brought my daughter all the way from Canada for this.

"I wish more people would take the trouble to learn their heritage. It is important that we remember. I am a chief from the Bulhoek area, and I am one of the organizers of tomorrow's festivities. I am meeting another elder so that we can go and prepare for tomorrow. This," he points to his uniform, "is an appropriation of the German Schutztruppe uniform. In pre-war times, the Herero working among the Germans began to mimic their drilling and marching. They took the uniforms that the Germans threw out and wore them. The Germans called it *kinderspele*, child's play, but the discipline stood the Herero in good stead when the war broke out in 1904." Welcome speaks with great pride of his ancestors' achievements. In an act of defiance, he tells me, the Ovaherero adopted the uniform and after the war continued to use it as a statement of resistance and of commemoration. "In those days, the Herero took whatever the German soldiers threw away. That is why it's a mix of things and why none of us look the same. We reflect the people who came here and ourselves. We have made it our own. It is ours now."

We are nearing the gate, but I take a closer look at his uniform. The cut of his jacket is clearly South African, but the medals are more interesting than he cares to acknowledge. One of the medals on Welcome Kalondungwe's chest is a German South West Africa Campaign Medal with a clasp indicating Omaheke; another is a World War II Service Medal like the one my father wore to Remembrance Day parades. The last medal is a South African Police Service badge.

Seeing the medals on Welcome Kalondungwe's chest stirs up a memory and his voices fades into the background as we continue our walk toward the gate. After class one afternoon in 1990 I walked from the old campus in Storchstrasse, down John Meinert Street toward the city centre. The main street, then still called Kaiserstrasse, was crowded with UNTAG troops. The United Nations Transition Assistance Group had arrived in Namibia in 1989 to monitor the transition to independence and to facilitate the withdrawal and demobilization of South African troops from the country. By early February 1990, their mission was scaling down and it was not uncommon to see soldiers spending a final few days in Windhoek before flying home. A medley of languages and laughter from the cafés and bars drifted into the streets. The presence of soldiers also brought with it a slightly more sombre side. Demobilized South West Africa Territorial Force (SWATF) troops and other troepies who had fought on the South African side during the war were eager to rid themselves of any traces of their involvement in the now-unfashionable South African Defence Force. Pawnshops and memorabilia stores were crammed with SADF uniforms and medals.

In one of the many side-alleys along Independence Avenue, a small pawnshop displayed its haul of medals in the window. It was hard to distinguish one medal from another, but I felt a sense of pride in knowing that I did not own any of them. It was the object next to SADF medals, set off ever so slightly from the rest, that held my attention. The swastika at the end of the ribbon was unmistakable. And beside it, a red, white and black bumper sticker bearing the flag of the *Reichskolonialbund* and the acronym, DSWA — Deutsch Südwest Afrika. It was a grim reminder that although Independence Day was only two months away, the past was still very much with us. A young Finnish soldier brushed past me and picked up the swastika and a bumper sticker and walked over to the counter to pay. I remained standing outside, riveted by the interaction that was taking place beyond that doorstep.

By the time we reach the gate, Welcome has moved on from military regalia and is talking about the women's signature Victorian dresses. "The otjikaeva, the headdress the older women wear, is an adaptation of the traditional leather *ekori*. When the missionaries came, the women gave up their traditional clothing and began to wear the long dresses. But they kept some of their traditions. They still wore the otjikaeva headscarf, but now it was made from cloth rather than leather. The two points represent the cattle horn, which are central to our culture."

"Welcome home, brother," he says as he leaves. "Welcome home."

I return to my seat under the camelthorn. A groundscraper thrush sits tantalizingly out of reach of my camera lens. Finally, it comes in close and sits within reasonable photographic distance of my perch. But even then, it is skittish, allowing me access under duress. It sits still for the briefest of moments before taking off again. Photography, like travel, relies on patience and serendipity. My patience pays off and I move on to lure the very shy crimson-breasted shrike from its perch at the top of the tree. It flits down for a split-second investigation and then hides itself among the tallest branches again.

A short while later, I walk over to the office to find out where our campsite will be for the evening. An old man walks in with me. The woman at the counter fawns over him. After he leaves, she explains. He's a senior *omuhona* and she's working with him and Welcome Kalondungwe to deliver charity parcels from children in the Netherlands. "They've agreed to give me a small slot during the festivities to hand over the packages," she beams. "It's all part of the

Apostolic Faith Mission endeavour. I don't believe in the upfront approach some people take. I'm more of a friendship missionary. I really try to get to know the people as *people*. If they happen to come to God in the process, that's wonderful. It's all about friendship and understanding."

"But it's difficult terrain," she whispers as she leans over the counter. "These Hereros as still so stuck in their ways. You know, the ancestor worship and stuff. The ancestor thing is so important to them. I can't understand it," she concludes, shaking her head. "I just can't understand it."

◆ ◆ ◆

While Welcome Kalondungwe and his cohorts prepare for the parade, Sinead and I follow the GPS to Moordkoppie. Listed high among the things to see and do in Okahandja, Moordkoppie lies by the roadside, caged in by a dilapidated fence. My first response is that it is just another hill in another town. There are no markers or road signs to indicate its location and if it were not for the GPS being uncharacteristically co-operative and accurate, we would easily have missed it.

The name is self-explanatory: Murder Hill. But whose? And when? The guide books provide little information. Neither do the people in Okahandja. I ask around town at the post office and in the streets, but no one can tell me. In the end, it takes a journey through several books to find the answer: Kahitjene, a chief at Okahandja invited the Rhenish missionaries to settle near his homestead in an effort to gain access to European guns and the economic benefit of increased contact with the traders who invariably followed the missionaries. The move angered Jonker Afrikaner, the Nama leader who controlled much of the region to the south and in September 1850, he attacked Kahitjene's homestead. At the Battle of Moordkoppie, Kahitjene lost about seven hundred soldiers and his homestead and the mission were both destroyed.

On the way back from Moordkoppie, we drive past the military museum we had noticed on our previous tour of Okahandja. It's an impressive building with a bold facade and a scattering of old vehicles parked inside the gates. Two guards sit outside, looking bored. As we turn into the driveway, the guards shoo us away. I think it's because it's a Saturday afternoon, but one of the guards walks over to me. "The museum will only open next year," he says. As we drive away, I make a mental note to come back and see what a post-independence military museum will look like.

Back at the camp, Sinead decides to attempt making pancakes. The pan is buckled and it produces scrambled crumpets rather than pancakes, but the variety is good, for our meals have been dull and repetitive. After dinner, I pour myself the last of the port from Lüderitz and we settle in with our books and read by the firelight. The camp security guard greets me loudly as he passes on his first round through the camp. He disappears, but I know I will see him again. On the second round, he stops and chats for a while. "No," he says, "I won't make any of the events tomorrow. I get off at six in the morning, so I'll sleep until two and then spend some time with the family before coming to work again." I thank him for looking after the place and politely send him on his way. He assures me that he has everything under control.

Later in the evening he comes around again. He walks straight over to me, brandishing a 12-gauge shotgun. He digs into his pockets and hauls out a stash of cartridges. I'm not sure whether this gesture is meant to put me at ease, or to intimidate me. He tries to load the cartridges into the barrel, but can't quite figure out how to get the cartridge in. For a moment, I consider showing him how to do it: You have to break the neck of the gun all the way until the cartridge clamp releases. I hesitate. Faced with the choice of an armed guard who doesn't have a clue how to handle his weapon, or one who does and brandishes it about to impress his guests, I find myself in a quandary. In the end, he stuffs the cartridges back into his pockets and stalks off. I suspect his proselytizing with a gun is no worse than the camp manager's own missionary endeavours. As he leaves, I head for bed. I fear for what I might be shown on his next round.

◆　◆　◆

Sinead and I amble our way through breakfast, reading and eating until just before nine, when we head out. We arrive at Nau-Aib just as the parade is about to start. The marshals on their horses display an arrogant authority that becomes equestrians. There is something from the Roman Republic about their actions — the *equestres* milling about the riff-raff, giving orders. They bark rudely at anyone who disobeys or strays from the pack and charge bystanders who won't move. There is no request: here you watch your step. They're bullying the troops into submission. Gradually order descends on the crowd and on the marchers. Platoons of youngsters wearing cardboard box caps drill imperfectly. They're a flurry of arms and legs whirling in total disregard for the whistle that attempts to set pace. Older, more practiced units make for more polished drills. The platoon leaders punctuate every step with a blast on their whistles. In the milling of horses and young recruits and military bands, the whistles become a sideshow and the marchers follow their own lead. A group of young marchers wearing kilts seem incongruous until you realize that this is an adaptation for a platoon of young girls. The chaos moves slowly and deliberately. This is serious business: Every town has its own commando unit and standards. Several marching bands offer accompaniment to different sections of the parade. It's a glorious cacophony that moves out of Nau-Aib toward the centre of town. As we go, the competition between platoons increases. A leader whispers something to a leader in front of him, then returns. He orders his troops to sharpen up and they hastily execute a series of about-turns before picking up the pace again.

Here and there, the call-and-response of freedom songs breaks out and the entire procession, including bystanders, begins to toyi-

toyi. Feet hit the ground in unison and the trademark "Hayi! Hayi!" of the dancers punctuates each step. They start singing an old protest song. Memories of anti-apartheid demonstrations flood into my head and, despite the heat, I notice goosebumps on my arm. But this is no protest and some of the women begin to ululate to express their joy.

Behind the platoons, there is a phalanx of women. Their dresses reflect their clan affiliation: red for the women from the areas surrounding Okahandja and Okakarara, green for the Ovambanderu and white for the women from Omaruru. The women have an air of sobriety about them that is completely absent from the men up ahead. Suddenly, one of the women breaks into song. Again and again, she repeats the same phrase, inviting the others to respond. Their hands rise to shoulder height in imitation of an ox horn and they clap to the rhythm of her words, repeating the refrain on her signal. It happens so effortlessly, so informally, that I almost don't recognize it for what it is: an *outjina*, a women's praise song. I do not understand the words, but I recognize the structure and the visual clues. As the praise singer nears the end of her song, she turns to the women behind her and fires off a closing salvo. This is how the women encouraged the soldiers during the Battle of Ohamakari, praising from the back of the battlefield, calling in bold defiance, "*Ehi Rovaherero!*" This land belongs to the Ovaherero!

Sinead and I fall in behind the women, darting forward every now and then to get to the front of the procession. I am intoxicated by the parade. The bands are playing and the marchers show off their drilling skills. The marshals on horseback move back and forth among the crowd, pushing everyone toward their destination. At times, the entire procession stops for no discernable reason. Everyone takes it in their stride. At the Fritz Gaerdes Public Library, the procession turns and crosses Martin Neib Avenue. At the bottom end of Martin Neib, they turn to their left and head down the narrow lane to the graves Sinead and I had struggled to find. This crowd knows instinctively where to go. Once there, they will settle in for a day's worth of commemorative speeches. One by one, people will pass by the graves and pay their respects to the departed.

Most of the events will happen in Otjiherero and I know that what lies ahead is the most significant part of the parade, but I also know that it will be hours of torture for a teenager. Already, Sinead is looking at her watch and calculating how long it will take to get to our next destination. She has us on a tight schedule, for she wants to go to Etosha National Park. We hang back and watch the marchers make their way to Maharero's grave, where the festivities will come to an end. As the parade disappears from sight, we return to the order of our bakkie and its cantankerous GPS.

11

Somewhere near the middle of one of my elementary school projects, a small slate brooch creates a lump. No matter how hard a person tries, the project always opens on that page. The dark grey of the slate draws the eye away from the writing, but not enough to distract you from it entirely: the deep blue ink lines reflect a child's genuine attempt at neatness, although the odd yellowed blotch reveals where the hand slipped and a correction was made. Over time, the spots where a Q-tip soaked in bleach was daubed on a letter to hide the wayward strokes of a fountain pen have yellowed faster than the surrounding sheets of paper, revealing traces of errant handiwork. The image on the slate, however, has remained as vivid as ever. On its greenish-grey surface, a tiny white figure dances across the stone, poised in mid-step, reaching, forever reaching beyond the confines of the page that holds it captive. The brooch itself is nothing special but the image on it lives. The figure that is forever in motion is a tiny replica of Reinhard Maack's watercolour of the White Lady of the Brandberg.

By the time we leave Okahandja and head for the Brandberg, the sun is already brutal. As we approach Uis, the fine white dust from the road and the tin-mine tailings has settled on just about everything.

We stop in Uis to refuel and to book a camping spot for the evening before continuing on our way. Our GPS doesn't know where we are and we abandon it. We have become used to its vagaries and now we travel as whim, or the map, takes us. The map is not very helpful either, but we know we're in the right area, so we decide to take a joyride toward Khorixas. At a small roadside stall, a young girl dances us to a standstill. Sinead runs over to their stall to look at the dolls on display while I try to get some directions from them. The small crowd of girls clusters around our bakkie and they become increasingly more animated as they provide information. It is impossible to take much from their spirited discussion and while they take to arguing the correctness of their instructions in Damara, Sinead finds a doll she likes and returns to the car. She pays one of the girls and we head back in the direction we came from.

As we finally turn onto the road that will lead us to Brandberg, the GPS splutters and announces that the visit to the White Lady involves a strenuous forty-five-minute hike. "Not recommended," it declares in its overstuffed American drawl. We opt to ignore the advice from the gadget and forge ahead. We park the bakkie in the parking space delineated by — what else — stones. This, after all, is Uis. And Uis, we have been told repeatedly, means "stone."

You could say that the White Lady descended upon Reinhard Maack, the first European to lay eyes on her, as he emerged from his dreams in a rock shelter in the Brandberg Mountains. Maack and his cartographer friend, Alfred Hoffmann, arrived in the Tsisab Valley after dark one night in 1917 and decided to spend the night under a sheltered overhang. Looking over them during their sleep was a group of shamans clinging to the rock surface as they had done for thousands of years. When Maack awoke, the White Lady smiled down at him. He drew his sketch pad closer and began to draw. Later, he created a watercolour of the rock image based on his initial sketch and the accompanying notes. Maack's sketches lay in the museum in Cape Town for twelve years until Abbé Henri Breuil found them.

It was Breuil who coined the misnomer White Lady, for the subject is neither white nor a lady, and history has proven his theory wrong many times over. But the name he gave the painting has stuck. And today, we have a date with this infamous Lady of the Brandberg.

At the conservancy office, we pay our dues and are assigned to a young guide, Michael. He bolts up the pathway that leads into the valley despite having done so at least six times today. As we walk along, Michael rattles off the scientific names of plants and shrubs. He's less sure when it comes to identifying the animals of the area and he confesses that he is still being trained and has just started taking the courses required for becoming a professional guide. Local plants are in the first unit and he is eager to display the knowledge he has gained. His enthusiasm, like that of the young girls at the roadside stall, is infectious. The colours of the veld and the diversity of the plant life are astonishing. There are hints of green everywhere. In the distance, the peaks of *Königstein*, the highest point in Namibia, are set off in the fiery glow that gives this place its name.

The view from the top of the Brandberg gives one the chills. On a clear day, the Atlantic Ocean shimmers in the distance to the west and the Namib stretches endlessly in all directions. In 1489, three years after Diogo Cão's voyage to Cape Cross, Martellus, the Italian mapmaker who accompanied him, marked a peak to the east of Cape Cross as Serra Parda, Black Mountain, suggesting that this is where Cão died. Later explorers identified the range as the Dourissa, a corruption of the local Damara name, Dâures, which means "burning mountain." Indeed, the Brandberg is visible from Durissa Bay, north of Cape Cross, yet it is hard to imagine a voyage inland from there. The Brandberg lies between the dry beds of the Ugab and Messum Rivers and the ninety-kilometre trek from the ocean would have been almost impossible for sailors who, by all accounts, were nearing the end of their rations.

The valley leading up to the Maack Shelter where the paintings are is an oven. The Tsisab River is a gentle stream that offers little relief from the heat at this time of year. I look back and see that Sinead is flagging, so I take photos to slow Michael's pace and give her time to catch up. My shirt clings to me and I watch in dismay as Michael hops from rock to rock, seemingly immune to the heat. Suddenly, we are at the Maack Shelter. I feel my heart pounding, and it is not as a result of the climb up to the cave. I have been here before as a child, I am told, but I have no recollection of it. All I have is the fading handwritten school project that provides a brief history of the White Lady and an additional sentence or two about the Brandberg. And a copy of a relief painted onto a slate brooch. "It's not much," Ma said just before I left for Windhoek, "the overhang is dark and everything is behind bars to prevent people from damaging it." At night, I had dreamt of seeing the White Lady break free from her imprisonment so she could wander the Tsisab Valley at will, and now I was about to behold her.

I fear disappointment more than anything, in the way that the *Mona Lisa* is a disappointment to those who are hurried past her in a tour group and are required to maintain the safe distance from the painting. The thought of staring at a distant, fading image of the White Lady fills me with dread.

We walk around the corner and the shaman appears in front of me in all his glory. He is covered in ceremonial ash from his transcendental journey to generations and places beyond his ken. I am a mere foot or two away from this sacred image and I am overwhelmed. Michael is talking in the background, but I barely notice. I am absorbed in the image sequence before me. Where to look first? The synapses have gone into overdrive and I take everything in, in slow motion. Transformations — half man, half beast — leap out of the ochre rock. The wildebeest stripes on the torsos resemble the streaking sweat of a shaman dancing his way into other worlds. He takes me with him. Sweat is transformative, a powerful muti and it runs freely down his arms and mine. He is half beast and half man, straddling worlds we only imagine. We are drawing the power of his universe into us and the sweat of the wildebeest is running down his arms. Dance beads and fly whisks sway through the air. The fire and white dust of this place, Uis, gathers around his legs and moves up his body, envelops him.

As we approach the overhang, the paintings in the Maack Shelter form a tableau that moves from the viewer's right to the left. On the right, a woman with shamanistic feathers on her upper arm leads the procession. She appears focused on what lies ahead, as a good leader should. Above the human figures, a herd of eland move with them. The White Lady follows toward the end of the procession, diminished by years of neglect. Indiscriminate visitors have poured water on the image in an effort to enhance the colours, but have succeeded only in washing the pigments from the rock. In the hundred years since Europeans came to this valley, the image has faded almost beyond visibility. It is the White Lady who garners the attention of the world, but that particular relief is not the focal point of the tableau. Above the White Lady, an antelope with the hind legs of a human hovers over the rest of the figures. In front of this, a ghostly figure looks back at the antelope, as if emerging from the body of the animal. It is such sequences that lend weight to the interpretation of these paintings as part of a transcendental experience.

The White Lady dances me into the overhang, and onto my back to capture the images that grace the roof of this place. I see the trans-forming shamans, each different, each a performer of magic rituals that captivate the observer. Together, we dance a dance of stone, becoming one with the surrounding hills. I am Peter, I am rock. Entranced. Slowly, I am transformed. Too soon, alas, too soon, the guide signals that we have to move on. Königstein looms up ahead of us, but I am soaring above that, in a trance of white engravings. Image upon image upon image flows through my head. The Damara call this place Dâures, after the geographical features, but the Ovaherero call it Omukuruvaro, the Place of the Gods, after their deity, Omukuru. I think they may be onto something, for this pile of stone, with its adorned overhangs and reed-embanked stream, verges on paradise.

We walk back at a more leisurely pace and I try to take in every step of this pathway. I want to remember it. I want to stay here and savour the route over and over again. This is the path that leads from paradise and I want to remain among these phantasmagorical images. As we walk down the valley in the late afternoon sun, I have some difficulty re-entering my own world. The streams and pools are a crucial part of the entire journey into the mountains: water and the scent of a million herbs fills the air. A grass snake darts into the bush to the right of us. A fleeting glimpse. Somehow, such lushness is fitting. All around us, patches of saltbush flex their succulent saline leaves in the breeze. This is the lifeblood for several herbivores that travel up this valley. There is grass aplenty for the wildebeest and eland that grace the walls of the shelters with their sweaty bodies. The gorge is a perfect natural press gang in which to corner herds of wildebeest. This is indeed a place of abundance and it seeps into your bones.

We reach the main office after closing time; they are waiting for us. The sun is fading and there will be no time to go and visit the rock shelters that lie obscured behind these buildings. I know what I will find there, for I have seen such shelters before, shortly before independence on the other side of the Brandberg: crumbling rings of rock, evidence of a firepit, shards of arrowheads left by hunters. And in front of the shelter, within range of the arrows, the eddies of an ancient riverbed, where the animals would have come to drink.

One of the older guides tears me back to the lengthening shadows of the present, "I want to go to Windhoek with you."

"Be careful what you wish for," I reply.

"See, you come here from Windhoek to see the White Lady. I want to go to Windhoek to see the city. I too want to see beyond my valley."

I find it strange that he should ask to leave the Brandberg when this place has transformed me, but I offer him a ride nonetheless. "I can't," he confesses, "I have to work."

On the way back to the main road, we pass a young family on their way home from their day's labours. The man is trying to tie their young child into his wife's abbavel. I stop. The mother looks at me gratefully. "Put my daughter in front with you; we'll hang onto the back," she says. I open the door of the canopy and the parents slide in, dangling their feet over the tailgate. The baby on Sinead's lap cries, but she rocks her gently and the little one falls asleep almost as soon as we start driving.

In the rear-view mirror, I watch the two young parents snuggle up to each other. She leans over tenderly and wipes the dust off his collar. He smiles bashfully. He rubs her neck, as if to rub the dust and the aches of the day out of her. Their hands meet and they lean their heads into each other. For them, the brief respite from walking and caring for a young child becomes an eternity in which they are suspended between worlds as they watch the Brandberg sink into darkness. I too do not want this moment to end for them, but about five kilometres down the road, the woman signals for me to stop. We say our goodbyes and I watch as the man ties the abbavel to her back. Then he picks up their bags and they head off down the footpath to their home. I watch them disappear around a bend before I get back into the car.

◆　◆　◆

When I wake in the morning, there is a haziness to the air and the Brandberg sheds its blankets slowly. I appreciate the coolness of the morning in Uis. Other campers begin to stir as the sun comes into its own strength. My German neighbour and I smile at each other and exchange pleasantries. Then we settle down with our books again. My body hurts from the exercise of the past few days — sandboarding, kayaking, climbing. Early mornings become long days and by nightfall, I appreciate being able to stretch out and sleep. Yet today, I am unable to concentrate on my book, for images of the White Lady still flash through my head. I pick up Luís Vaz de Camões's Os Lusíadas in an effort to quiet my mind, but the White Lady pushes the white sailors aside and re-enters my head. A man comes around to collect garbage at the bin across the way from our campsite. He rummages in the bin and removes a five-litre container. Here, people still collect gourds, as they have done for millennia. Anything that stores water is a valuable commodity. The early Europeans came down this coast, trading pots and beads — trinkets. The coastal traders knew better. It was the Europeans, blinded by their lust for gold, who could not tell the real value of things. In the desert, a pot to hold water is worth more than a fine china plate.

We leave for Twyfelfontein right after breakfast. The GPS doubts the existence of such a place, but we forge ahead. As we head toward the parking lot near our destination, the GPS spits out a final burst of gibberish, insisting that we make a U-turn. We ignore it and eventually it pouts and says, "Drive straight, and in two kilometres reach your destination on the right." Then it retreats into an ethereal silence to lick its wounds. We stop and begin the short walk to buildings that occupy the centre of an unassuming valley. Perceptions are deceiving, though, for Twyfelfontein contains the largest collection of rock engravings in southern Africa. Although the local people call it ǀUi-ǁAis, which means "permanent spring," the farmer who settled here as part of a war veteran's concession in 1947 found the water flow less reliable and settled on the name Twyfelfontein — Doubt(ful) Fountain. He farmed in the area for twelve years, until, encouraged by an expropriation deal when the area was included in the Damaraland territory as part of the apartheid-ization of Namibia, he sold the land he had been given and left again for South Africa.

Our guide, Sylvia Thanises, is jovial and articulate. She leads us on the Lion Man Route toward the engraving that gave the route its name. Although reading the rock engravings at Twyfelfontein as sha-manistic or ritualistic has come in for much criticism, I do not believe that they are merely depictions of daily life, as these opponents of the shamanistic theory suggest.

The Lion Man is a complex work of art. The shallow pecking technique, so common in many of the other petroglyphs, is used only in part of the image. The centre is left untouched, creating a defined, hollowed centre. There are five claws on the tail, one for each digit of the shaman's hand.

Along the way, we pass several images of giraffes with five horn-like protrusions on their heads: the sign of the shaman again. A lion for the courageous and a giraffe for the far-sighted, perhaps? In the engraving, the giraffe's legs taper to signify the sensation of elevation, or levitation, that accompanies the trance-state. The engravings signify both the process of reaching a trance-like state and the details of the transcendental journey. I am easily transported into other realms by these works of art. The creatures of the earth and the sky and the oceans lie side by side on the rocks. Here and there, we encounter broken circles or drawings that span fissures in the rock — deliberate interruptions in the continuum of the trance.

Before leaving Twyfelfontein, Sinead and I take a look at the map. We could take the main road to the Petrified Forest to see the remnants of trees that were washed down from Central Africa at the end of the ice age, before the separation of Gondwana, but Sinead wants to show off her new-found navigation skills and sends us along a shortcut. The road is a sandpit and I long for the added traction of a four-wheel drive. Since we don't always get what we want, I lock the differential. Now that both my back wheels are forced to turn at the same speed, we gain a little traction and inch our way forward. Every now and then, I get out to investigate the best possible route around obstacles and washouts.

The jumble of rocks we pass along the pathway through the forest reveals only fragments of its secrets. Large portions of the trunks remain underground. What is visible crumbles slowly in the elements. These are small shards of ancient history from the depths of this land, but the dense stone weighs heavy in the hand. The guide points out a small patch of *Welwitschia mirabilis*. I am glad we do encounter this ancient plant, as we had not done the Welwitschia Drive while we were at Swakopmund and it is something I wanted

Sinead to see. The welwitschia, Namibia's national plant, is an extraordinary thing. Adapted to desert conditions and thousands of years old, welwitschia are hardy survivors in a hostile environment. Just past the welwitschia, we see some hoodia, the latest miracle crop from the desert. Our guide can barely hide his excitement. "They're planning acres of hoodia plantations from here to Khorixas. It will bring work to the people." Hoodia contains all the promise that jojoba held not so long ago. Its appetite-suppressing qualities have made it the darling plant of the moneyed, who can never be too thin. They come to the desert to hide in its fortified spas. There, they hope this elixir of the desert will show them the path to eternal youth. Our guide seems keen to help them on their way.

Back at the parking lot after our walk through the forest, our guide approaches us with a request: Could we give one of his colleagues a ride into Khorixas? He needs to go to Swakopmund to write his field guide exams, and so we make space for Salmon !Nawaseb. Salmon knows the road intimately and talks incessantly about a wide range of things. He's a trainee guide at the forest. He is on his way to Swakopmund to write his final guiding level 3 exams. After this, it is one more set of exams before he can become a freelance guide and have the ability to travel anywhere in Namibia to work as a trained guide.

"People skills," is what Salmon defines as the key characteristic of a guide. He speaks English well, but he is more comfortable speaking Afrikaans with us when he wants to explain an intricate concept. Even better would be if we understood Damara, but Afrikaans will do. Sinead understands the broad strokes and when she gets stuck, I fill in the gaps in English.

"Move over to the right of the road," Salmon declares suddenly. I follow his instructions, and as we head over the crest of the hill and into a sharp dip through a dry riverbed, the left side of the road disappears.

"Lucky you know this road," I say. "We would've gone straight into that hole."

"They should put a warning sign up," Salmon says. We drop Salmon off at the entrance to Khorixas and wish him well in his exams. The sun is hanging low on the horizon by the time we get to our campsite on the other side of town. The rundown dustiness of Khorixas disappears as soon as we enter through the gates of the camping grounds. Inside, the pathways are neatly manicured and patches of grass indicate suitable campsites. While we register, a family wanders passed us on the way to the camp restaurant. Sinead and I find our spot and set up the tent. The two young women camping beside us are already having supper when we arrive. By the time we're ready to make a fire and start cooking food, they've crawled into their tent. Beyond the walls that enclose the camp, a party has started at the local gas station. Sinead and I have our dinner and settle in to play a game of cribbage. While we play, the night air tosses snatches of music and conversation over the walls, assuring us that there is life in this town.

Later on, while Sinead showers, I refill our water bottles at the tap beside our stand. The tap leaks profusely and I attempt to stop it by retying the rubber tubing that is meant to cover the hole in the pipe. I manage to stem the flow, but for the rest of the night I can hear the low hiss of water escaping from under the rubber. Sinead settles down for the night when she gets back, but I rekindle the fire and set up the table and a lamp to write. Dogs bark aimlessly and incessantly as I transcribe my thoughts and notes on the day. As the last embers die out, I pack up for the night.

In the morning, I crawl out of the tent and look for the water bottle so that I can fill the kettle for coffee. It is gone. As I walk over to the tap to fill the kettle, a swallow swoops into the little pool that has formed where the water from the leaking tap has gathered overnight. Another joins in the fun. I drink my coffee and watch the swallows enjoying the water before the sun dries it up. This is a strange world, I think, where a plastic water container is worth more than most worldly goods.

12

The first European explorer to see the Etosha Pan, Francis Galton, estimated it at fourteen and a half kilometres wide, but could not determine its length due to the shimmer off the surface of the pan. Galton only saw a small part of the pan and his estimates were woefully inadequate: it stretches for one hundred twenty kilometres from east to west and another sixty kilometres to the north. In the dry months, the Etosha Pan is a massive salt flat and the water recedes underground; in the wet season, it is covered in a shallow film of water that runs into the basin from the northern flood plains. Then, the flamingos from Walvis Bay head to the pan to escape the icy Atlantic winter winds; animals from across the entire region gather here to savour the abundance of water. The traders too converged on the pan to replenish their stocks of water. Thure Gustav Een, a Swedish trader, describes how, on their way back south after a long and successful trading mission, he and his entourage reached Ekuma on the northwestern edge of the pan and, finding no water there, dug some weak wells in the clay banks to slake the worst of their thirst. A group of local San, possibly members of the Haillom who lived in the area of the Etosha Pan before they were forced to move beyond the park boundaries, led them to a stable watering hole at Okaukuejo.

"Here," Een writes in his diary, "we said farewell to the boundless plains of Ovamboland. The landscape now assumed a different character, small rocky hills arose here and there, the stony ground was alternatively covered by thorn-bush and omatatti trees." From Okaukuejo, Een and his wagons headed south past Outjo and on toward Omaruru and Walvis Bay, where they could trade their wares along the coast, as people had done for centuries before them. And off to his left lay the peaks of Mount Etjo.

For a short while on our journey north, we follow the path Een took on his way south. From Khorixas we head toward Outjo. The bakkie has a full tank and sounds content. A vehicle with a full tank always sounds content and sits well on the road. A short way out of town, we turn off the main road onto the D2743. Korhaans pick roadkill off the ground like vultures, and a lone grey loerie flops its way across our path. I drive carefully, since the road is stony and I am wary of getting another puncture. We are driving through the rocky debris of the Ugab Terrace, the remains of a prehistoric river that lie about one hundred sixty metres above the present-day Ugab River. The expansive plains and straight pathways Een described in his journal have temporarily given way to a series of twists as the road makes its way between the hills that form the outer edges of the ancient Ugab River Valley. Here, after the last ice age, the Ugab had scoured away the sedimentary rock, leaving towers of sandstone. As we come around a corner and emerge from a dip, I feel the bakkie lurch to the left and skid.

I stop the car and Sinead and I get out. "Back left," she says before I have even adjusted to standing outside the car.

She reaches for the cross wrench and the jack as I begin to unpack some things to get to the spare tire in the back. An inquisitive go-away bird settles into a tree. It peers at us, wondering whether we're going to be roadkill for the korhaans soon. Just as a precaution I listen for cars. "See, nothing coming!" I yell at the bird as I tug at the resistant lug nuts.

"Go away," is its curt response. It watches us the whole time as we unpack the bakkie and repack it.

Eventually, we're back on the road. A kilometre or so further lies the most famous of the ancient exclamation marks, the Mukarob, the Finger of God.

The Mukarob as it stands today marks the end of a saga that stretches back into the Pleistocene era when the ancient river subsided and the erosion of the sedimentary layers began. By the time modern European travellers first came to see the Mukarob, it was a needle that reached impossibly into the sky, a twelve-metre sandstone pillar resting on a narrow mudstone neck. Below this shapely neck lay a broader mudstone base that rested on the top of a small hill. At the height of its glory, the precarious structure rose some thirty-four metres above the bed of the prehistoric river. In the 1950s, at the start of the apartheid government's efforts to colonize Namibia and fill it with Afrikaner settlers, the Finger of God seemed as bullish and indestructible as the apartheid regime.

Nature and history, however, had other plans. Toward the end of 1987, the South African Defence Force made a push to capture Cuito Cuanavale, a strategically important town in southern Angola. The battle for Cuito Cuanavale ended in March 1988, when the South Africans withdrew after a seven-month siege. A new battle ensued as diplomats haggled over the details of an agreement. Finally, on the thirteenth of December 1988, South Africa, Angola and Cuba signed the Brazzaville Protocol, which determined that UN Security Council Resolution 435, the resolution that would facilitate the transition to independence for Namibia, would be implemented. The formal treaty was signed in New York a few days later, on the twenty-second of December. Impossible as it may have seemed at the time to the handful of soldiers who crossed the Kunene River in 1965 to start the War of Independence, the apartheid monolith had collapsed and Namibia was finally on its way toward becoming a nation.

The import of the negotiations sent reverberations throughout the world. Even nature played its part. As if in anticipation of this epoch-changing event, a violent windstorm had toppled the upper pillar of the Mukarob one night early that December. Although scientists have postulated that seismic activity somewhere across the ocean provided the tremor that had shaken the Mukarob off its pedestal during the windstorm, others took a more metaphysical approach. I was sitting in the inner courtyard of the Thüringerhof Hotel in Windhoek one afternoon early in February 1990, enjoying a Tafel Lager with some friends and talking about a future trip up to the Mukarob, when a man reached over from the table next to ours. "Let me tell you about the Mukarob! It was not the winds of change that brought the Mukarob down, I tell you, nor some tremor. They've got it wrong! God got wind of what the politicians were planning and sent them a warning. A warning. He told them about the end of the world and they didn't listen. Now here we sit with the *gebakte patat*, the hot potato. This place is going to go to shit." Having prophesied, our neighbour returned to his drink.

"It looks a bit like a dehorned rhino," I say to Sinead as we walk up to the base of the mudstone horn. "Still a majestic creature, but not quite the stuff of mystery." From the Mukarob, we head for Outjo, where all roads converge. Around us, the landscape changes again. Mustard trees, *Salvadora persica*, give way to grassland and camelthorn. We are back in the hinterland, where the water is sweet and the grass is tall. Anthills gradually change from the desert white to an inland red. Beside the road, cattle mill around in search of coolness and shade under the mustard bushes beside a borehole.

In Outjo, I take the tire to the garage to be repaired. The attendant shows me the many previous cuts and patches and declares solemnly that the tire cannot be repaired again; I am compelled to buy a new tire before we head north to Etosha. At Etosha National Park's Anderson Gate, we pay our entry fee and enjoy the late afternoon drive up to Okaukuejo, the southernmost rest camp in the Etosha National Park. For many Afrikaner families, the annual pilgrimage to the national park is a way to return to a version of a past rural idyll, to live once more the illusion of what their forebears saw as they

trekked across the land. For two weeks of every year, there is a reaffir-
mation of their sense of belonging to the land. Over the school
holidays, the park will be filled with families spending their evenings
by the campfire, recounting numerous hunting trips or family lore.
Storietyd. Storytime. In the hushed sunset beside the watering hole,
stories emerge from the shadows of the night that will scare children
from their sleep. Stories of the demons that haunt people still emerge
from what the playwright H. I. E. Dhlomo once called the "aromatic
hours" of the evening.

By the time we arrive, the sun lies low toward the watering hole and
we have about an hour before the gates close for the night. There is one
person ahead of us in the queue at reception and when my turn comes,
I ask for a camp spot. "We're full," the woman on duty informs me.

I ask whether there is anything at any of the other rest camps?
Halali? Namutoni? If we leave now, we have an outside chance of making it there on time. "All camps are full," she repeats. To the one side, a
man leans against the counter, watching us. He leans over to his son
with a bemused smile and comments, loudly enough for us to hear,
"They should have booked in advance. Tourists never learn."

"Overflow campsites?" I venture.

"Only for Namibians."

"I am Namibian." She demands to see my documents, but I have
nothing but my word, an entry in my South African passport that
identifies my place of birth as Okahandja and a birth certificate. I
show her everything I have and I explain that my identity was stolen
and that I am at the mercy of the Namibian Ministry of Home Affairs
and Immigration. She is unmoved by my plight.

"They could turn your application for citizenship down, you know."
Not likely, I want to protest. I already am a citizen; I just need the
papers to flash around. Namibian courts have ruled repeatedly that
Namibian citizenship is an inalienable birthright. I am Namibian,
with or without the documents to prove it. "Until you have the papers,
you are not Namibian," she reiterates firmly.

It's pointless arguing with her, so I reach for my passport and papers. The man with the smirk looks at me, but his expression changes when he notices my name on my passport. "Are you related to Dave Midgley?"

"The vet?"

"Yes."

"He's my brother."

"Wihan Brand," the man says and offers me his hand. Then he turns to the woman behind the counter. "He's Namibian, I'll vouch for it. I know his family. Find him a place." The woman glares at me, then smiles at Wihan and assigns us a place in all of the Etosha rest camps for the following three nights, at Namibian rates.

"In Africa, it helps to know people," Wihan remarks dryly to Sinead. He proceeds to tell me about my brother and how the two of them worked for the same employer for a while. Now, he runs a chemical cleaning company with a contract to service Namibian national parks. He's here to do overnight training with the staff. We chat for a bit more before parting ways — Wihan promises to put me in touch with some of his friends who had been in the war and who want to tell their stories. Sinead and I head off to set up our tent. There's still a bit of sunlight left, so we go for a short drive. When we return to our campsite, I see the rear tire I replaced earlier in the day deflating before my eyes.

After dinner, Sinead and I retreat to the watering hole to read and write while watching the animals approach for their evening drink. A lone blue wildebeest, shaman stripes and all, arrives ahead of the herd. The elephants arrive and hold sway over the water for more than an hour as they play and settle themselves for the night. Sinead has taken the camera and photographs the animals as they mill about. Every now and then, I glance up from my writing to enjoy the sunset activity. Other people are starting to leave when Wihan appears beside me. He's being housed in one of the luxury suites beside the watering hole — "One of the perks of the job" as he points out. "I'm a bit busy tonight, but my son and I are taking a break in Halali tomorrow night. Find me there and we can talk some more about the war." He leaves to start his night's work. After a while, a man comes and sits beside me. "Johan," he introduces himself. "I heard you saying to that other guy that you're looking for stories about the war."

"I am interested in hearing some stories, yes," I confess.

"I was with the Panser Div," he says. "We left the base in the mornings looking for people to shoot. That's not war, you know, but that's what we were trained to do. We weren't trained to question our actions. Now that's all I do. Question my actions."

Johan's pride in serving in the army is visible in the animated way he talks about the good times they had at base and on leave; his disappointment at the aftermath is palpable. "We were trying to make a better world, you know. To prevent the Communists from taking over. What for? Look at them now. Mugabe and his clowns. And these corrupt people here in Namibia." No matter how hard I try to lure the specifics of these corruption allegations from him, he only speaks in circles, always returning to the futility of it all. Johan looks at me with tired eyes. "Is this what we fought for? Is this where it ends up? Why did they send us up there if they knew we were going to lose — and believe me, they knew."

He gets up to chase away a bold jackal that is sniffing at the garbage can just to the right of us. "I should head off to bed," he says. "Tomorrow is going to be a long day."

◆ ◆ ◆

The next morning we pack up the camp and I drop the tire for repair at the camp gas station before heading out with Sinead for a game drive. In the early morning light, a steenbok darts across the road and makes its way through the bush beside us. We stop and watch. The ewe is nervous about our presence, but after a while, she seems to relax. Then, a soft whistle and her kid bounds out of the bushes next to the car. It wastes no time before latching on and suckling. At

Olifantsbad, we turn around and start heading back to Okaukuejo to collect the tire. A herd of impala rams to the left draws our attention. Two stroppy males stare at each other. We stop right beside them, but they're oblivious to our presence. They snort and pose. Their heads move around, but their attention remains focused on the other's movements. The rest is all for show. And I see again two young boys on the school playground. "*Kôkkie! Kôkkie!*" the bystanders yell. A cockfight. Gert moves in and Iulius simply closes up. He falls to the ground, where Gert kicks him repeatedly. Iulius doesn't move, refusing to be drawn into the fight. It's not as if he couldn't: he's a champion martial arts fighter. He chooses not to. And Gert kicks and kicks and the boys egg him on, closing the circling, baying for blood.

The two rams lower their heads and charge. I snap them right at the moment their horns lock. Yet I feel empty as the victor trots off, all full of himself, and the other young male is left to pick himself up out of the dust. Off to the side, I see a third ram, puffing and snorting in the aftermath of testosterone, watching, disdainful but offering no challenge.

Back at Okaukuejo, we discover that the deflated tire is also irreparably damaged. I load it into the back of the bakkie. We make our way to Halali, taking all the detours we encounter along the way. It is late afternoon by the time we drive through the gates. Halali, the cry of the hunters as they corner the beast. Halali, the favoured hunting grounds of German settler elites. We set up our tent as the sun is setting. When we're done, we head straight for the watering hole. The infrared lights of the viewing site give the people waiting for animals to arrive a spectral glow. The shadowy figures move slowly and speak in hushed tones. The animals are slow in coming and the more impatient souls wander back to the camp for dinner and a fireside conversation. Soon, only a handful of people wait with Sinead and me. Two eyes gleam at the edge of the bush. They hover at the periphery of our sight for a while before slinking cautiously toward the water. The leopard crouches and starts drinking. If it were not for the eyes, you'd barely notice it. So unlike lions, who announce their presence with the grunts and roars of the bullies that they are. When it has finished drinking, the leopard pads quietly into the bush to our right and the watering hole is silent once more.

A few minutes later, a short squeal penetrates the night.

"What was that?" Sinead asks.

"Which way did the leopard go?" I ask her in return. She points in the direction of the sound as it dawns on her. "Death comes quickly in the dark," I say.

The woman beside me has been listening in to our conversation. She turns to me and asks, "Is this her first time? It's rough on them when they hear the death cry. Is she your only child? Where's her mother?" She fires her salvo of questions with a hunger for personal information that seems to be part of holiday conversations. The ones where you bleed strangers for information. Occasionally, the friendships you form in these few days last a lifetime, but mostly the intimacy is fleeting. I give her the basics of returning to show my daughter the country of my birth.

"It's good that you're writing it all down," she latches onto the topic that interests her. "It's important that our children know their heritage. I'm married to a German, a descendant of the Schutztruppe who stayed after the war." She talks about the closeness these soldiers developed for the land and how it has passed on through generations. "It's not that different to the love of the land we Afrikaners feel." She has opened a sluice and as we walk back toward the camp, she talks freely. "They're different, these Germans. I'm having to learn to speak German so that I can communicate with my husband's family. They won't speak Afrikaans to me. My son's grown up German. He speaks German fluently and is proud of his heritage. As he should be. He even insists that the farm workers speak German to him because he's German! He even wants me to speak German to him now."

Her pride in her son's awareness of his heritage is a scab, underneath which festers a deep wound that tears open as we walk. "You must make your daughter speak Afrikaans. Tell her about our Afrikaner history too. That gets forgotten, the struggles of our people. Surely our history is important too? It gets lost in this new Namibia." What part of that history do I tell my child? Do I tell her only of the Trekkers and their determination, or do I tell her about the sadness that envelops the Johans of this world? How do I tell her what our generation has done? What about the histories that lie buried here in the park? Stories about the spectres of history that emerge in the dark? We part ways with so many questions unanswered.

She rejoins her husband and her son while Sinead and I head toward the main administrative buildings, where we will meet a guide who will take us on a night ride through the veld. We squeeze in along the wooden benches in the back of the modified Land Rover. The guide provides us with blankets, for the night air can cut to the bone. The night creatures are skittish, so he drives with the headlights off, swinging his infrared light back and forth with practised ease, stopping whenever he spots an animal in the dark. An African wildcat. A marsh owl. Noises that awake images of warthogs and other animals feeding. Spectres in the dark, dyed a dull reddish-brown in the light of the infrared lamp. As we pass Rietfontein, the light flashes briefly on a stone marker bearing the inscription "Graves." Back and forth we go in the dark, repeatedly crossing intersections with stone markers. Each one contains a ghostly reference to the untold stories that haunt this place, waiting for someone to listen: Rietfontein, Goas, Noniams, Xamarob, Charitsaub, Nuamses. Little remains now but these names of places to remind us of the Haillom who lived in these parts. The spirits of their ancestors and the stories that remain on the tongues of the disinherited still wander through these plains, but the Haillom themselves huddle in shacks along the outskirts of the towns that surround the park. There, they form part of the masses that crowd the road allowances, the landless, jobless invisibles who blot the landscape. Yet they hope the government will give them some land to call their own, a place near their ancestral lands where they can once more appease their restless spirits. The shadows of their ancestors blow cold against us as we drive across their land in the night.

We stop briefly at a riverbed where a pride of lions lies. We see eyes and ghostly shapes in the night. "I want to see lions in the day," Sinead says. "Not these shapes in the night."

I too am tired of ghosts.

Silently, right behind me, a hyena emerges from the dark. Danger lurks everywhere in these parts. That is the history we have wrought. Beyond the park boundaries, to the west, lies the road to Kamanjab and from there northwest into the Kaokoveld and on to the Kunene River and the Epupa Falls; on the right the road runs north to the Caprivi Strip, through Tsumeb, Grootfontein and Otavi — the so-called Triangle of Death, where People's Liberation Army of Namibia (PLAN) soldiers wreaked havoc among the farmers of the region during the war years. Every year, Danger Ashipala and the members of his Typhoon Brigade would walk eight hundred kilometres from deep inside Angola, make their way through a host of South African bases and troops, and fight their war. They came when the annual rains started; when the rain dried up, those who had survived the season of war made their way back to the bases and refugee camps in Angola. A few stayed behind, working undercover to recruit more troops for an insatiable war. The main road north, the B1, follows the western route, for it was a road built and tarred to carry South African troops and materiel north during those years. And hovering indecisively in the middle is the Etosha Pan, a salty refuge for the war-weary.

The hyena disappears in the dark.

In the morning, we return to Rietfontein. In a small clearing, some springbok graze in the background; a lone hornbill hovers over the brush and meerkats play in the bushes. There is a single grave, sunk low into the ground. A marble headstone erected in 1955 gives the name of the deceased as Johanna Alberts, wife of Gert Alberts, leader of the Dorsland Trekkers, who died here of fever as he and his followers made their way north.

In the last quarter of the nineteenth century, a group of Afrikaners from the South African Republic, the land of newly discovered gold, grew disaffected with the greed and alleged immorality of their leaders. Why, their president even travelled on a Sunday and tolerated dancing in the beer halls of the Witwatersrand! Driven by their conservative faith and a Zionistic impulse, they headed out from the Zoutpansberg area in search of their New Jerusalem. When they reached the sands of the Omaheke, they turned north. Along the way, they left their wagons and the graves of their children. By the time they reached the Etosha Pan, more than half of their number had died or turned back, disillusioned. Yet the faithful remainder trekked on. At the Etosha Pan, they found good water and stayed for a while, until the local chiefs, fearing that they would lay permanent claim to the land, hurried them on their way. North of the pan, Gert Alberts and his people trekked, north and west until they crossed the Kunene River at Swartbooisdrift, and then they trekked on to Humpata in Angola, where they settled. The grave at Rietfontein is the only trace of their presence here and every now and then their descendants, like the descendants of the Haillom, make a pilgrimage to the land their ancestors once occupied near the Etosha Pan.

History and politics and animals merge in the night and flood our sight in the light of day. As Sinead and I have made our way north, the land has become more unfamiliar to me and my thoughts have become more hostile. I grew up in the south, and the stories of my memory seldom reached beyond Otjiwarongo. For two days, Sinead and I have been wandering the southern reaches of the pan, searching for a way around it. Beyond Etosha lies the region in which the War for Independence was waged and I know that is where I must go next, yet it feels as though I keep butting my head against obstacles, battling setbacks. It's as if the north doesn't want me. *Things will change when you get to Ruacana*, I tell myself. Just get to see the Kunene and the border post; that will shift your mood. Still, I cannot shake the feeling of being in no man's land, in an artificially created paradise where displacement has been the norm. Beyond the pan lies a new world, a world of battle zones. In an effort to delay our deployment, we scurry for the safety of Fort Namutoni, just like those who came before us: the traders and the Trekkers, the German troops who build their fort here at Namutoni during 1902 and 1903, and the South African soldiers who pursued them here during the First World War.

Fort Namutoni, an outpost of the German empire, had seen plenty of action before the South Africans arrived. There were always small skirmishes with local kings. In 1904, Chief Nehale Lya Mpingana and his troops attacked and destroyed the fort. The names of the seven German soldiers who defended the fort until they could withdraw under cover of night appear at the entrance, but the names of the Owambo soldiers who died during the battle have disappeared into the soil. The Germans had barely finished rebuilding it when the South African troops chased them out of it. The pan and its environs became a park in 1907 and Fort Namutoni fell into disrepair and was only restored in the 1950s, when the park was opened to tourists.

We arrive just before the gates close and pitch our tent in the dark. It's been a long and dusty day of driving around the edges of the pan and we spend the evening trying to relax around the fireside. For the first time since coming to Etosha Park, I sense the perimeter fence of the rest camp caging me in. It is there for our safety, I know, but I need space. Three days of being cooped up in the bakkie have left me irritable. I sense Sinead is frustrated too. She has receded into herself and has barely spoken in the last two days. That alone is a troubling sign. We need to leave this place and the ghosts that haunt our thoughts here.

We get up early and as soon as the gates open, we set out along some of the shorter loops that surround the camp. We stop for a while at a watering hole and photograph some giraffe and elephant. Then we are on the move again, through the dense forests of the Dik-Dik

Loop, scouring the verges for the tiny antelope that give the drive its name. They are elusive, shy creatures, but today they have graced us with their presence in abundance.

We head back toward Namutoni, but just before the gates, we turn off and skirt the perimeter fence of the rest camp on our way to Fischer's Pan. The pan is dry and looks like the scarred landscape of a post-apocalyptic movie set. Baked salt deposits and knolls of grass lie clumped together on islands stranded in the middle of a barren expanse. In the distance, I spot a Verreaux's eagle on a treetop. Sinead sighs as I stop to attempt yet another photograph. "It's a bird!" she says. Her irritation is palpable. I should feel relaxed and refreshed after the diversion of looking for animals, but I too am agitated. We drive back to Namutoni in silence.

Right outside the camp, there are signs to two gravesites: on the one side of the road there is a memorial to the nameless Owambo soldiers who fell in the battle of 1904; on the right, there is a grave for Peter Emil Bähtz, a German soldier who died at the rebuilt fort in 1907. The two markers for the fallen soldiers lie on opposite sides of the road — Germans to the right as you exit the camp and the Owambo to the left.

Back in the rest camp, we make breakfast and pack up the tent. The last item in our routine is cleaning the dishes. Sinead snaps at me: "If you move the knife, you'll stack the plates better!" She yanks the knife out from between the plates and throws it in the washing bowl. She and I seldom fight and she regrets her action instantly. We agree that it is time to move on. "I feel cramped in my seat," she whispers after a long, uncomfortable silence. We rearrange our luggage to create a little more room for her. "That's better," she acknowledges, but then retreats into silence again.

With the car packed, we decide to take a walk up to the fort before picking up our laundry. The rest camp is set off to one side, so we have to follow the plank walkway that keeps visitors off the soggy soil around the watering hole. Along the way, several pieces of art make

up a series of installations set up in 2007 as part of the park's centenary celebrations. Sinead walks ahead, determined to reach her
destination, while I try to spend time at each piece of art. The installations are not clearly marked on the map and I miss a few.

We enter the fort and wander through the tourist shops and stalls
that have been set up in the rooms that surround the courtyard. In
the one corner of the courtyard, a peephole allows us to look into an
old cell containing a work by Hercules Venter. We enter the corner
where the holding cell is and bend over to get in under the stairwell.
Already, I feel enclosed and claustrophobic. The peephole for the cell
reveals nothing but a blackened room. I step back and look around
me. To the right, there is a light switch. I flip it on and peer through
the peephole again. Inside, the ultraviolet light grows brighter, revealing bits and pieces of the image. Ghostly figures in an otherworldly
hue — soldiers and shamans, ancestral spectres, barbed wire and disembodied guns seem to drift in space. The deep blue and black of the
installation sears the eyes. It is not just a celebration of the park. It is
a testament to the centenary of the Wars of Resistance that officially
ended in 1907, the year the park was declared. The trance-figures
awaken an awareness of the Haillom who inhabit the area, of the
soldiers who died in battle here and further north during the War of
Independence. For someone who is heading north, this sets the mood:
this is what the fighting was for. Freedom is an ethereal construct
here. I feel myself drawn into a netherworld of spirits and ancestors.
I hear their cries of lament and defiance beat against the doors of the
cell. Alarmed, I retreat, battle-weary from unearthing gravestones.

A tok-tokkie — a scarab beetle — scuttles into the shadows.

I try to escape the onslaught on my senses by taking a walk
through the little museum at Fort Namutoni. Against the wall hangs
a trove of rifles used by King Nehale's troops during the attack on the
fort in 1904. I notice that many of the guns were only accessioned
after independence, which means that throughout the War of Independence, the descendants of these warriors had hung onto them,

hidden them, even as the SADF did their rounds and confiscated any firearms they could find.

Outside the museum, there is another site-specific artwork, *Weeping Women*. Imke Rust's fading evocation of one of the foundational myths of the Etosha Pan stands in contrast to the starkness of the guns on display at the museum. According to San legend, when strangers invaded this region, killing all the men and children, the women who remained behind wept for their lost ones. It is their tears that created the great salt pan and cleansed the earth. The seven salt-pillar women stand there, waiting for the rains that will once again let their tears fall on the land.

The tears of the women who wept at Etosha mingle with the tears of those who stayed behind while their husbands, sons and daughters made their way up the long road across the Namibian border to Cassinga, and on to Zambia. From there, those old enough and fit enough to fight would be sent for military training; those under sixteen would be sent to school, either in Zambia or in sympathetic European countries. Eventually, they would make their way back to Angola, where they assisted in the refugee camps or helped to clear a safe route for their strike brigades to cross the Namibian border. Back inside the borders, the women who had stayed behind would provide their war children with sustenance, bearing the brunt of the violence the South African forces unleashed on them when they came in search of the shadows that were slowly sapping the souls of the apartheid government and its puppet army.

The next stage of our journey is to travel north toward the Angolan border at Ruacana. I linger, for I know it will be a hard road. Finally, I have to face the demons of the past. Ahead of us lies the war zone, where most of the fighting during the War of Independence occurred. I fear what we might see there, the spectres that will emerge, but go we must, for this is why I have come here in the first place. We collect the laundry we'd dropped off at the main office the night before and set out. The early morning light reflects gently off the pan. Sinead and

I both retreat into silence. As we head north toward the King Nehale Gate, a throwaway remark from Francis Galton's *Narrative of an Explorer in Tropical South Africa* flashes through my mind. Just north of Namutoni, which is marked on his map as "Omuchamatunda," his rendition of Omutjamatinda, the Otjiherero name for this place, he writes, "We passed the grave of the god, Omakuru [sic]; the Damaras [Ovaherero] all threw stones on the cairn that covered it, singing out Tati-kuru! Tati-kuru!" I have a desire to visit the grave of Omukuru and to lay a stone on the ombindi, but I cannot find any trace of it on the maps. As if to taunt me with the vagaries of history, the gate to the east of the park is called the Von Lindequist Gate, named after the governor whose legacy will haunt this place forever.

When the disgraced General Lothar von Trotha was called back to Germany after his genocidal campaign against the Ovaherero, it was von Lindequist who replaced him and who was tasked with setting up and administering the allegedly more humane alternative of concentration camps. As we approach the Nehale Gate with its barbed-wire fence reaching out beyond sight to the left and the right, a uniformed guard steps out into the sunlight.

13

Bart at the call centre was filling in time: "You're pretty far from home with an accent like that," he said as he muddled through his computer system to update my contact information.

I knew where this was going: Australia? New Zealand? In the end I'd politely say something like, "It's the other one."

Instead, he says "South Africa." Then after a moment's hesitation, he adds, "But it could be Namibia . . ."

"Not bad," I acknowledge cautiously. "How did you guess?"

"I'm from that part of the world myself."

"Ah, so you might know Okahandja." Small talk. Does it really take this long to change an address?

"That's where I was born," Bart announces.

I hadn't seen that coming. I'd been living in Canada for more than a decade and the closest I'd come to a Namibian was during the 2001 World Athletics Championships in Edmonton. Sinead and I had woken early to go and cheer on Sandy Jacobson, a local Edmontonian, when I spotted a Namibian flag among the runners. It was Elizabeth Mungudhi. She smiled and glanced at the crowd when I called out "Go Namibia!" And now here I was talking to a guy in a call centre who not only knew where Namibia was, but could pronounce the name of the town I was born in. We talked for a bit about Okahandja, and then came the inevitable question: "Have you been back?"

"Not since independence," I tell him. "And you?"

"Nah. Never went back once my folks moved in 1970." That's about the time my parents moved to South Africa. I don't mention that. Instead, I ask him where they went.

"Angola. We're Portuguese. Bart. That's short for Bartolomeu."

"As in Dias?" I have a knack for stating the obvious.

"The very same. That's me. Bartolomeu Dias. The things parents do to their kids, you know."

I do know, but instead I remark that I have always had a fascination with Angola. Names of cities and places linger in my mind. There was a time in 1976 when these names echoed through the elementary school playgrounds as the boys shouted, "*Wie wil saamspeel Kaptein Caprivi?*" Who wants to play Captain Caprivi? Captain Caprivi, the gun-toting hero of government propaganda films had penetrated the psyche of every young Karoo lad, where he blended with Grensvegter — Border Fighter — the hero of a series of Afrikaans photonovels. In the photo stills and captions of these books, they saw a sleeveless elite soldier hunting for terrorists, not the man with the impressive lineage who originally bore that name: Georg Leo Graf von Caprivi de Caprera de Montecuccoli, the German chancellor who bestowed his name on Namibia's Caprivi Strip. On the playground, these young soldiers-to-be hunted for victims they could torture using the innovative practices they gleaned from the movies.

And beyond the playground, newly conscripted teenagers gathered at the station alongside middle-aged men. They were all preparing to leave for the border, the Namibian border to be precise, as part of the military force that was invading Angola at the time. They would return from the Caprivi months later — some hardened by the experience of war in Angola and northern Namibia; others simply shell-shocked. They would drive through the town's adulation and remain on the farm for months, staring at the cannon shells on their mantelpieces. The names of these young men have receded in my memory, but the names of the places they visited remain.

There was war all around, it seemed. In Angola, in Johannesburg and Cape Town, where schoolchildren threw stones at police. And sometimes, like Hector Pieterson on a cold June morning in Soweto, they threw their frail bodies against the wrath of apartheid guns. This was a time when parents would lower their voices discreetly or turn a newspaper upside down to hide the photographs of yet more dead bodies or more burning vehicles. They would talk of their sons who were on the border, of Tannie Annette and Oom Richard, who worked at the mines in Daveyton. Wondering whether they'd be safe.

The remnants of war were never far away. After school, I would look up from my homework and stare at the British fort on the hill, still offering safe passage to the trains crossing the railway bridge above our house almost a century after the South African War had ended. When my homework was done, I'd explore the trenches that ran along the length of the rail line between the two forts that guarded the bridges on opposite ends of the town. We grew up amidst a history of war and we travelled up and down the broken trenches every afternoon after school.

On my way back to my room at night, I would walk past the mantelpiece where Uncle Bobby's photograph stood alongside his medals. Dad too had fought in North Africa and in the Italian Campaign. But Dad came back; not like Uncle Bobby, whose journey back from Abyssinia ended in the Heroes Acre at Mombasa. And for the rest of his life, Dad remained a loyal member of the Memorable Order of Tin Hats (MOTHS). Every Armistice Day, Dad would shine his medals and join the parade down the main streets of Burgersdorp. By the end of 1976 the boys returning from Angola had joined the veterans of two world wars, and photos just like Uncle Bobby's had begun to appear in other houses in town.

Bart Dias's voice catches me unawares. I'd almost forgotten that I was on hold. He's telling me about Luanda and how post–civil war reconstruction efforts are slowly bringing the city back to life. I inter-ject: "I really want to go to Cuito Cuanavale."

Bart's blunt "Are you nuts?" just about says it all. It's not one of those places that leaps out as a prime destination in the glossy mag-azines you find at travel agents. Truth be told, I had barely heard of Cuito Cuanavale before it became a household name in Namibia in the months leading up to independence. At every event and party, Cuito was on people's lips. Slowly, a complicated story emerged from these conversations: South African troops, funded indirectly by the United States, had been assisting Jonas Savimbi's UNITA (*União Nacional para a Independência Total de Angola*) in the Angolan civil war since 1976. This was, in part, why all white South African males had been called up for military service. In 1988, after more than a decade of fighting in which the war had reached a virtual stalemate, South Africa decided to launch Operation Modular. It was a last-ditch effort to wrest control of Cuito Cuanavale from the FAPLA troops — the *Forças Armadas Populares de Libertação de Angola*, another party to the Angolan civil war. FAPLA, I knew from conversations on school playgrounds, was the military wing of the MPLA, the *Movimento Popular de Libertação de Angola* that had won the election in 1975.

The water-rich town of Cuito Cuanavale, situated in the fertile soil of the Cuando Cubango province in southeastern Angola, lay roughly halfway between Luanda and Jamba in the southeast of the country, where Jonas Savimbi had his headquarters. Most signifi-cantly, Cuito had an airport that lay within striking distance of Jamba. A strong FAPLA presence there would make life difficult for Savimbi and his South African backers. After all, Savimbi's continued free rein in southeastern Angola prevented PLAN soldiers from penetrating into northern Namibia. And that suited the South Africans just fine.

During the Angolan civil war, the fortunes of all three countries that had a stake in the war — South Africa, Angola and Namibia — became ever more closely knit. Matters came to a head in the mid-1980s. South Africa wanted to make one final push to destroy

PLAN and to bolster UNITA's chances at gaining access to Luanda — and having control of Cuito Cuanavale was essential to that plan. Moreover, the ANC's military wing, *Umkhonto we Sizwe* (MK), had training bases in the area. This could be a victory on many fronts for the South Africans.

At best, what happened at Cuito Cuanavale in the closing months of 1988 remains cloaked in ambiguity. It all depends on how you define victory in war. Initially, the South Africans advanced on Cuito and managed to take a strategic bridge across the Cuito River, some twenty-three kilometres south of the town itself. The joint FAPLA, PLAN and MK forces at Cuito dug in and the battle seemed over when Cuban reinforcements arrived. The Cubans' air power, combined with the determined resistance offered by the combined ground forces in Cuito Cuanavale, forced the South Africans to retreat . . . all the way to the negotiating table in Windhoek.

PLAN claimed victory, for their struggle was won at Cuito; the Cubans claimed victory for the Socialist International; FAPLA claimed victory over Savimbi's UNITA forces, because with the South Africans out of Angola, it was merely a matter of time before Savimbi capitulated; and MK claimed victory, for they had helped bring the mighty SADF to its knees. The South Africans claimed victory too: their aim, they said, had been to keep control of the bridge, not to invade Cuito Cuanavale. Anyway, they argued, just do the math: 4,785 Cuban/FAPLA soldiers killed; with ninety-four tanks and hundreds of combat vehicles destroyed. Only thirty-one South Africans killed in action, with the loss of three tanks and eleven armoured cars and troop carriers.

And so the stalemate continues beyond the war.

Through it all, the people of Cuito Cuanavale remained part of the war's grim statistics. During the 1980s, South Africa was one of the world's largest producers of land mines and they knew how to deploy them. As Johan had explained during our conversation in Etosha, "The claymore was my favourite — the South Africans made the Mini MS 803. It was a claymore, really. Because it's a directional fragmentation mine, you get a lot of blast. It's a bit like a poppy seed, you see. When the lid pops off, the shrapnel sprays in all directions. More bang for your buck. You could lay it in the ground as a conventional mine. You could string several together in a necklace or tie them to trees in an ambush. It could be detonated by command or by trigger. A beautiful thing." The Russians supplied FAPLA with liberal quantities of mines for their own use. And so the only crop that blossomed in the fertile fields surrounding Cuito was land mines. Today, despite extensive mine-clearing operations, Cuito Cuanavale remains one of the most land mine–ridden areas in the world.

Bart's reservations about Cuito are well-founded.

"Why would anyone *want* to go to Cuito?" he asks.

It's hard to explain. Especially over the phone, to a complete stranger.

"There," says Bart. "Address updated. Is there anything else I can do for you today?"

Bart had done more than he realized. It was because of that conversation that Sinead and I were now travelling on this road. It forms the artery around which the South Africans built their war machine. All along it lie the remains of old army bases and many of the towns we pass through owe their existence to the military. Sinead stares out of the window as I drive on in silence and let my thoughts wander. I worry about her, for over the past few days in Etosha, she has withdrawn and lost her spirit. At the same time I am glad for the silence as I drive north toward Ruacana. The road signs along the B1 north become a litany of military bases ripped from memory: Oshivelo, Omuthiya, Oshakati, Omega, Eenhana . . .

In all likelihood, I know, I am not alone in my quest to explore the north. Every year, busloads filled with ex-troepies gather for pilgrimages to the shrines of their war. They wind their way up through Namibia, stopping in places like Tsumeb to visit the remaining legends of their time, like the German soldiers who came to live here after the Second World War and who helped to organize civilian defence units during the war years. They gather in the old canteens and reminisce about the Iron Crosses they received from their heroes as tokens of appreciation. Then they skirt the Etosha Pan and head north along this road we are on now, stopping at the ruins of the bases where they spent their days on the border. They open cans of beer and pour libations to their memories. Some, the diehards, push through into Angola, to Cuito, to search for answers and, sometimes, to make amends.

Perhaps we are not that different, they and I, with our pilgrimages to the graves of the deceased, with our illusory hopes of finding answers here among the *oshanas* and *mahangu* fields of Owamboland.

I really have no need for road signs or maps here, even though I've never travelled to northern Namibia before. The names of these towns were my constant companions as I grew up. Between the reams of military bases strung along almost every road in northern Namibia lie hundreds of tiny villages, some consisting of no more than a handful of houses, places where the PLAN soldiers would hide on their way south. I recognize them too. They are from the table of our caravan. My sister and I would pick the most obscure names we could find and challenge each other to find them in record time, or to string them together like nursery rhymes: Omugulugwombashe, Onamandongo, Opuwo, Onesi, Ondiva, Ongandjera. At some point in the next few days, I know we will pass by or near most of these towns.

I know also that most of what I will find along these roads will be ghosts and memories, for the South Africans left little physical evidence of their presence when they departed. Unlike their predecessors during two World Wars, they did not bury their dead on foreign soil and they took care to demolish all but the most permanent of the bases. On their patrols, they also left little evidence — a trampled ring of huts, smouldering ashes, the buried remains of the people who died at the hands of bloodthirsty young troops.

The bumper-to-bumper traffic from Onyati to Oshakati pulls me out of my reverie and into the present. Here, I have to pay attention to the road. Small villages cluster around the road and wherever you look, there's a pub with a name like Arsenal, Lucky No. 2, Emporium Delight or Long Road Bar emblazoned across the front. At Ondangwa, we drive past the sign for the border post at Oshikango, and my mind starts to wander north again toward Cuito, but my thoughts hit a roadblock before they get there. The road is being repaired and cars are only allowed through the construction one at a time.

In Ondangwa, we learn that the cause of the congestion is the annual trade fair at Ongwediva. We press on through the cars and street markets that have overflowed onto the road and livestock and children on their way somewhere, with their teacher leading the way. Here and there, graveyards lie by the side of the road, completely unfenced. People and animals wander among the graves, grazing on whatever stubble they find. In this world, the living and the dead mingle shamelessly.

I hand the tire that could not be fixed in Okaukuejo in for repair at the TrenTyre in Oshakati. While we wait, Sinead and I cross the road and settle in at the Low Life Bar. It's as if the saloon from the set of a spaghetti western has been dropped next to the road in northern Namibia. There are no seats inside save the handful of stools chained to the brass footrest that runs around the edges of the room. A solid brass grid stretches the length of the counter, separating the clients from the booze. Only when she's certain that we are indeed entering the establishment does the bartender heave herself off her perch and lean on the counter with all the overstated panache of a bored youth. I order a Windhoek Lager and a cool drink for Sinead. We sit outside at a fold-out table with plastic chairs. It's cool in the shade, but I can feel the heat of the day pounding on the awning. In the open space in front of us, passersby grab a quick meal from the assortment of vendors who have gathered along the roadside. Sinead and I have a sandwich with our drinks.

A man pulls up in a van and a lanky youth who's been hovering around opens the back and starts off-loading the evening's stock for the bar. The driver jumps out and introduces himself as Isaac. We chat for a bit about the roads and the traffic. "It's because of the Mahangu Festival," he says as he heads inside to talk to the bartender. "Business is taking off in the Oshana Region." Sinead and I continue to eat in silence as we watch the traffic go by. Mahangu, pearl millet, is the staple crop for subsistence farmers in northern Namibia. The Mahangu Festival is just another part of the government's efforts to increase awareness of the industry and to streamline production by introducing milling facilities like the one at Ongwediva. On his way out, Isaac joins us again. He pores over our map and shows us where to go. "Opuwo is a must. You have to see the Himba," he says. "And the craft market."

"I want to go to Ruacana and to Omugulugwombashe," I tell him.

"But there's nothing at Omugulugwombashe. Nothing. Go see the waterfalls at Ruacana. NamPower has built an impressive electric plant there."

"What about the royal palace at Tsandi?"

"Sticks. Go to Ruacana, then come back here and experience the Mahangu Festival. For your daughter's sake."

"We'll see about being back for the Mahangu Festival," I tell him. "I'm going to Ruacana on my way to Swartbooisdrift."

"Ah the Dorsland monument! With that bakkie, you can do the trip from Ruacana to Swartboois no problem. Just over the mountain. Then you can come back through Opuwo. They've set up an entire Himba cultural village there just for tourists. Now you don't have to go out into the middle of nowhere to see them."

"We were thinking of heading up to the Epupa Falls too." Isaac glances at me. He hesitates before he responds.

"Yes, go see them while you can. Then come back for the Mahangu Festival!" He calls to the youth and jumps into his van before I get a chance to ask him about that moment's hesitation. Is it just that he doesn't particularly like the falls? Does he mean that we should visit them while we're in the region, or is there something that he isn't sharing? The Epupa Falls have been a source of contention for almost as long as the country has been independent. An uneasy stalemate has developed around the development of the Epupa Dam Project and the Ovahimba, for whom development means the loss of their way of life. The proposed dam would flood the falls and the fertile plains that surround it. It would destroy a large portion of land reserved for communal grazing among a people whose lifestyle depends on cattle and it would cover more than a thousand ancestral graves. In turn, the government offers economic development and a hydroelectric station that would, in good years, produce a portion of the power needed to drive the increased agricultural production in the north. For the rest of the time, the catchment area would be a vast, sterile mud flat. But Isaac has fled and I am left to ponder the possibilities on my own yet again.

Sinead's take on the proposed development is simple: "Who would want to destroy the Ovahimba culture? I like waterfalls, we should go see them."

It is mid-afternoon by the time our tire is fixed and we decide to head directly for Ruacana. Even before we've left Oshakati, I spot the turnoff to Endola, where I know Meme Priskila Tuhadeleni lives. Meme Priskila, who sacrificed her children and her marriage to the war. She and her husband, Kaxumba kaNdola, the Pipe Organ of Endola, opened their home to the Mesah yaVictory and his five companions when they entered Namibia after three years in exile. Kaxumba, Mesah yaVictory and the other men left and fought at the Battle of Omugulugwombashe, but Meme Priskila stayed at home. When the police arrested Kaxumba and sentenced him to life imprisonment on Robben Island, she stayed at home to raise their children. And when the police and the army kept returning to her home, beating her and asking her where her husband was, she stayed. And when her children left to become soldiers too, she stayed at home. As her own children left, others came. Some were family, others were strangers who had lost their own homes, but they had heard that Kaxumba kaNdola's home was open. Even now in her old age, when she is impoverished and too old to earn money, there is a house full of children who have wandered into her home for refuge. "My husband welcomed everyone and this is the legacy he left me to deal with," she said in an interview with Ellen Namhila reproduced in *Tears of Courage*, a collection of women's stories about their role in the struggle. "I cannot let him down. I cannot disappoint the dead or myself."

In the canal by the side of the road, youngsters swim in the late afternoon heat; some lather their naked bodies with soap. Others, younger ones, play in the oshanas behind the canal. A few young girls lean over the edge of the canal to draw water for their homes. A man wades through the muddy water to inspect his fishing nets. At every bridge across an oshana, children offer fish for sale. A young girl reaches into the road with her string of fish, hoping to catch our attention, but I hurry along: Ruacana beckons.

We drive over the hill and descend into the town just before sunset. In the distance, the Kunene River cuts through the swaths of deep green. There is nowhere to go once you're in Ruacana, I realize. The road ends along the banks of the Kunene and the only way out of town is to retrace your steps. On the Angolan side of the river, mountains guard the banks, thick and heavy. Ruacana was a perfect place to situate a military base from where the SADF could patrol the banks of the Kunene toward Swartbooisdrift.

As we stop at the campsite just outside of the town, two women come running down a pathway from the house set back in the bush at the top of the hill. They are very friendly, and remark how pretty Sinead is. "Another man and his young lady came here a month ago. We're seeing more of that."

I tell them she's my daughter. "Can't people see we're related?" Sinead asks as she closes the door of the vehicle behind her.

"Where's the mother?" they demand to know and I explain that she decided not to make this trip with us. I show them a photo of Julie, which satisfies them. We chat for a while and the women tell us how peaceful it is here now. The campsite belongs to the community and they are slowly getting more tourists to come here. "It is better than it was during the war," says the older woman, and shrugs her shoulders.

I probe her a little more. "Oh, the soldiers, you know." She refuses to be drawn out further on the matter and I let it go.

"Look after that child," they shout as they head back to their home. "She looks sad." The campsite is spartan. The smell of creosote and lye from the newly built pit latrines and shower cubicles hangs in the air as we drive down toward the river. Sinead chooses a place right beside the river overlooking a deep pool with reeds. It is completely secluded and the serenity of our surroundings soon washes the last of the day's journey off us.

We set up the tent and I am adding wood to the fire and getting things ready for supper when Julie calls. Sinead answers. I can hear her telling her mother about the long distances we have travelled to get here and how the time in the bakkie is wearing on her. She is sitting with her back to me and her voice drifts over the water at Hippo Pools.

Julie is busy at home. Even from a distance, I can hear dogs barking in the background. "Are those our puppies?" Sinead asks. Julie puts the speakerphone on so that she can continue getting ready for bed — after all, it is after midnight in Canada. The dogs become more animated at the sound of her voice.

Sinead's defences crumble. She has not been home in almost two months now and without warning her stoic silence of the past few days gives way to waves of homesickness. I pry the phone from her hands and huddle beside my daughter on the stone ledge overlooking the Kunene River. There is little I can do but hold her close.

In the gathering shadows, we watch the sun set over the Kunene. African sunsets are not the long drawn-out affairs of the northern hemisphere. Here, the sun explodes into a dramatic flare of orange. The whole world is ablaze briefly before the shadows bloom and night descends. Sometimes, a furious outburst followed by silence is all that is required. It is well after dark before we begin to make supper.

I dig in the food box for whatever scraps of comfort we find there: potatoes, carrots, chickpeas and a stray tomato. As our limbs stretch after the day's inactivity in the car and her stomach fills with food, Sinead's mood thaws a little. We play cribbage in the semi-dark of the fire and complete our daily routine of checking through the day's photographs and writing up diary entries.

The older Omuhimba woman walks by to check on us. She sees Sinead's tear-stained face in the light of the fire. "*Sy's so mooi, maar sy lyk ongelukkig. Jy moet haar mooi oppas. Sy's jou kind,*" she tells me for the second time that evening.

"She's so pretty, but she looks unhappy. Look after her well. She's your child," I translate for Sinead. She cuddles in a little closer. "In Etosha, as we were sitting at the watering hole in Okaukuejo, a woman asked me if I was an only child," she whispers. "I told her 'No' and she wanted to know where my mother and sister were. I told her it was only the two of us. The woman smiled at me and said, 'I like it when one parent and a child travel together — it's always a special time.'"

◆　◆　◆

The doleful "whea-whea" of a piccolo enters my dreams. For a while, I simply lie and listen to the bird, trying to figure out what it is. When the call switches to a very distinctive "di-di-di-diderick," I know: it's a Diderick cuckoo — the male varies its call in the breeding season. Two laughing doves join in, andante molto mosso. I stir into action as a clash of finches and passerines rebel in the reed bushes in a rush of percussion. I emerge from the tent to the sound of the river flowing gently and the sight of the morning sun just catching the sandbank on the Angolan side of the river. All night, the bray of donkeys and the echo of human voices talking until the early hours of the morning have drifted down the valley and into the campsite. We are alone here, but the disembodied voices of our neighbours and of the people across the river have comforted us. The discussion from the valley was not exuberant partying, nor was it an angry, militant salvo of words. It was simply a group of friends laughing and chatting the night away. How could such tranquillity arise from the violence that tore the country apart for decades?

On the sandbank, I notice two logs sunning themselves. I set up my camp table and a chair right by the river's edge, make a cup of coffee and settle in to read or write while I make the transition into the day. It is this simple pleasure that consumes my efforts now, as the turtledoves flutter off with a faster-paced trill of coos and the finches drop off into silence at my approach. They will resume their noise, and the cicadas will join them as soon as the sun hits the trees on this side of the river. I revel in the calm that exists where once freedom fighters crossed the river and where the night was punctuated with the staccato of machine guns, not the gentle voices that kept me awake last night. There is barely a trace left of the SADF troops that amassed here to cross over into Angola.

More human sounds intrude and one of the logs stirs and slips into the water. As I begin to ready myself for another day in the car, I mull over how my borders have expanded — north initially meant anything beyond the Gariep, with the lights of Goedemoed Prison shining across the river; at university the border meant this border, the Namibian border. And yet I knew that beyond that world lay other borders that would tear apart my insular existence. On days like these at the Gariep River, Dad would relax enough to give me glimpses of his life as a soldier in World War II. He was reticent to talk about what had happened, always intending to spare us the horrors of war. "I've seen it and I don't want to go back," Dad would say whenever the topic of European travel came up. What he meant is that he was there in the war, that he had seen Europe all beaten up and destroyed, that he had been part of that destruction. "Who returns willingly to the places of nightmares?" he said once.

Here I sit, having coffee on the northern border of my country, the home I barely know. My world has become porous and I seep across its borders in body and in mind. The people who live here move along either bank of this river, oblivious to passports and controls. I am reminded of what one of my students, Mr. Huiseb, told me once: There were no terrorists that crossed these borders, only fathers and sons and daughters and mothers, lovers and family and friends. I begin to recognize that Salmon, the trainee guide from the Petrified Forest, is seeking to be a freelance guide so that he too can expand his horizons in the way I have. He wants to extend beyond Khorixas, just as I now want to extend my horizon beyond the Kunene. The Ovahimba on these roads, who travel or seek lifts seemingly to nowhere in particular, are also on a quest to expand their horizons.

As we set out to leave Hippo Falls, a man on his way to work poles his way around the island in a *mokoro*. At the island, he stops briefly, reaching into the reeds and lopping off a bunch with his panga. He swishes the long flat blade from side to side with an effortless flick of the wrist, scooping up each handful of reeds as they tumble beneath the force of the sharp blade. When the bottom of the mokoro is filled with green reeds, he returns to poling. He lands at the bank and waves at us just as we drive off.

We do not head into the town itself, for it is still early and, besides, we have a long day of travel ahead. The sooner we get on the road, the better. We take a short detour to the border post and the NamPower reservoir. From the border post, we walk to the viewing point. From where we stand, we see a glimpse of the Ruacana Falls in the distance and a vast rocky expanse where water flows in the rainy season, or when the authorities open the sluices at the Calueque Dam to let the water run freely. Then, the Ruacana Falls are a sight to behold, but now they're a trickle of water dripping down into the valley on the other side of the gorge. We sit and watch the falls for a while. Only the river now lies between us and Cuito Cuanavale, I think. The river and a few hundred miles of minefields.

14

We have not been able to get visas for Angola and so I am left to my own imaginings. I try to imagine my way up through the old neutral zone, past the Kavale Rapids and up to the Calueque Dam, for in a way this is where it all started, these border wars. The Kunene flows south from the highlands of Angola until it approaches Ruacana, where it makes a sharp turn to the west and heads toward the ocean. The original border agreement between Imperial Germany and Portugal simply stated that the boundary lies in the "rapids south of Humbe." To the Portuguese, this meant that the border lay at the top of the falls at Ruacana and stretched east to Nkurenkuru; the Germans, however, held that it lay some sixteen kilometres north, at the upper reaches of the Kavale (Kazambue) Rapids, just below Erickson's Drift, and that it stretched east from there until it hit the Kubango (Okavango) River at Katitwe. While the dispute was being settled among diplomats in Europe with only the vaguest sense of where these places were, a neutral zone was set up between Ruacana and the Kavale Rapids.

Although Portugal had controlled the coastal sections of Angola for centuries, their interest in the hinterland lay only in its major exports: ivory and slavery. The trade routes ran straight west and then reached south toward the Okavango River, where the slave trade had become endemic by the late nineteenth century. It was only after the southern port of Moçâmedes came into existence in the 1840s that the Portuguese began to show a sustained interest in the south of Angola. Most of the slaves captured in the lands surrounding the Okavango River were put to work on local plantations and farms, and when slavery was finally abolished in 1879, the farmers traded the old ways in for a contract labour system in which former slaves became indentured servants. Their day-to-day lives barely changed.

As the Portuguese pushed into southern Angola, local resistance increased. King Mandume ya Ndemufayo of the Kwanyama repelled the Portuguese time and again, but despite his military prowess, Mandume was caught in the middle of a battle beyond his making. As hard as the Portuguese pushed from the north, the Germans were pushing from the south, for they too needed access to African labour.

For the Germans, access to Angola gained an additional urgency when the South Africans invaded German South West Africa from the south. The German commander, General Victor Franke, realized that he had a shortage of food brought on by a severe drought, and the only way to secure food was by gaining access to the crops in southern Angola and to direct imports from the Angolan port of Moçamedes. General Franke attacked Cuangar and Naulila late in 1914, thus gaining control — such as it was — over the entire Humbe region. The occupation lasted less than a year, until the Germans surrendered to the South Africans. No sooner had the Germans left than a Portuguese force under General António Pereira de Eça attacked Mandume and reoccupied the Humbe area. Mandume burnt his palace at Ondjiva and retreated south, across the neutral territory that lay between the two disputed colonial borderlines, and settled among his people in South West Africa.

Mandume had been on good terms with the Germans, allowing his people to enter the colonial workforce. Now, he needed the South Africans as allies in his fight against the Portuguese, who were squeezing him from his territory north of the border. Such help was not forthcoming. After his defeat at Ondjiva, Mandume's authority was challenged, and hunger and famine made it difficult for him to restore the faith of his people in his leadership. Mandume remained defiant, refusing to accept colonial authority, or to recognize the borders that divided his kingdom. He moved across the neutral zone to restore unity among his people, and in so doing angered both colonial administrations. His relations with the new South African authorities south of the border soured rapidly and early in 1917, they sent a large force to attack him. On the fifth of February 1917, Mandume made his last stand at Namakunde, which lay in the neutral zone. When it became clear that he had lost, he took his own life rather than surrender to colonial rule. As he lay dying, the legend goes, he took off his necklace and asked his aides to give it to his mother as a symbol of continued resistance. The Kwanyama people lost their king and their freedom on that day, and to this day families remain separated by a border imposed on them by two colonial powers.

It was only in 1936 that the decision was finally made to recognize Ruacana as the border, and a relatively peaceful period ensued that ended only when South Africa invaded Angola in 1975. Once more, the area just north of Ruacana became the pretext for war. While Angola was still a Portuguese colony, the Portuguese and the South Africans had reached an agreement to build a dam at Calueque. A series of water tunnels would bring water to Ruacana, where the South Africans would set up a hydroelectric station and a series of canals that would take the water further south. The dam was completed in 1975, just as the transition to Angolan independence occurred. Using the strategic importance of the new dam as an excuse, the South Africans invaded Angola.

The South African troops stationed at Ruacana either marched west toward Swartbooisdrift, or forged the river into southern Angola to guard the Calueque Dam.

In 1988, the Cuban soldiers fighting in Angola opened a second front against the South African forces. They pushed south toward the

Calueque Dam, forcing the South Africans to retreat to Ruacana. As they retreated, Russian MiG-23s destroyed part of the dam wall.

In a way, the war that started here also ended here, for it was this Cuban offense that forced South Africa into its last-ditch effort to capture the strategic transport hub of Cuito Cuanavale. The Namibian War of Independence ended, but the Angolan civil war would drag on for another decade, and the damage to the Calueque Dam remained. Since then, it has operated at about two-thirds of its capacity, straining Namibia's access to water and electricity. It is this lack of water that spawned the idea of a dam at Epupa.

◆　◆　◆

From the Ruacana Falls, we head out toward Swartbooisdrift. "No problem," Isaac at the Low Life Bar had said, "you don't need a 4 × 4 to get to Swartbooisdrift." About two kilometres down the road to Swartbooisdrift, we come up against the side of a mountain. The goat path that apparently doubles up as a road swings around the edge of a steep gorge. About halfway up, the bakkie groans to a halt and begins to slide back toward the drop. I let it roll, looking for traction as I steer it away from the edge, down the track until I find solid ground. I engage the diff lock and start up on my Sisyphean task again, this time veering to the left in search of anything other than loose shale. We hug the stone along the edge of the road furthest from the drop. The engine strains and I wish for the added traction of a 4 × 4, but it is not needed. At the top, I stop for a second and let the cool morning breeze blow across my back. I'm sweating. I glance over at Sinead. She says nothing, but I know that she is nervous. There's a sense of accomplishment, but I know too that there is a long way to go still: we have barely started. What goes up must come down, and I have to head down into the valley that stretches to the horizon. I work my way across the little plateau and ease my way onto a good stretch of road. A short way further lies a small drift with about two-

and-a-half feet of water. I feel the engine lurch as the exhaust gets submerged and I keep the revs up so that there can be no back-suck. Beyond the drift, I smell wet dust, like earth after the first rains, and life seeps back into my bones.

I keep moving through the low-lying pass that winds its way into and thorough the hilly valley. From the high points along the way, the tops of the makalani palms along the Kunene are just visible. I know that although I cannot see the river to my right, we are following the run of the water, for we are driving on river sand and the bakkie slips and slides in it, sometimes right up to the chassis. We didn't have breakfast before we left, so I pull over to get some food from the back. As I get out, I spot another bakkie, a 4 × 4, coming around the bend. This is the only other traffic on the road today. As the bakkie passes me, I spot two old tannies with *bollas* in the back seat. It's a hunch, but tannies with their hair done up in a tight bun and wearing their *kisklere*, their Sunday best, on the road to Swartbooisdrift can only mean one thing: A pilgrimage.

I follow them closely. The driver obviously knows this road well, for he swings left and right in anticipation of holes and in search of hard ground. I match his movements. The one time I do miss a beat, I feel the tires sink into a patch of loose sand. I pull out and make a note to stay on the tracks he makes. We pass the Kunene River Lodge and he veers to the right, onto a track that looks even less like a road than what we've been on for the past three hours. I glance at the dashboard. We have travelled little more than forty kilometres. I follow instinctively, even though we could be headed anywhere. After another three kilometres of drifts and sand and rocky roads, I spot the sign for the Dorsland Trek Memorial and Swartbooisdrift. My hunch has paid off and my marker has led me straight to the monument. Below me, I see the shallow river heading west toward the ocean. Somewhere down there in the valley, lies the drift where the Dorsland Trekkers crossed on their way to Humpata, which would become their home for several decades.

"I thought we might be heading for the same place," I say by way of introduction. We begin chatting almost immediately. They insist on speaking Afrikaans even though I try to keep the conversation in English so that Sinead can follow. But it's always back to Afrikaans. I focus my attention on the three older people. From the corner of my eye, I notice a row of graves just below the monument. Our bakkie is parked beside one that reads "Petrus Johannes van Eck." This is a surprise: I take my name, Peter, from the anglicized version of my uncle's name: Petrus Johannes van Eck. And suddenly, there is a connection between me and this place, however tenuous. I too appear to have had family on both sides of this border.

The older man introduces himself as Eric Peters. I recognize the name. It belongs to one of the stalwarts of the Monitor Action Group, a conservative political party that calls for the reinstatement of capital punishment and corporal punishment, that insists on a meritocracy that will advantage those who, historically, had access to superior education and calls for the right to self-determination — a thinly veiled adaptation of apartheid policies.

"My grandfather was Otto Peters, the German consul general in Angola. He married a woman, a van der Walt, from Humpata. Otto and his wife returned to Namibia in 1927 along with a bunch of other Trekkers. On Otto's death, his widow married a Chapman who was a direct descendant of James Chapman, the nineteenth-century traveller."

"Yes, I know the traveller. I've read his account of his travels to Lake Ngami."

"That's the man," Eric says. "But did you know that one of his sons went to Humpata with the Trekkers? They suffered there. The Angolan government didn't care for them and ostracized them and forbid them from practicing their religion. Wanted to turn them all into Catholics. And that despite the Boers helping them fight against the Germans."

"The Angola Boers did more than fight against the Germans," I start to say. "They also fought against Mandume during his last stand," but one of the tannies has joined the conversation and interjects.

"My grandmother was born on the way to Humpata," she remarks. "She was born in the wagons. They came back with the 1927 returnees and settled in Gobabis. That's where we're from. The remainder of the Angola Boers struggled on, never quite gaining a foothold. When the civil war broke out after independence in 1975, the last of the Trekkers were repatriated to South Africa and Namibia."

"But they haven't forgotten their past. There've been several commemorative treks and gatherings," Eric picks up the narrative again.

"Yes," echoes the other tannie. "Every three years, the living descendants of these Trekkers come to the monument and they have a *fees*, a festival. We've been to every one of them. A large part of the gathering is to add more stones to the cairn beside us to acknowledge those who have made the pilgrimage."

Each of the stones on the pile has a name on it and I step closer for a look. "This is the only history we have left in this place," Eric Peters laments. "We have to preserve it."

The most lasting way they could find to do this was to build an ombindi. The stones are piled shoulder-high. The tannies have busied themselves with wiping the dust off the outer layer of stones, taking note of the new names they see and sketching out where each one fits into the broader community of trekker descendants.

"No need to add our names — they're there already. See?" They point to one of their names. "But we come anyway. We come to remember our forebears." All the while, the younger man who drove them here hangs in the background. Now he steps forward and introduces himself as Karel Bredenhann.

"I'm an army brat. My mother was stationed in Ruacana. I did my service in 51 Battalion. Patrolled Sector 10 and west to Swartbooisdrift. I did my officer's training in Okahandja in 1989," Karel tells me. I do a quick calculation. Had I responded to my call-ups, Karel and I may have been cohorts.

I look down toward the river. "Is that where the Dorsland Trekkers crossed over the river?" I ask.

"No," Karel tells me. "The drift isn't here. That's a mistake everyone makes. It's only the tourist monument that's here. The real drift lies about a mile back, where 51 Bat had its outpost. Follow me." He leads the way back along the road to a small hill by the side of the road. "The drift is just over the hill," Karel shouts as he waves us through. The tannies open their windows and wave at us at they take their leave.

Sinead and I walk to the top of the hill. Rusted ration cans mark the way to the first set of ramparts. Here and there, we spot an old cartridge. Together, they are the only visible evidence we see of the old military outpost. Where once soldiers' bodies had cleared the interiors of the ramparts with their continuous abrasive presence, grass has now reclaimed the earth. Traces of the old footpaths that once linked these shelters reveal themselves to the careful eye. To the right of the ramparts lies a large rock. Inside, all along the rocky overhang, ex-soldiers from the 7th South African Infantry Division have left a wall of graffiti. Where the ancient artists at Twyfelfontein and other places throughout the country left enduring works of art but no names, the conscripts left their names but no art. Just a hollow attempt to leave a trace of their presence. No exotic animals for them, no dream carvings or trance circles and carefully prepared dyes and paints. Simple scratches and black camouflage paint smeared into letters is all that remains.

Ramparts mark the way down to the drift itself. We stand on the small sandy beach and look out over the rocky crossing and the swirling white water. Only the desperate would try to cross here. And yet the Dorsland Trekkers, in search of their own freedom and independence, faced north and ventured into the crocodile-infested waters with their wagons and their livestock to reach their promised land. A century later, PLAN troops plunged into these same waters. They did not have to worry about crocodiles. The troops of 51 Battalion, bored by the endless hours of staring at the rocky drift, had dealt with them over the years. But they did have to worry about the barrage of gunfire they could expect as they made their way back into Namibia.

15

As you meander through the folds of the mountains that stretch west from Swartbooisdrift, you rise over a crest that leads into the valley beside the Epupa Falls. A swath of blue-grey makalani palms lies beside the green of the mopane trees and the stunted yellow winter grasses sough in the wind. Set off against the russet stone of the mountains, the Kunene lures you into its timelessness. This is an ancient river, forged by the passage of glaciers through the rocky landscape. As the memory of dusty roads fades behind you, a series of lodges and campsites on the riverbank rises into view. This is a paradise where visitors can forget, if only briefly, the worries of their daily lives. Epupa lies about two-thirds down the course of the Kunene, and the falls are the last big drop before the river makes its final push through the Kaokoveld and into the northern reaches of the Namib.

A few feet away from the edge of the river stands a large thatch-roofed enclosure. There is no one at the reception desk, so Sinead and I wander through the *lapa*, past the bar counter, and stand at the water's edge. Just downstream from the lodge, women wash clothing in an eddy above the falls while a group of youths dive into the cluster of pools. "We don't have time to do it again," I hear the desk manager at the lodge call to someone in the kitchen as she heads toward us. "Make something else. Time is money. And go slow on the rations. We're only going to town next week." Epupa is several hours' drive from Opuwo, the administrative capital of the Kunene Region. It takes careful planning to run a hospitality business in such a remote place. Benita wipes her hands on a kitchen cloth before realizing that she's made the remnants of her labours visible to the public. She hides the cloth sheepishly and smiles at us. "You've come to escape the rush of your world, and here I am creating a fuss. Forget it all and don't worry. We run on African time here. Only meals are served at a fixed time."

African time. The panacea that explains all conceivable evils — from failure in business to a lack of attentiveness to the future and a failure to understand the importance of dividing the course of human existence into fixed segments of time. "The kitchen staff burnt one of the dishes I had planned for tonight. Ag, but we'll think of something else for you. Nothing for you to worry about. We don't have any more campsites available, but I can offer you the last of the chalets for two nights." Benita doesn't seem to breathe once words begin to cascade from her mouth. She continues to chatter as she books us in, but my mind has wandered beyond the thatched open-air dining and reception area to the garden that lies beyond it. The blades of the young makalani palm leaves protrude from their quivers on the river banks. Above them, the leaves of full-grown trees hang like limp swords. The meandering footpaths and the taut canvas walls of the chalets stand out against the small copse of corrugated iron shacks that lie beyond the perimeter of this place. That is where many of the staff who work at the tourist concessions have settled. There, life continues as children dart between the houses and mothers carry water to their homes.

While Sinead showers, I sit on the *stoep* outside our room. I start reading, but I am easily distracted. For a while, I watch the lazy flow of the river around the island to my left. There is barely a ripple as the river widens in preparation for its descent. What water doesn't flow down the large cataract close to the Namibian shore will tumble down the tangle of forty-plus smaller cataracts that spread for almost a mile to the north. I take a sip of my beer and close my eyes in an effort to relieve the tension caused by the day's driving and to push the day from my mind. Just for a few minutes, I'd like to forget about what brought me to the north. To forget that since leaving Etosha, I have constantly been reminded that I am part of a generation bred for violence. To forget that this violence we have perpetrated on a new generation was imprinted on our DNA and thrown in our faces at every opportunity. It was cultivated inside of us and now we reap the harvest.

I open my eyes and watch the water gather speed as it nears the falls. Resentment keeps surfacing. Resentment that my education came at the cost of a generation of barely literate black children; that time in my schooling was set aside for playing soldiers. Some of my friends from my school days are among the wounded and dead who float through the underworld of my skull. Lives were wasted and destroyed. Resentment that while I sat in a classroom, young black children of my generation felt compelled to walk hundreds of miles across borders in Botswana and Namibia to fight the injustice that made my life possible. Regret that I did not know enough then, or have the backbone, to join them. Resentment that the letters I received from friends stationed in places like Omega during the Namibian War of Independence were as broken apart and redacted as their minds.

I no longer feel guilt about the privilege of my past, for that serves little purpose. I cannot change what has been. I can only use what I have learned to good effect in the future. Now, there is only anger that a callous regime made my generation pay for their ignorance and hatred, left us broken and our lives filled with their lies and residual hatred. I am angry that as Eric Peters spoke at Swartbooisdrift earlier in the day, I felt myself being drawn back into the narrow Afrikaner shell from which I had struggled to emerge.

The lies of my generation and the generations before us are finally being exposed, along with the bodies in the mass graves that litter this landscape. I am disturbed that Isaac at the Low Life Bar in Oshakati, like so many others during our trip, so readily dismissed the cultural and historical heritage of this land during our conversation. *A hard day's driving has worn you down*, I tell myself. *Let it go. You are tired and disappointed.*

But it is too much, these lies and the deceptions of the past. I am part of the muddled generation, the lost generation, the wounded generation. I am exhausted by the thought that we are squandering the legacy of the people who died to secure basic human rights. I have tried to raise my daughters with an awareness of the prejudices of my past, and seeing these old lies in the flesh at Swartbooisdrift thrusts them to the fore again. The visit to the ramparts at Swartbooisdrift has upset me more than I imagined it would. I have been conditioned to feel nostalgic about these remnants of a war I didn't fight in. I came here, in part, to see for myself and to recover some of this history that others tell me is part of who I am. I do not doubt them: it is part of me. But as we drive past the ruins of old bases, or find the barracks turned into nondescript NamPower lodges and corporate training sites, I realize that I can't. I feel nothing for these dilapidated structures. I may have been bred for this violence, but I cannot commit to it. *You are not like the others*, I try to remind myself. *You resisted.*

But for now, along the banks of the Kunene, I am just exhausted. How do we pick up the shattered pieces of this community and rebuild it? How do we move forward from this — this war? I have tried for twenty years to understand. It is not about understanding, I sometimes think. It is beyond comprehension, this fatigue that is compounded by every image of gratuitous violence from the wars in Iraq or Afghanistan. It is as if the walls of Berlin and the apartheid wall of Israel that come weighing down upon me. When? When? When will we stop this madness and give our children hope for their future? How do I convey this past to my daughters? How do I make them remember without filling them with anger and resentment and despair?

Sinead emerges and settles beside me with her book. Since the phone call from her mother at Ruacana, she has been even quieter than usual. I let her read in peace. Eventually, I can stand it no longer.

"I've seen this before," I tell Sinead. "From Lüderitz on, everywhere, people don't seem to care about the past.

"Just like they don't care about the future. They want to build a dam here. How can they just flood these falls? This place would be nothing without them! I've heard it all before."

Sinead says nothing. When she eventually does respond, she redirects the conversation with skill acquired over many years. "These days are mine, you said. We're not talking about those things now." She wants to draw me out of the past to things that matter here and now. Sometimes, I need her to help me forget.

"Benita mentioned river rafting. I'd like to do that," she adds after a short pause.

In the late afternoon, we walk up the hill to watch the sun set over the falls. A faded handwritten sign at the summit reminds visitors that this viewpoint is on communal property and that they are here at the invitation of the local community. Visitors are asked to pay a nominal fee, but there is no one around to collect money. A group of trans-Africa backpackers are settling in with their drinks. Their raucous mating calls echo through the valley. Sinead and I linger a while and then walk down toward the bottom of the hill, closer to the falls, where we can be cloaked in silence. We both need silence now. Behind us, the backpackers also grow silent and contemplative as the alcohol washes through their bodies. Tendrils of mist, fingers from an unknown past, from a world beneath the water, reach out to us. Out of nowhere, a stray dog appears. Only when we reach the gates of the lodge does it retreat, driven back by the snarling heads of the lodge pack.

We head over to the lapa for dinner. A few feet away from us, in complete darkness, the Kunene flows swiftly in the night. After dinner,

Sinead heads for bed. I settle in at the bar counter beside the river. Tonight, I will continue to wrestle with Lethe's quarrelsome siblings who threaten to become my permanent companions on this journey. I order a drink and begin to write up my notes for the day. In the background, the duty manager, Shaun, is talking to a group of men and I hear the concern in his voice. "Someone drowned," he tells me when he returns to the bar. "One of the herdsmen saw the body floating a few miles upriver." The Kunene has claimed another soul. "Tomorrow, we'll start searching." I offer to assist, but he assures me that they have enough helpers from the surrounding villages to walk the banks.

Benita joins us after her kitchen duties have been wrapped up. As Shaun pours himself a beer, a man walks in, asking for money. "But we gave you money yesterday." There's a heated discussion, at the end of which Shaun returns to the bar and starts counting out some cash. As soon as the man has left, Shaun turns to me. "We share part of our revenue with the local conservancy. The conservancy leaders are meant to distribute the money to the community, but this guy's forever coming in here at night, demanding revenues. He takes the money and the community doesn't see much. There's little we can do. The whole system is corrupt." I think again of the sign on the hill, but I know too that what Shaun says is not entirely true. We have visited several conservancies that run very effectively and where the benefit to the community is visible.

Shaun takes a long drag at his cigarette and lets out a slow trail of smoke. "The conservancy boards are turning to hunting to make money for their people. They invite foreign hunters and sign away the animals faster than they breed. They ignore the advice of conservationists. Take the shooting of the last Hobatere male, which was reported as taking care of a problem lion." Scare quotes scatter with animated abandon as his hands take flight. "Bull. The GPS in the lion's collar tells a different story: the animal spent the night running along an erratic path that suggests it was being followed and herded into an illegal trap. The last signal from the GPS tracker is at three in the morning. Night shooting is illegal. The area around the shooting site also has signs of baiting, another illegal method. There's corruption everywhere." Shaun downs his drink and pours another. Then he lights a cigarette and sips his drink while we listen to the sound of the water falling a little way to our left. I finish my drink and bid him goodnight. He forces a smile. By the time I get to our chalet, Sinead is fast asleep.

16

I wake early. The birds are not as noticeable as they were in Ruacana, but the view of the fast-flowing river just above the Epupa Falls makes up for the lack of wildlife. Over at the lapa, Shaun and two men are busying themselves around a rubber dinghy. Across the river, I see a chain of men walking along the bank. I walk over to Shaun and again offer my assistance. They thank me for my offer, but decline. Instead, they invite us to visit a nearby Ovahimba homestead with a group of residents at the lodge.

We leave for the village shortly after breakfast. Time, it seems, has little meaning here. A woman heads into the kraal at the centre of the homestead to begin the milking. She settles herself and pulls the flecked red rump of the Nguni cow toward her. After a few tugs at the teats, she hands the container of warm milk to one of the toddlers hanging around at the entrance to the kraal. He drinks thirstily. Just outside the gate of the cattle enclosure, lingering wisps of mist lick at the smoke from the *okuruwo*, the eternal fire that maintains the peaceful relationship between the people of the village and their ancestors. A young boy draws a blanket around his shoulders to stave off the lingering chill of the night. As the sun strengthens and the mist disappears, he will discard this encumbrance and run after the dog.

It is easy to be lulled into the illusion that life has continued in this way since these people settled in the Kaokoveld region during the sixteenth century on their migration south from Angola. But that would ignore the recurring migration of people and herds across the border into Angola in search of good pastures in the traditional lands of their forebears. To think that life in the Kaokoveld remained in idyllic stasis would also ignore the split that occurred at the start of the nineteenth century, when the bulk of the Ovaherero continued their migration south, leaving behind a small remnant, the Ovahimba, to farm the pastures of the Kaokoveld. It would ignore too the forced retreat of the Ovahimba across the border into Angola as the Topnaars and the Nama sent their cattle-raiding parties north during the middle of the nineteenth century.

Most significantly, it would ignore how the lives of the Ovahimba have changed since the first European colonists arrived. One man who embodied this change and who would play a decisive hand in shaping modern Ovahimba identity was Vita Tom, the son of Tom Bechuana and a woman known to us only as Kaitundu. Vita was born during the Battle of Otjimbingwe in 1863, which was perhaps a sign of how war would come to govern his life. As a teenager, Vita travelled into Angola with his father and the trader, Axel Eriksson, to visit King Mweshipandeka sha Shaningika of the Uukwanyama at Ondjiva in present-day Angola. Thus began a relationship with Angola that he would maintain for the rest of his life.

A few years later, in 1881, Vita Tom fell in with the Dorsland Trekkers who crossed the border at Swartbooisdrift and settled with them at Humpata. Vita Tom soon gathered a band of fellow exiles around him as more and more people were displaced in the wars. He and his followers fought for the Angola Boers and they fought for the Portuguese. And when it was expedient, they fought for King Mandume as well. During the genocide that accompanied the Wars of Resistance, many of the fleeing Ovaherero headed north and found refuge with Vita Tom and his people. It was during this time that Vita traded bellicosity for politics.

At the end of the Wars of Resistance, Vita Tom and his people returned to Namibia, settling near Epupa. Back in the Kaokoveld, Vita used his military prowess to establish himself as the leading omuhona in the region. He confronted other Ovahimba leaders and he confronted the colonial authorities, always insisting on the retention of the Ovahimba lifestyle. Much of the lifestyle of today's Ovahimba exists because of Vita Tom's efforts. Epupa and the village we are visiting fell under Vita Tom's command in those days, and as the Epupa Dam project illustrates, their descendants are still fighting a central government for the right to maintain their lifestyle.

Today, there are only women and children present in the village. The lone exception is the head of the village. However, as soon as the omuhona has completed the customary greetings upon our arrival, he too takes his leave to join the others in their search for the missing body. I look around. At several places throughout the village, the skulls of departed cattle adorn the trees and shelters, emphasizing yet again how central these animals are to the Ovahimba and much of their culture. A young Omuhimba man's close association with cattle and with the ancestors starts at birth, when the father gives his son a heifer from the matrilineal herd. It is a gift, or a loan, which the son will use to build his own herd. When the father dies, the son slaughters a beast from this herd, symbolically returning the gift to the father and completing the link between generations. Still the connection does not end there. Regular sacrifices to the ancestors reinforce this relationship, reminding the living that the ancestors are always with us.

The women have gathered at a home furthest from the road to begin the painstaking daily task of applying otjize, the distinctive ochre that covers their bodies. The villagers are used to intrusions from tourists and for the most part they ignore us as they go about their business. A puppy scavenges. The group of children who tag along behind him show little interest in our presence, either. A young boy tires of running after the dog and approaches us. Sinead and I play with him for a while. He takes a piece of paper I have torn from my notebook and runs to his mother, trailing the page in the wind behind him. She looks up and smiles at us. She beckons to the interpreter who has accompanied us as our guide. "She looks like you, but where is the mother?" he translates her question.

"She stayed at home," I reply. The woman nods and leans over to pull her son toward her. She hugs him and blows onto his stomach. He cackles with laughter. "It is a dark day for us," the woman tells me over the giggles of the next generation. "We need to feel our children near us. Your daughter needs to be with her mother."

She invites the women in our company to smear some of the otjize on their arms, but Sinead is distracted by the boy who has left his mother's side and is playing with her bracelet. One of the other women steps forward and smears the paste onto her forearm. "It smells a bit like camphor," she remarks. The interpreter repeats her comments in Otjihimba and the woman nods.

"It is red, for life," he hands back the woman's response. With those simple words, she shifts the conversation away from the scent of the otjize to its symbolic value: life and beauty. The red ochre symbolizes life, and on a day like this, where the community has suffered a loss, it is important that we be reminded of that. She indicates that we should enter one of the huts nearby. Inside, the smell of camphor hangs in the air. A bushel of herbs lies on the stone pestle beside the woman. She reaches over and adds a few more coals from the fire to the smouldering herbs. A few gentle puffs send the smoke billowing into the crowded space. "This is *omuzumba*," the guide says, pointing to the herb, "the plant that gives the otjize its aroma. It belongs to the genus *Camphora*."

When we emerge from the house, the mother has gathered all her children around her. They bid us a safe journey and we take our leave.

Our guide stops beside a copse of mopane trees. A few carefully placed piles of stones indicate that this is a burial site. Cattle horns curl like withered aloe fronds above some of the graves. Our guide tips a small libation of milk onto one of them. "When we visit the graves of our ancestors," he informs those of us who have gathered, "we have to pay our respects." It is only when the living pay due respect to the deceased that the ancestral spirits are released and become free to dwell among the living. Most of the graves in this small cemetery are unmarked and so as the generations pass and new ancestors join the ranks of the deceased, individual names of the ancestors will be forgotten and their spirits will belong to the entire community rather than to individual lineages.

As we look at these graves and observe the obvious respect our guide has for these resting places, Sinead turns to me. "Will these graves be covered by water if the dam gets built?"

I whisper a subdued assent. "The six-hundred-foot dam wall will span the narrow gorge below the falls and will drown every bit of land we now stand on."

"I don't understand why they'd do that," she replies as we turn away from the graves.

In the afternoon, we go whitewater rafting. We return to a sombre campground shortly before sunset. The body of the drowned man was found among the rocks at the edge of the falls and Shaun and the men are busy making arrangements for the body to be returned to the village. Chris Mueller, a German tourist, joins us at the bar while we wait for dinner.

Sinead tells him about the rafting. "The rapids weren't as bad as I'd thought they'd be," she says. "I was more scared of my guide. He kept pretending to tip me out of the raft. There are crocodiles in the water!" Chris laughs.

"The animals are slowly returning after the war. We saw a baby crocodile hanging just above the waterline in the roots of a makalani palm. I could barely tell the difference between it and the roots of the tree! Other than the crocodiles, we saw a leguaan. But the guides say they've seen antelope and even the odd elephant on the Angolan banks."

"I shouldn't have taken my glasses off," I say. "It was all a blur to me."

"Well, I went on a one-on-one guided tour of a Himba village today," Chris reports on his day.

"I really liked the cultural tour of the village," Sinead says. They compare notes.

"I've been coming to Namibia every year for eighteen years now," Chris tells her. "I've been on these group tours. They are nice, but sometimes I feel that they turn the people into objects. You come in, look around and walk away. Going on a personal tour like I did allows you more time to get to know the people. You spend an entire day with a community."

Sinead thinks about it. "That would be nice. I wish we had time to do that, but we have to get on the road again tomorrow. Maybe next time."

The guests at other tables finish their dinner and leave the lapa. I ask for some coffee and listen to Sinead and Chris. The last of the other visitors have left and their voices carry into the night and mingle with the sound of the water flowing by. "I come back to this community every year and over the years I have made many friends. This morning, I saw some of the girls from the community I visited getting ready to walk to their mobile school. It's miles away, so I gave them a ride."

"Mobile schools?" Sinead frowns.

"It's a program developed by the Norwegians," Chris tells her. "Because the Himba are semi-nomadic, it is very difficult for the children to attend school regularly when the community moves. The Norwegians helped to build small classrooms that can be moved with the community. Once a week or so, a teacher comes to the mobile school and gives them classes and assignments for the next while. That way, only one person has to travel. It is an attempt to educate children in a way that respects their culture and their lifestyle."

"Cool!"

"It is," I say, "but there are problems and concerns. The Norwegians have handed over administration of the project to the Namibian government, and they have started turning many of these mobile schools into permanent ones."

"That's just wrong. If the schools stay in one place while the Ovahimba keep moving, kids won't be able to attend school."

The servers start cleaning the tables around us. Chris takes this as his cue to leave. Sinead goes to bed as well, but I stay behind again to write up my notes on the day in the brighter light of the lapa. Shaun does some admin work while I write. Once her chores are done, Benita joins us at the bar counter. In the background, a slight breeze blows the moisture from the river over us. Shaun is in a sombre mood after the day's events. "Imagine this place without the falls. Just imagine water where we are sitting now. Because that's what you'll get if that bloody dam gets built. All this will be gone and then there will be nothing left for tourists to see." His ire grows more animated with every sentence. He lights a cigarette before launching into his next salvo. He has every right to be angry, as do the Ovahimba and every other member of this community. Ever since independence, the *ovahona* and other concerned citizens have resisted the government's efforts to build the dam at Epupa. Over the years, an uneasy stalemate has developed.

"It was the South Africans who first came up with the idea of building a new dam below the falls. After independence, the Namibian government took up the idea again as a way of breaking Namibia's dependence on foreign power supply. The problem with the whole scheme starts at Ruacana. The hydro scheme there only runs at about seventy percent capacity because the water supply from Calueque is so erratic. But in the end it's not the dam that really counts," Shaun says, "it's votes." I can see his point. In the elections that have been held since independence, the Kunene Region has consistently voted in members of parliament from opposition parties. Some see the push to build the dam as a way of breaking the political hegemony in the region by forcing the Ovahimba out of their lifestyle.

Shaun pours us both another drink before he continues. "If the bloody government just helped the Angolans fix the Calueque Dam, it would provide enough energy to supply the needs of both the Angolans and the Namibians. There is no need for this idiotic scheme." Shaun does what he does at the end of every outburst: he lights another cigarette. "You know, they can build solar panels on nine hundred hectares — a fraction of the area the dam would destroy — and produce the same amount of electricity as the proposed dam every year and not just in years with a good rainfall." He closes his eyes and sucks the smoke into his lungs at a leisurely pace. Time is suspended as he holds his breath and lets the nicotine seep into his body.

"The Himba have been protesting the new dam," he says eventually. "They've even been to the UN and other international bodies, but the government is insistent. Now they're talking of moving the dam site further down the river, to Orakawe. But the same problems exist there. It is Himba land, even though the government disagrees."

Benita interjects. "The Himba have other questions. Why are the medical facilities in the region so poor in comparison to other regions? Would the government be supplying the farmers with subsidized fodder in this time of drought? As always, the government avoids these questions. But that's in the future. We can't predict what will happen."

There's a brief silence as they search for less controversial topics of discussion. We are on the banks of the Kunene, after all, and here we are meant to forget the troubles of the outside world. I steer the conversation to the fertile soil of Namibian archaeology. Shaun perks up. "They've found some new sites near Rundu."

"I've heard rumours that they have discovered sites that reveal something of riparian culture in the region, yes."

"Ja, but they're in areas controlled by the National Defence Force," Benita interjects. "I doubt very much that the public will be granted access to those sites."

"Those aren't the sites I'm talking about," Shaun remarks casually. "I'm talking about the new sites. Not only the ones from the colonial era, but the other, more recent ones." Benita gives him a look. Clearly, we're back in territory everyone shies away from, so I prompt him.

"You're not talking about the graves at Eenhana and the ones outside Lüderitz and Swakop, I presume?" A few years ago, developers uncovered a large mass grave at Eenhana, a former South African military base and the site of the final skirmish between South Africa and Namibia. Since then, several more graves have been uncovered, some containing the bodies of civilians, others the bodies of SWAPO soldiers. In 2008, the government unveiled a shrine to the fallen at Eenhana, but visitors seldom go there, whether it is because the shrine is unknown or that they don't want to be reminded of the past is unclear.

It is a pity, for like the Holocaust memorials, these places of suffering should be made visible; they should stand as reminders to our generation of what we did. They should not be hidden behind the gates and barricades of military bases and paraded for political gain at opportune moments and then forgotten. There needs to be an openness and a willingness to discuss the events that surrounded these acts of horror.

And it is openness that I seek: stray news reports on the Internet or a dropped comment during conversations over the past few weeks point to the existence of new mass graves in the Kavango Region. Graves that look as though they date from the post-independence era. I want to hear more about them, yet I know from the past few weeks that there is nothing that makes people clam up as quickly as dredging up the graves of the past. Tonight proves no exception. The generally forthcoming Shaun pauses to take the last drag on his cigarette. Benita watches him carefully as he completes his ritual. Shaun takes his time stubbing the cigarette out and exhales the last lungful of smoke onto the counter as he does so. It billows up and he waves it away from me. Only when the air has cleared, does Shaun speak again. "Do you remember the SADF poaching scandal that led to the eradication of so many species in southern Angola and the Caprivi? It's happening again." It's barely after nine. Shaun swings his head around and looks at the empty chairs beside me. "Last round," he says.

17

Sinead and I leave for Opuwo early in the morning. About fifteen minutes out of Epupa we encounter a blue Toyota bakkie at the side of the road. The hood is up and two young men are peering into the abyss. I pull over. One of the men ambles over to me. "I'm out of petrol," he says.

The nearest gas station is in Opuwo, so I begin to offer to give them some gas from our jerry can, only to realize as I open my mouth that it's filled with diesel. Instead, I offer to take him to the nearest gas station. He glances over at his companion, then at the girl sitting in the bakkie. He thinks hard before declining my offer. He scribbles a short note on a piece of paper I hand him: "Innocent is about 10km from Omurundu, Dave. Plz send me 20L." Then he draws a map and explains to me how to find his friend.

"At Oukango, just where the road turns off to Opuwo, there's a café bar. Go straight. About three hundred yards further, you'll see a yellow Golf — that belongs to Dave. If you carry on and follow the curve of the road, you'll see the gas station. They have diesel too," he says, glancing at my fuel gauge.

I wave goodbye and set off to help Innocent and his friends. It's about seventy kilometres to Oukango, where the road makes a sharp dogleg and disappears into the distance. A small two-rut track leads to a motley assortment of houses strung to either side of the road. I spot the bar Innocent mentioned and a little way ahead, there's a second bar. A handwritten sign announces: "Petrol/Diesel." Half a kilometre further, the road makes a U-turn and heads back on the other side of the row of houses to my left. We have still not seen the yellow Golf. Right in the bend, a sign indicates again that there's diesel for sale and so I continue on the assumption that if Dave isn't there, then at least I can get some diesel. At the gate, I turn in, get out of the bakkie and walk over to the woman sitting on her chair. A man is fiddling with an engine part for the government vehicle parked to my left. The woman leafs through an invoice book and doesn't so much as look up when I approach. "Do you know Innocent?" I ask her. "He's from Oukango. Lives right beside the petrol station." She shakes her head. I explain the predicament and show her the piece of paper with the note on it. She and the youth at the engine enter into a lengthy discussion in Otjiherero before she turns to me: "I know Innocent. Dave is out of town."

"Well, can you try to organize some petrol for Innocent?" She shakes her head.

"And can I get some diesel?" I ask. She shakes her head again. I look around for a pump of sorts, but there is nothing but a pile of scrap metal behind me. I can see a 200-litre drum sticking out from behind the building and I suspect that may contain the diesel.

The woman sees me looking at the drum and replies hurriedly, "The guy who does the diesel isn't here."

"Is it Dave?" I ask.

"No."

"Well, can you get him to come and help me with some diesel?"

"I'll call the guy for the diesel." She reaches into the folds of her dress and hauls out a cell phone. She dials a number and speaks for about ten minutes.

"He's coming."

Sinead and I wait in the bakkie for just over fifteen minutes before she tells me that he has decided not to come after all. With no access to any gas and just enough diesel in the tank to get us to Opuwo, I give up on Innocent and trust that someone else will stop to help him.

Opuwo is overrun by hawkers selling tourist trinkets. We have barely stopped at the gas station when the first hawkers find us. By the time the tank has been filled, about thirty of them cluster around the bakkie, trying to sell us some fresh fruit and vegetables. I take a quick look, but their wares have wilted in the sun and I know the vegetables won't last in the heat of the car. For anything to last in our small cooler, we need to get goods that have had the benefit of spending the night in a store's refrigerators. We nudge our way back into the main road and head to the local supermarket to restock our supplies. Just out of town, reality and the map clash. The map indicates a crossroad, but at the junction, it is clear that no such road exists. The road to the right leads to Kamanjab; the road to the left heads back to Ruacana. In the middle, straight ahead of us, should be a road leading to Tsandi, but instead Sinead and I find ourselves staring at a barricade. There's a small cluster of road workers' houses at the junction and a man wearing a reflective vest steps out into the sunshine. I ask him for directions. He points in the direction of the shantytown that lies beyond the T-junction and laughs. "I'm heading for Tsandi. Give me a ride and I'll take you there." He introduces himself as Wilbald Shingweda and squeezes in beside the bags on the back seat of the double cab. As soon as he has settled himself, he reaches into the folds of his overalls and hauls out his identity card to show us. Wilbald uses his insider knowledge of the area to guide us through the shantytown that has developed opposite the T-junction. Directly behind the houses, a beautiful new tarred road materializes out of nowhere. Wilbald smiles. About five kilometres down the road, he asks to be dropped off. "Just head straight along this road — it will take you right into Tsandi," he says as he waves through the window.

I can hardly believe our luck. The map had indicated a minor road and I was expecting little more than two ruts. I do not complain and enjoy the opportunity to drive on a brand new tarred road. The bliss does not last. Not long after we've dropped Wilbald off, the tar ends, and so, for all intents and purposes, does the road. A new road is under construction, but for the next fifty kilometres, we bump along the potholes beside it. The GPS cackles advice about going through Kamanjab — a detour of more than three hours. The GPS is generally about five years behind in its analysis of the terrain; now, it revels in being right for once and does not let us live it down. Eventually we do hit a road and take the turn to Tsandi, where we turn left and set out for Omugulugwombashe. Mopane trees and goats mingle with scattered homesteads and oshanas by the roadside.

We drive through a number of small, unnamed villages that hug the roadside, following the road until it ends in a clump of mopanes about two kilometres beyond Omugulugwombashe. We can see a clinic to the right, but there is no monument in sight and no direction markers to indicate one. The clinic looks deserted. I turn around and drive back to the bar in Omugulugwombashe to confirm the directions I have. In the bar, an old man sits by the table, clutching a bottle of Tassenberg. I ask the young man leaning on the counter where the monument is. At the mention of the monument, the old man turns around and stares at me. Then he turns back to his bottle and swigs the last mouthful from it. His head sinks to the table. I want to talk to the old man, but the bartender hustles me back to the car.

"This is Omugulugwombashe," he says pointing to the dot on the map. "The monument is just outside town, at the clinic. You stop and walk four hundred metres."

"Which direction?" I ask. He seems unsure and busies himself with looking at the map again. The map doesn't indicate the road out of town, so he points again to the dot that is Omugulugwombashe and repeats himself. Then he retreats to the safety of the bar. The old man staggers into the sunlight and walks aimlessly down the deserted street. I call after him, but he has retreated into a private, drunken world in which he sings a doleful song to the goats that have decided to accompany him on his wanderings.

Sinead and I head back to the clinic. This time, there's a sign of life, so I go in and ask the nurse on duty. "The gate is open." She points to a gate behind the clinic. As we exit, I notice the posters inviting people to come for free HIV testing on Namibia's national HIV awareness day. Other posters alert people to the different ways in which to keep your environment as germ-free as possible when you're infected — and even when you're not: "Staying germ-free helps you fight HIV," one poster rhymes.

At the gate, we find everything locked up. There is a handwritten sign with a cell number on it. I dial it and a man answers. He assures me he'll be there in ten minutes. Half an hour later, no one has appeared. I walk to the road to see whether someone may be coming from the town. Two goats tethered to the washing line in the back-yard of the clinic bleat at me as I pass. Another fifteen minutes pass without interruption. I call to make sure he's on his way. "I'm just on patrol," the man tells me. "I'm walking in now. Ten minutes."

And so we wait at this place that ignited a revolution. On the twenty-sixth of August 1966, the South African Police launched an attack on the PLAN soldiers here at Omugulugwombashe, including Meme Priskila's husband, Kaxumba. Over the preceding year, soldiers had crossed the Namibian border and had begun recruiting foot sol-diers among the local population. As police surveillance increased, they left their homes and settled here in the heart of Uukwaluudhi, where King Shikongo shaTaapopi had offered them a safe haven. The men hiding in the bushes were unprepared for the wrath of the apart-heid machine and their first battle ended in a disaster. Those who were not killed during the battle fled underground, avoiding the police for as long as they could, but in the end they were rounded up and sentenced to imprisonment on Robben Island. Their resistance inspired others, who continued to flood over the border of Namibia and engaged with the South African forces. And with every setback, their strength and resilience increased until they learned how to win the war, if not the battles that comprised it.

It's hard to imagine this small clearing behind the clinic as a battle site when the biggest battle Sinead and I face is staying awake. The midday sun is killing us and though it's only early spring, even the ants seem lethargic and reluctant to set foot on the soil. I drift in and out of wakefulness. An hour later, Sinead nudges me. A man appears from the bushes to the left toting a 12-gauge shotgun over his shoulder. He introduces himself as Matheus Jonas Kahumbe and shows me his PLAN combatant card. I notice that his date of enlistment is 1979. Right after the Battle of Cassinga.

Matheus unlocks the gate for us and as we walk down a footpath that leads to the monument, he tells me he trained in the Soviet Union and that he was stationed at Cassinga until the end of the war. Cassinga is one of those names that drifted through my childhood as I became aware of the world beyond my immediate borders. For months from the end of 1977 onward, the adult men of Burgersdorp had been called up for military camps. Those fresh out of school became the first set of teenagers who were called up for two years of compulsory military service, to be followed by a further eight years of annual camps lasting thirty days each. Teachers appeared in uniform and the old jail beside our house was transformed into the commando headquarters. In April 1978, the men left in droves, only to return months later bearded and with eyes dulled by combat. Early in the morning of the fourth of May, the South Africans descended on Cassinga, a town located two hundred fifty kilometres into Angola. Initially, Cassinga had been set up as a training base for PLAN soldiers, who received logistical support from the Cuban forces located at Tetchamutete. As more and more refugees from Namibia crossed the border, Cassinga transformed from a military base to a refugee camp. Or both. The details are not always clear, but what is clear is that by the end of that fateful day, the bodies of the dead were stacked high in Cassinga. The South African government claimed they were all soldiers, but the photographs of children and unarmed civilians splashed across the papers around the world made mockery of their claims. Cassinga was a defining moment in a war that otherwise continued by stealth.

Matheus's grasp of English is minimal and his Afrikaans is only slightly better, but we manage to communicate well enough by meandering among islands of language.

"So you fought at Cuito Cuanavale?"

"Yes, I am a man," he responds. It is not a statement about his prowess, or his perception of masculinity. It is an observation that he has been through a rite of passage and that he has been changed by it. There can be no return to the time before the war. I look at Matheus's face. There are no scars, as I have seen on so many older men in these parts. For many Namibians, scarification signals their transition into adulthood. Matheus points to his leg. There is a small entry wound just above the knee where a bullet entered his body. Lower down along the calf, the exiting bullet has left a mangled welt. This wound is his initiation scar, marking a transition into manhood that had started at the Battle of Omugulugwombashe and that ended when he was wounded in the last major battle, at Cuito. He, like me, is one of the wounded generation.

"Cuito is always with me," he says.

Matheus and I talk for a bit more. I ask him about the battle at Omugulugwombashe. "I am from here," he says.

I do a quick mental calculation based on the dates in his identity card. "Where were you when the battle happened?"

"I do not remember much. I was about six," he says. "I only remember the helicopters. *Hulle praat elke aand met my.* They talk to me every night." The sounds of sunrise etched into a child's mind; an initiation rite that set him on a journey north across the borders in search of freedom. As Matheus lay awake, listening to the sound of helicopters and bombs breaking in the day, I lay swaddled in the safety of my crib in our home in Okahandja.

Years later, while Matheus Kahumbe lay in the trenches waiting for the battle at Cuito Cuanavale to begin, I was lying in bed, contemplating a decision I had just made. It was August 1988 and the End Conscription Campaign had recently been banned. Despite having been banned, the ECC had organized protest marches and was launching a new protest campaign. Around the country, thousands of young men added their names to the list of those who would not serve. Earlier in the month, the local campaign organizer, Darryl Maclean, had asked me whether I would be willing to make a public statement about my refusal to serve in the army. There could be no return after a decision like that. The sentence for draft evasion was six years. I knew I objected to the war, but was I prepared to go to prison? It was different for others, like Charles Bester. He was the poster case, the objector whose trial was headline news. Charles had objected on religious grounds and in the time he spent in prison, it was his faith that sustained him. I did not have that security. All I had was a conviction I did not yet understand in its entirety. What I did know was that two of my friends, Edwin Prins and Robert Mopp, had been detained without trial the previous year. I had seen what prison had done to them. I reread the letters from a friend who had been stationed on the Namibian border. They oozed despair. That was enough. I knew I wanted no part of a system that did such things to people, so on the day of the campaign, I went to St. Andrew's College in Grahamstown. In one of the classrooms set aside for this event, Daryl read the generic End Conscription Campaign statement:

- We live in an unjust society where basic human rights are denied to the majority of the people.
- We live in an unequal society where the land and wealth are owned by the minority.

- We live in a society in a state of civil war, where brother is called on to fight brother.
- Young men are conscripted to maintain the illegal occupation of Namibia, and to wage unjust war against foreign countries.
- We call for an end to conscription.

And so on. After reading the statement, each one of the objectors walked up to the podium to state publicly their right to conscientious objection and to sign the declaration. I remember little of my time up there besides fear. My hands were shaking as I signed my name. I recall saying something about two unjust wars and not being willing to fight against my own countrymen. I hope that I mentioned that I was opposed to the illegal occupation of Namibia, the land of my birth. I think I did. It's a blur. I do remember people in the streets telling me how disgusted they were and how violently they disagreed with my actions. I remember telling them how much I didn't care. But inside I was trembling. It was a small gesture, but I believed those words then, as I do to this day.

I look up from Matheus's wounds and read the inscription on the obelisk in front of me: "The torch of the armed struggle was lit and the path to liberation was illuminated." Standing here at Omugulugwombashe, looking at Matheus's wounds, I realize that believing and having conviction in what one says is one thing. Understanding the implications of those words is something else.

We both returned, Matheus and I. The difference is that I came and left again. Matheus returned, and every day he still returns to this place of memory on his rounds. I thank him for his contribution to securing the freedom of this land. As we leave, I see Matheus walk back to the monument and stand in silence before it. He is still standing there as I turn into the road that leads back to Omugulugwombashe.

After the battle at Omugulugwombashe, the South African Police set up a permanent base in the nearby town of Tsandi, from where they could conduct regular patrols to surrounding areas. In the shadow of that police station lay the royal palace of the Uukwaluudhi, where King Shikongo shaTaapopi lived and which is now a museum. Sinead looks at the clock on the dashboard. "We have time to make it," she says. "Drive."

It's almost closing time when we arrive, but as soon as we stop, a woman walks over to the bakkie. "I'm Elizabeth and I will be your guide today. Welcome to the royal palace!" Her slight lisp bubbles through the smile. It doesn't take her long to lead us through the compound. We move through the various sleeping quarters for the king's body-guards, the protocols involved in meeting with the king, the sleeping arrangements in the royal homestead. Elizabeth stops in front of a small enclosure near the middle of the compound. "This is where the king would meet with his generals before they went into battle," Elizabeth tells us.

A shiver runs down my spine. "Did any of the PLAN soldiers gather here before going into battle?" I ask, since I know that King Shikongo shaTaapopi, the reigning king of Uukwaluudhi, was sympathetic to the Struggle and it was he who had given permission for the original group of PLAN combatants to set up a camp at Omugulugwombashe.

Elizabeth just laughs. "You'd have to ask the king, but he's not in today."

As we drive away from the royal homestead, an old man appears on the stoep of the house beside the palace. King Taapopi smiles and waves at us. Sinead turns to me.

"I really liked Elizabeth. This was the best part so far. It's such a complex country and I don't always understand the history, but I like it." I can't expect her to understand what I haven't been able to grasp in more than double her lifetime, and I tell her so.

"It's a bit like apartheid," she continues. "I was born at the end of it and I can't comprehend the full impact of what it was like living through it. Or of the impact it had on peoples' lives. I just know it was wrong." I have little to add. The longer we have been in Namibia, the more I have sensed this born-free generation gap. "I still tell people

I'm South African even though I've spent most of my life in Canada. It is my special place, my heart-place." That I understand. Namibia is my story-place, my heart-place. Just as I can't explain how Namibia remains such an important part of me, so she can't explain to others how South Africa remains so strong in her, and why she still insists she is South African.

"I sometimes feel I've missed out on something important by not living in South Africa." Again I can only nod in understanding.

"I have that feeling about Namibia," I tell her. "There's a hollow that I have come to fill, and it's overflowing. This is my country even if some idiot stole my passport and my identity card and I cannot haul it out and prove it. But it will always be part of me."

And yet I sense as we leave the royal homestead, that I do not have to say this. Sinead understands.

At dinner in Oshakati, a man sits at the other end of the stoep. His silhouette against the sun makes it impossible to see the details, but even from here, I am struck by the familiarity of the figure. I walk over to the bar and exit through the doors behind him. Even up close, I am shocked. For more than a second, I stare: he looks like my brother. The echoes and ghosts of my family have haunted me all along the way. Etosha, Namutoni, Naukluft. The Van Eck Grave. Physical points that tie me to this place.

◆　◆　◆

Oshakati is a military town that has been abandoned. The shopping centre in town looks like it is falling apart and all around it, street markets have appeared. It's shortly before eight, and the vendors are setting up. The half-drum braai grills are out and lengths of log are already burning to coal to supply the day's customers with food. I see some kids carrying fish on strings; others have bowls of meat on their heads. A young couple walks by, hand in hand. One of them stops and drops off a bowl of meat at one of the vendors — her mother, by the looks of things. The mother says something to her. She smiles and walks off to school, still holding her boyfriend's hand.

We have chosen to take a southern route to the Caprivi Strip, our next destination, but closer to the border, a road runs east toward Rundu. I would have loved to travel on that road, but the barman at Oshakati had said the road was really bad this year and he had recommended 4 × 4 traffic only. It's a pity, for that road was built to carry troops from base to base just south of the border — from Omafu to Rundu. I try to run my mind through the bases along the road, but my mind gets stuck at Eenhana. The first contact between PLAN and South African forces happened at Omugulugwombashe, but the horrors of Eenhana, where the last skirmish took place, are just beginning to surface. It was after the Mount Etjo meeting and the UN was already monitoring the transition. South African troops were slowly being demobilized and were confined to bases all along the border. PLAN troops were tentatively beginning to return to Namibia. They began their final march from deep within Angola toward the border, passing through Namakunde, King Mandume's old capital and on to the border at Oshikango. As they approached the Eenhana base to be demobilized and turn in their weapons, the South Africans cried foul. It was a breach of the treaty, and they insisted that the PLAN soldiers return north of the border. The UNTAG force was still unprepared for a large-scale operation of escorting the soldiers back over the border, and agreed that the South Africans could do it. But they did not escort the troops back over the border. Instead, they engaged them in combat, killing three hundred PLAN soldiers. They bulldozed the bodies together and pushed them into an unmarked grave near Eenhana. It was only in 2007 that road crews uncovered this mass grave and the slow task of trying to identify these bodies began.

If only those were the only graves. Meme Priskila says with confidence in her memoir that there are other such graves along that road. Many of them. And other oral accounts support her claim, for stories of Koevoet units wandering into villages and wiping out the inhabitants abound. After that final skirmish, the peace accord was renegotiated and the SADF retreated back to their bases, gloating about revenge for Cuito. The PLAN soldiers limped back into Angola and waited for the elections.

There is a constant stream of vehicles heading north along the road between Ondangwa and Oshakati. Fortunately, we're moving against the flow of traffic. I wonder why the road is so busy, for the school holidays are over. Eventually, I see a billboard advertising the Mahangu Fair in Ondangwa. I point it out to Sinead. "That must be what has generated this onslaught of vehicles." She nods and settles down for a snooze. She'd slept badly and we were up early. She dozes off and I retreat into my own thoughts about how people seem to show little interest in the monuments of the past. It is the present that seems to consume their thoughts. To the younger generation, the born-frees, these monumental money pits bear little relevance to their lives. Perhaps the two women at the coffee shop in Lüderitz were correct: We don't need more things to remind us of the past. We need a future and a way to give people their humanity back. More than anything, they have sacrificed their dignity and their humanity and they need it back.

Only, I've discovered that it is not that simple to leave the ghosts of the past behind.

18

The main road that traverses northern Namibia swings in a slow loop southeast from Oshakati, down through Tsumeb and on to Grootfontein before it bends back north again toward Rundu and the Caprivi Strip. Once the early morning traffic from the trade show has thinned, Sinead and I settle into the dull routine of watching for stray animals on the road. There's plenty of that. Road, that is. A full five hundred kilometres of it set out for the day's travel. Sinead chats for a while about the past few days in the Kaokoveld, about the animals in Etosha, the places she'd like to visit on a return journey. Gradually, the monotony of the road lulls her to sleep. About ten kilometres outside Tsumeb, I am startled from my reverie when a road worker steps into the road, pointing to the right front tire. As he does so, I feel the bakkie lunge slightly to the driver's side. I pull over and watch the tire shrivel into a limp mess before my eyes. The next steps have become routine: Sinead reaches for the jack behind the seat while I haul the spare tire out of the back.

The hard, whitened earth by the roadside drops steeply. Sinead joins me as I wriggle under the vehicle. Together, we push and shove, weighing our options in search of a place to position the jack. By now, a cluster of road workers has gathered around us. Two of them join

us under the car. They too can't find a solution. One of them crosses
the road and returns with a *real* jack, the one used to raise the road
workers' truck. We now have another problem: the jack is too big to
fit underneath, so Andimba, for that is the name of the man who has
come to our assistance, helps me push the car back onto the camber
of the road and gain a few inches. This time, we manage to squeeze
the jack in and the bakkie rears up on its back wheels, baring its fangs
above us. I can hear the GPS chuckling to itself in the car as it makes
a helpful suggestion. One of the road workers is already tugging at
the wheel lugs. Two new hands appear and remove the tire. Another
set of hands puts the brand new spare on and again within a minute,
the bakkie is dropped back onto all fours and our volunteer pit crew
has us ready to leave.

"Where are you headed?" asks Andimba as he picks up the jack.

"We're hoping to make Rundu tonight. But first we'll have to see
to this tire."

"Grootfontein. There's no tire place in Tsumeb." We shake hands
and Andimba rejoins his colleagues.

"People here are so helpful," Sinead comments as we drive off.
"Everyone helps. And people still find a reason to smile, even though
their lives are hard." We settle into silence again, counting down the
remaining miles to Grootfontein.

"I'm hungry," Sinead says. "The GPS says there's a tire place down
the next road and a café nearby." I follow her directions. The woman
behind the counter continues to click the cards on the computer
screen and barely lifts her eyes when I walk in. I wait patiently for
her to finish her game. When she's done, she starts another. I ask for
assistance. She doesn't even flinch as the bomb on her screen explodes.
She reaches out her hand and takes a sip of Sparletta Cream Soda and
restarts her game. Still no acknowledgement of my presence. Smoke
from her cigarette forms a screen between us. Eventually, one of the
repairmen from the workshop sees me. The woman barks at him in
Afrikaans about forgetting a detail on the work order, then returns to

her game. When I ask for the bathroom keys, she flicks her wrist in the direction of the counter. I lean over and search for it. She offers no assistance.

"My turn," says Sinead when I get back to the bakkie. While she's gone, I drop the tire at the workshop. When she returns, there is a look of indignation on her face. "She told me I had to pay! I told her you hadn't, but she just stared at me. So I just took the key anyway." We cross the road to the café. It takes a while before the waitress drags herself from her friends and approaches us. When the food appears on the counter, she collects it and throws the plates onto our table without a word. "I take back what I said about helpful and friendly," Sinead says. "Does anyone here smile?"

I've begun to wonder that myself. I ascribe much of it to the peculiar history of this town and its place in the war. "During the War of Independence, people referred to this area around Grootfontein and Tsumeb as the Triangle of Death," I start to explain to Sinead. "When the PLAN soldiers crossed the border into Namibia, they'd head toward the area between Tsumeb, Grootfontein and Otavi. Much of the fighting inside Namibian borders took place on the farms that lie between these towns. Grootfontein also had a large South African military base. Basically, the locals and farmers circled their wagons and they've never really left the protection of that circle."

"That's no excuse," Sinead says.

"It could just be the weather, but I suspect the truth lies deeper. It's a century's worth of resentment, combined with hereditary conservatism and belligerence. The Trekkers and traders who passed through northern Namibia in the late nineteenth century included several groups of Dorsland Trekkers. One of the main routes for these Trekkers ran north past Lake Ngami and up through the Omaheke, past Grootfontein and Etosha, and on to Humpata in Angola. At Humpata, they clashed with Portuguese authorities over the right to retain their language and their Calvinist beliefs in a Catholic world. Dispirited, they returned the way they had come, settling in northern

Namibia. Grootfontein became the centre of government for the Boer Republic of Upingtonia.

"The Trekkers built homes and began cultivating farms, but their utopia did not last. Within two years, the Trekkers asked the German colonial authorities for protection and they became part of German South West Africa. Some of the farmers moved on in search of greener pastures, but some remained, and so did their descendants. It's more than just the War of Independence," I tell Sinead.

After lunch, we head over to the post office. Sinead has had enough of Grootfontein rudeness and opts to wait in the car. I leave her there and run inside. A knot of human bodies clogs the entire passage, but as I enter, people find space to move aside. I step forward and the gap behind me closes. An amoeboid bubble opens ahead of me and I feel myself gliding effortlessly toward the counter. An old woman in front of me struggles to drag her bags out of my way. I stop her. "No need to move out of the way for me."

"Ouma only speaks Ndonga," says a voice from within the crowd. I cannot see anyone, but I can tell from the sound that the owner cannot be more than five or six. I bend down and search among the legs and bags around me. A boy steps forward. "I'm meme's helper." I smile at him, but the woman puts a protective arm around her grandson and pulls him toward her. I hold the boy's gaze and remain on my haunches. Around me, people have started to move again, but the boy and I remain fixed in our bubble on the linoleum floor. Barely a minute has passed since I walked into the room. A deep sadness enters my bones: this is how long it takes for two decades to disappear. I am the only white face in the building. This parting of the seas, I realize, is occasioned by my whiteness.

"What is your name?" I ask of the boy.

"Elias."

"You speak English beautifully, Elias."

"We learn it at school. But we talk Afrikaans to white people here. I can count to a hundred already."

"I don't mind which one you speak to me," I tell Elias. "But show me how you count." My heart warms to this child who has not yet learned the inhibitions of race or language.

Elias rattles off a string of numbers in Afrikaans, English and, I presume, Ndonga. Every now and then, he needs a prod. I help him with the English and Afrikaans; his meme helps with the Ndonga. She has relaxed enough in my presence to let him go. He shows me the treasures in his pockets; I show him mine. Meme reaches into one of her bags and pulls out a small container of *oshifima*, porridge made from mahangu maize. She offers me some before holding it out to the boy. Although I have just eaten, I realize that she is extending her friendship. I dip my fingers into the bowl and rake a small dollop of oshifima onto my hand. Her face lights up. And so we nibble our way to the front of the line, my new-found friend, Elias, his grandmother and I.

The rich taste of the oshifima lingers for a while after we leave Grootfontein for the second leg of our trip up to Rundu. At Mururani, we cross from the Otjozondjupa Region into the Kavango Region. The policewoman at the disease control post approaches and asks for my driver's licence. I hand her my passport and the international driver's licence. She looks at the papers carefully.

"I see you were born here in Okahandja. Why don't you have a Namibian passport?"

I explain to her that my papers were stolen. She nods. "You have applied for your passport while you're here, né?" I assure her I have. She folds my papers together again neatly and hands them back with a smile before waving me through. Just outside Rundu, we get pulled over at a checkpoint. A Namibian Defence Force officer steps into the road. His bandolier is heavy with ammunition and an AK-47 dangles disquietingly in his hands. He approaches us and throws out his hand as a signal to produce our papers. I hand him the documents. He fires a few single-shot questions at me before flicking his hand again to release us from his interrogation. I drive slowly down the gauntlet of camouflaged vehicles behind him. Casspirs. The mere sight of them is enough to take me back into the days of protest marches. Rows of Mellow Yellows, the yellow police Casspirs, pocking the roadside as we marched. Policemen lazing against the sides of their patrol cars; young troops poking their helmets over the top, curious to see the spectacle unfold before them. Some were hoping to see action, as they had on that day in Langa in 1985, when South African troops fired at the mourners who had come to attend a funeral. And those of us in the march would toyi-toyi and wave flags of red and black and green and gold. It takes a while to shake the memory.

We arrive in Rundu near the end of day. There's an orderly bustle as hawkers pack up their roadside stalls and head home for the evening. Sinead catches the GPS in a moment of co-operation and directs us to a lodge with a campsite. We enter through a set of large black iron gates hung on imposing white pillars. An elephant statue guards each side of the gate. The bungalows all face the reception like the ranks of a well-trained army. Along the walls, austere masks and statues salute visitors in an overbearing show of African kitsch.

Sinead and I move through the stark parade of masked buildings and park beside one of the tenting spots in the open space that lies beyond. I try to find a secluded spot in this wasteland of camping pads, but even among the trees it is impossible to hide the eight-foot barrier of concrete and razor wire that runs around the perimeter of the compound. From where we stand, the land drops away toward the banks of the Okavango River. I draw Sinead close to me and together we look out over the throng of workers making their way home to the shacks that crowd the banks of the river below us.

Dust. Not even in the desert did I have this overwhelming sense of dust pervading my body. In desperation, I clean out the back of the bakkie and wipe down everything, but the camp dust dries right through the wet streak left by the cloth. Dust is ingrained in the concrete of this place. There is no wind. Oh for a bit of wind. There is only the muggy heat of the day settling into the darkness.

Around five in the morning, an incessant roundel of dogs and roosters penetrates my dreams. I lie for a while immersed in that shadowy netherworld between sleep and wakefulness, listening to the dogs barking. An insect hovers around the tent. It flies into the canvas and rolls down the side, stunned. There is a brief silence before it picks itself up and the buzzing starts again. Again and again, it beats against the canvas, trying to force its way in. I want to sleep in. I want to sleep and to forget.

The assault on the tent is relentless. The bug and the baying dogs have lodged in my head and I feel a sense of unease growing in me and I try to force myself back through that illusionary portal that separates the realms of sleep and wakefulness. Alas, it is too late; I cannot fall asleep. My mind fills with thoughts. Today, we will leave Rundu and head into the Caprivi Strip. The Caprivi, the place of childhood stories. The stories I'd overheard from the adults; the stories that were translated into playground games; the stories that emerged from the photonovels about Grensvegter; the place where Buffalo Battalion had its headquarters; the place where the war started. Lines from the end of Book Six of the *Aeneid* drift into my head: this is the dread that Aeneas must have felt as he stood at the portal that would lead him out of the underworld and back into the real world to face the trials and battles that would secure a place in Italy for his descendants. I cannot remain besieged inside this tented netherworld forever, so I emerge to a cloud of mosquitoes that have been waiting in ambush. Behind the tent, the main gates gleam ivory in the morning sun and the day appears young and vigorous, but on the table beside our tent, the *nachtreste*, the remains of the night, linger in a layer of dust.

The Caprivi has always been an oddity, I think as I prepare breakfast and listen to the sounds of people walking to work from the shacks that lie between our campsite and the Okavango River. It was tagged on as part of the continental horse-trading that took place among European nations after the Berlin Conference of 1884. In 1890, the German chancellor, Leo von Caprivi, received this strip of land from Britain in exchange for giving up Germany's claim to two islands: Heligoland in the North Sea and Zanzibar off the east coast of Africa. Germany was largely an absentee landlord. A small contingent of troops was stationed at Nkurenkuru, a little way northwest of Rundu, and another at the eastern end of the Caprivi Strip, at a place they called Schuckmannsburg. These two outposts were not really intended as administrative centres; rather, they were there to keep an eye on Portuguese activities north of the Angolan border. When the South Africans took over after the First World War, they continued the trend of being absentee landlords, governing the region from Bechuanaland. For the most part, the local peoples remained nominally independent, but as both the ANC and SWAPO began to use the Caprivi Strip to give their troops access to South African territory in the early 1960s, it became necessary to gain firmer control.

The Caprivi Strip was the location of the playground wars South African boys of my generation staged. This was where the playground hero, Kaptein Caprivi, fought his battles. Schoolboys would re-enact his feats; playground equipment became the base camps in Rundu and Katima Mulilo. Katima, where many of their fathers were stationed in those times. Katima, in the heart of the Caprivi. Katima, where some people argue the War for Independence started.

Sinead crawls out of the tent to a squadron of mosquitoes. "Go away!" she complains as she swats the air. She lathers herself in repellent until even my cereal tastes of citronella. It works for a few minutes. Sinead has a quick shower at the restrooms nearby while I strike the tent and pack up. When she returns, she grabs a granola bar and an apple. "Let's get out of here! I can't stand these mosquitoes."

We drive back along the phalanx of bungalows toward the gates, which by now have lost their ivory sheen.

"*Ne, pueri, ne tanta animis adsuescite bella / neu patriae validas in viscera vertite vires,*" I intone solemnly as we drive through the gates.

Sinead furrows her eyebrows and shakes her head. "That's a little random, even for you."

"Not really," I tell her. "At the end of Book Six of the *Aeneid*, Aeneas's dead father leads him through the last few fields of the underworld, where Aeneas catches glimpses of the future. 'Never inure yourselves to civil war, never turn your sturdy power against your country's heart,' Anchises says to his son just before he sends him through the gates that lead from the land of spirits."

"And you're telling me this, why?"

"Because you should know about the War of Secession in the Caprivi. In 1985, the vice president of SWAPO, Mishake Muyongo, was expelled from the party. He subsequently formed his own party and after independence, he became a member of the National Assembly. It all seemed to be going well until 1999, when members of a group calling themselves the Caprivi Liberation Army attacked government buildings in Katima. The government retaliated by arresting hundreds of people. They have been in detention since then and their trial is still ongoing."

"Twelve years later?"

It's a fair question and I don't have an answer for her. The government's inaction during the trial has been a major concern to human rights groups from around the world.

"So the war's over now, right?"

"For the most part. Mishake Muyongo went into exile in Denmark and he continues to advocate for Caprivian independence while the government tries to soothe the tension and create a sense of national unity. But it's difficult."

"Why? What's so difficult about not fighting?"

"It's not that simple. Around 2007 or 2008, they discovered a whole bunch of mass graves just across the Angolan border and also just north of Rundu. All told, about one thousand six hundred bodies. These graves date from around 1999, when the Namibian Army helped the Angolan government attack UNITA forces in southern Angola from bases within Namibia. At the time, there were reports of human rights abuses and many people were reported missing. The government claimed they had deported illegal immigrants back to Angola. The Caprivians claim these were their supporters who had been executed by the Namibian government. It's left many people angry and bitter."

We hand in our laundry at the cleaners and then head into town.

"But there are graves," Sinead picks up the conversation. "The Namibian government can't deny that."

"They don't. They claim these are graves dug by South African forces in 1972."

Our discussion is interrupted by the sound of drums and singing. Soon, a small procession of nurses and health professionals bearing a banner passes. Today is National HIV Testing Day. They are bringing the battle to HIV, the silent insurrectionist that has turned on the citizens of this country. It is clear that the government sees it as a war: the parade is headed by a small platoon from the 261 Battalion. I find the exuberance and festivity of this event oddly reassuring, yet discomforting. The marchers sing revolutionary songs, reminding bystanders that this battle is not that much different to the long battle for freedom. And a battle it is. In 2002, twenty-two per cent of the country tested positive for HIV. Unlike in some of the neighbouring countries, the Namibian government responded with a range of programs, including surveys, testing and treatment programs, and orphan care. Despite the difficulty of reaching rural areas in one of the most sparsely populated countries in the world, they had managed to bring the figure down to about seventeen per cent in 2008. In every town we have passed through on the way — from Omugulugwombashe to Rundu — we have seen posters and billboards.

All this pageantry taking place before us cannot erase the unease I feel at seeing the military presence here. Little effort has been made to conduct an in-depth forensic study of the graves. For the most part, the government has avoided talking about the prolonged trial, instead focusing the public's attention on the return of the Namibian skulls from Germany. In the Caprivi, they remind the locals of the balance of power by making the military visible at roadblocks and public events like AIDS Testing Day. Behind the importance and the urgency of the battle against HIV, is a government that is flexing its muscles as a warning to any potential dissenters.

We leave the revellers and find our way to the open-air market. Several younger travellers we have met in the course of our journey here have told us that this is the most exciting market in Namibia. It is certainly unlike any other market we have encountered. At the entrance, there is a display of handcrafted yokes and picks, traditional handmade knives and an assortment of knobkieries. The knobs on most of the walking sticks are simple, for they are intended as utilitarian objects for the locals, not as tourist collectibles. Among this array of hoes and knives, there's a hand-carved crucifix. It is made from a light wood, almost white. The face strikes me instantly: the nose and the full beard are surrounded by braided cornrows. The serenity of the image is compelling, but I find the juxtaposition with the traditional weapons beside it disturbing. Beside this display, a woman sells an array of dried legumes. A subtle reminder that this is one of the poorest and least developed regions of the country.

At the hub of the market, two women sit beside their gas stoves, dropping lumps of *vetkoek* dough into the heated oil. One of the women stirs a bucket of *oshikundu*, a millet drink made from mahangu. She does not break her rhythm as she leans over and takes two vetkoek from the enamel dish beside her. She calls to her son and hands the vetkoek to him. He grins as he runs back to his friend with a lump of deep-fried dough in each hand. The boys continue their games between bites of vetkoek. I walk over to the woman. She offers me a mugful of oshikundu and a vetkoek. I accept. Sinead does not feel hungry and declines the offer of a vetkoek, but she does lean over to smell the liquid in my hands. She pulls back as soon as the mixed aroma of fermented millet and milk hits her nostrils. The women laugh. Sinead sees some scarves at a nearby stall and wanders over to look at them while I finish my drink.

It is still early in the morning and although all the stalls have been set up and the wares are on display, there isn't much traffic. "People will come later, when they have finished in town. It will be busy this afternoon," the woman says to me as she watches Sinead wandering among the stalls. "They will bring out more things then for the tourists and the young ones. Now, it is just our people. Our stuff this morning." I take a sip of oshikundu and look around. I prefer the quiet.

"Where are you from?" she asks.

"Okahandja."

"And she's not in school?" The woman points to Sinead.

"No, she's finished school now."

"Hayi! She's isn't old enough." I laugh and tell her that Sinead is eighteen. She shakes her head. "That one is the youngest of five," she says, pointing to the youngster stuffing vetkoek into his mouth.

"And where are the others?"

"The girls help in the fields and the boys help with the cattle."

"No school?"

"No, no school. They do not need school."

"Those girls need to be in school," I insist, but she simply tells me that her children are needed at home.

I finish my oshikundu and head off to find Sinead among the stalls. I stop at a rack of bright scarves. A few schoolgirls walk into the market and start to browse. "Look at them," I say to the woman standing beside me. "Those girls should be in school."

The woman pushes her sunglasses into her blonde hair to keep the breeze from blowing strands into her eyes. "I'm on holiday. I don't look at such things!"

Eventually I find Sinead caged in a central African Dollar Store. Beyond the local craft market lies an emporium of mass-produced

Chinese goods and piles of hand-me-down clothes sent here by relief agencies in North America.

"This is disappointing after all the hype we've heard from other people," Sinead says. "I'm not looking for things I can find in any store around the world."

"Yes, China shops everywhere," says one of the craft market attendants resentfully as Sinead and I turn to leave. The Chinese have invested heavily in Namibia. They have built roads and buildings and have drilled boreholes, but it has come at a price. Cheap Chinese goods are flooding the local markets and local traders are feeling the pinch as they get pushed to the periphery of their own economy.

Shortly after noon, we collect our laundry and set out for Bagani. It's an easy drive on an old military road. The road is long, straight and wide enough to allow convoys coming from opposite directions to pass each other easily. The names of South African military bases and field hospitals confront me every few miles as we head east along the road to Katima Mulilo. Small villages cluster against the main road. As we approach the larger towns along the way, the number of villages increases and the tropical forest that encloses us recedes. After weeks of seeing birds all along the roads, I am struck by their complete absence along this one.

We spend the night at the Popa Falls, a lone tent in the campground at the edge of the Okavango River. As I sit in front of the tent, drinking my coffee, a giant kingfisher lands no more than a few feet away from me. It cocks its head and peers into the water. Slowly, I reach for my camera, but it flies off before I can focus properly. There's a chill to the morning air and I button up my jacket. After breakfast, Sinead showers while I take my turn washing the dishes.

The camp kitchen is dirty and neglected. A congealed mass bubbles in the bottom of the sink. I open the tap and it gurgles water through the sludge. I wash and rinse in stages, racing to complete a dish or two before the flotsam of cockroaches and congealed fat rises too high in the sink. Then I wait for the sludge to recede before scurrying through another round. At least the water is hot. The kingfisher taunts me by sitting on a nearby branch. It doesn't move, even as I take my seat beside it and reach for my camera. As soon as I point the lens in its direction, it flies off again.

19

The glimpses of the Okavango River just above the Popa Falls make it easy to forget that this was once a war zone and that this river defined the battle lines. I know that hidden in the bushes on the opposite bank lies Buffalo, final home base of the notorious 32 Battalion, but from where I am standing, there is little to see beyond a small herd of Cape buffalo and a copse of indigenous forest.

The *Os Terríveis*, The Terrible Ones as they were known in Portuguese, were known colloquially as Buffalo Battalion. They were the scourge of the Namibian War. The unit came into existence when members of the FNLA, the National Front for the Liberation of Angola, sought refuge in northern Namibia after the MPLA forces routed their opposition during the civil war that ensued right after independence. The South African government spotted an opportunity and directed Colonel Jan Breytenbach to form a unit from among these soldiers. The result grew into the dreaded 32 Battalion, where black FNLA soldiers fought alongside elite South African troops. Many of 32 Battalion's operations were clandestine and took place in Angola while the South African government publicly denied having any military presence there. Toward the end of the war, the soldiers of 32 Battalion were deployed as a buffer between regular troops and the advancing Cuban troops. Their methods were brutal. Conversations with ex-members of the 32 have revealed stories about the thousands of mines that were planted indiscriminately along the way out of Angola after an operation. At the Battle of Cuito Cuanavale, the FNLA soldiers sat on the front of troop carriers as the SADF bludgeoned its way through the minefields around the town. The official death toll South Africans have given for that battle — thirty-one soldiers — excludes the hundreds, perhaps even thousands, of FNLA troops who died there as members of 32 Battalion.

We cross over the Okavango just north of the Popa Falls. The bridge is being repaired and we have to use the pontoon tracks that have been laid there as a temporary measure. Just beyond the bridge, we turn off onto a dirt road that leads to Buffalo. The initial stretches of the dirt road have been cleared to allow guards to see any approaching vehicles clearly. A few miles down the road, we come across abandoned guard posts. The stonemasonry of the guard posts at the edges of the cattle gate remains solid; off to the left, the brickwork of the guardhouse has started to crumble. Beyond these gates, the road has not been cleared and the forest closes in oppressively. Some five hundred metres further, we come across more overgrown ruins. A small herd of buffalo lazes in the shelter of the bush beside them. We watch the buffalo for a while and then drive on until we reach a locked gate. There is a buffalo skull mounted on each of the gateposts. Beyond these gates lies Buffalo base. A sign informs us that we need to purchase a permit for entry and I look around for somewhere to buy one. There is an administrative building on the right, so I get out and walk over. The door is open, but there is no one on duty.

I have come this far with only one purpose in mind: to view the graves at Buffalo base. We have followed a trail of death and graves in our travels through Namibia. Scattered throughout the country are the graves of the German soldiers who died during the colonial wars. At Aus, the graves of the South African soldiers who died at the concentration camp in the First World War lie beside those of the soldiers they once fought. Throughout Namibia's war-torn history, the bodies of the colonizers have remained as a testament to a history that has become part of this land. However, among all these graves, there is not a single one that belongs to a member of the South African Defence Force who fought in the Namibian War of Independence. Every single South African casualty was flown back home for a full military funeral.

Well, not quite all. The FNLA troops who fought with 32 Battalion lie buried here at Buffalo base. Too black to be buried in South Africa and treated as pariahs in their own country, these soldiers found their final resting place here in Namibia, where their presence was widely resented. I look for a sign that will provide a contact number or the address, but I see nothing. Sinead and I sit at the entrance, considering whether to head back to Rundu to get a permit. It's a two-hour drive there, so by the time we get back to Buffalo, it will be late afternoon. The thought of retracing our steps fills me with despair. I am tired of turning back along the paths I have trodden. Sinead wants to get to Zimbabwe. She and I talk about Buffalo Battalion and the futility of war. We talk about bodies seen and unseen and the scars they leave behind. Seen and unseen. When we have exhausted ourselves, we just sit. Then we turn around and head back to the main road to Katima Mulilo.

We have been out of Rundu for barely a day, and already I feel as if I have left the sadness and malaise of the town behind. The drive into the Caprivi has lifted my spirits somewhat. As we drive, I continue to see efforts being made — houses are painted again and there is a pride that was absent in Rundu. Rundu just seemed tired and paranoid. At Kongola, we fill up. A teenager lurks off to one side of the gas station, but when he catches my eye, he moseys over.

"*Loop! Voertsek!*" the attendant yells at him. "He's a skelm. All these youngsters just hang around. They should be in school, but they just sit here looking for trouble. They're skelms. Crooks." He turns on the hapless youth. I catch only one fragment from the torrent of Kavango words that follow, *Mishake*, but it is enough to capture my attention.

"I heard you saying something to him? What did you call him?"

"I called him many things."

"But I heard the word *Mishake*."

"I called him one of Mishake Muyongo's children."

I try to get a bit more information from the attendant, for, in these parts, the name Mishake Muyongo has developed an aura of myth. Popular histories of the War of Independence tell us that the first battle in the war was at Omugulugwombashe. That is not untrue, but this version of history ignores the raid on the Caprivi African National Union (CANU) headquarters in Katima Mulilo on the second of August 1964. A few days earlier, the South Africans had arrested the CANU leader, Brendan Simbwaye. He was never seen again. At a special meeting of the organization's leadership on the second, Mishake Muyongo was elected as the new leader. The election was barely dealt with when the South African Police entered the building and a skirmish ensued. No one was injured and the CANU leadership escaped. In exile in Zambia, Mishake Muyongo and his colleagues negotiated a merger with SWAPO and, over the course of the years, CANU was largely forgotten as Mishake Muyongo rose to become vice president of SWAPO. The same Mishake Muyongo who incited the brief War of Secession in 1999 and who has been blamed for the post-independence political tension in northern Namibia. After a short silence, he says, "I'm SWAPO. Those children of Mishake Muyongo just cause trouble. They have no place here at my work. I have no time for their war stories."

Then he goes silent. There are things we do not talk about.

After the war, few of the villages that cluster around the main roads of northern Namibia remained. Members of Koevoet, the notorious counter-intelligence unit comprised of black Namibians, had razed most of them to the ground. The bodies of the villagers killed during Koevoet and SADF raids may well share the graves of those civilians discovered in the mass graves allegedly dug by the Namibian Defence Force around the time of the War of Secession. Whatever the truth might be, people have been slow to return and for large stretches, the country seems deserted. For much of the way to Katima Mulilo, the Namibian Defence Force is a visible presence. They patrol the roads and they have occupied the bases vacated by the South Africans. It seems that not much has changed since independence.

From the get-go, I feel at home in Katima, the Gateway to Central Africa, as it announces at the entrance to the town. That is exactly what it is: every tour company, every backpacker, every tourist and self-driver heading up or down Africa seems to take the road through Katima and on to Windhoek or Livingstone or Kasane. It is the last big town at the end of the Caprivi panhandle and it is surrounded by border posts. We too are here only to refuel and leave the country. Our destination is Ngoma, where we will cross over into Botswana.

Katima has seen itinerants since the middle of the nineteenth century, when David Livingstone passed by here on his way to the Victoria Falls. The tourist information shops have honed their skills over many years and quote exchange rates like weather reports. All along the route through northern Namibia, we have been warned about money troubles in Zimbabwe. "They only accept US dollars" said one self-styled expert. "Stockpile SA rand," said another. "You can only pay in pula at the border," his friend opines. "Hoard your cash. You'll need it." I had my doubts about these snippets of advice, but even so, we went to the bank in Oshakati to get some dollars. The woman behind the counter refused to exchange any currency for us. "You should plan your trip better. You should have brought dollars with you if you knew you were going to Zimbabwe."

No amount of logic can sway her. She remains immune to any suggestions that these were last-minute plans. "That doesn't matter. You have to plan everything ahead of time." I try another tack, asking for SA rand. She will not exchange Namibian dollars for rand, either.

"But rand is legal tender here," Sinead said.

"Yes, it is."

"Then why can't you give us any?"

"We just can't." Or won't. Having been unable to get foreign currency at the exchange, we resorted to asking for change in rand at every opportunity. By the time we'd reached Katima, we had collected a wad of South African currency. The one thing we still needed was pula to use in Botswana.

"The hawkers in Zimbabwe will charge you a ten to one exchange on the South African rand," says the travel agent at Katima. "They won't take pula. Don't try to find US dollars here. Zimbabwean prices are all in dollars and the cash machines dispense dollars. In Botswana, draw pula from the ATM." And so she dispels every rumour that has followed us since Opuwo. "Pay in Nam dollars at the Ngoma post. At the Zim border, pay in South African rand and pula."

We leave Katima mid-afternoon, hoping to cross the border before it closes. As we approach the border post, I remember that we had arranged to call Julie before we left Namibia, since we would not have access to a cellular network until we returned to the country. There is no reception at the border post, so we turn back and find a place to stay at the Caprivi River Lodge, the first place that offers telephone and Internet reception. There is no camping, so we rent a small bungalow for the night and spend the evening watching the sun set on the banks of the Zambezi. A horde of kids swim in the river and laze on a sandbank that runs far into the main current. In the background from across the river, we can hear constant drumming from the village that lies hidden in the bushes. As the shadows lengthen, the throng of kids thins out. The ferryman takes them back to the mainland ten at a time. Only the diehards remain and the ferryman pulls his mokoro up onto the bank and lies back, waiting for the kids to let him know when he can begin his last trip of the day.

He is just starting to push his mokoro back into the water when I receive a short text from Julie: "Check email." I leave the ferryman to cross the channel once more and go to check my email: our credit card has been suspended. The good folk at the credit card company had noticed strange spending patterns emanating from the heart of Africa and, in the best interests of their client, had suspended the account. Julie tried to get them to lift the suspension, but they wouldn't let her. I check my records. I had informed them that I'd be travelling well in advance, so this is their error. I count the cash on hand. There is enough to get us through the border posts at Ngoma and Kazungula and into Zimbabwe, but I worry about having enough money for the rest of the trip back to Windhoek. I weigh the options.

Sinead has been reading and writing in her journal. I let her read her mother's text before I make a suggestion: "Let's skip Zimbabwe, head back to Rundu and take the road down into Botswana on the other side of the Okavango Delta, past Tsau and through to Gobabis. That way, we won't need to get foreign currency or draw money until this mess is sorted out."

Sinead is resolute. "You said that Vic Falls would be vacation time. For you and me, and I really want to see them. You also need a break sometimes."

I count the money again. "There just isn't enough for both."

Sinead logs onto the Internet and does a quick search for accommodation at the Victoria Falls and in Botswana. She fires salvos of information at me and throws down a small brick of notes in front of her. "Katie at the travel agency said they exchange SA rand at ten rand to the US dollar, so that gives us enough dollars to stay at this campsite. I don't care if all we do is see the falls! We're. Going. To. Zimbabwe." Each word another brick of notes on the table.

I drop the topic temporarily, but back in our cabin, I ask her about food. Sinead digs through our camp fridge and the tins in the food box behind her and stacks them in a row in front of her. "There's enough to last us three days. By then mommy will have sorted something out." I look through the rampart of money and tin cans that has risen on the bed and stare at the impenetrable face of a teenager.

We have some dinner, play a game of cribbage and go to bed. Charging such defences is futile.

20

At the border post at Ngoma, a National Defence Force official saunters over to the bakkie and points two fingers at the tiny office by the gate. I get out and walk over to him. It is a beautiful spring morning in Namibia and, despite my concerns over money, I'm feeling relaxed after an evening on the banks of the Zambezi. I spent a fair portion of my day in Katima Mulilo phoning the rental company and getting an official release document that would allow me to take the vehicle out of the country. Armed with my papers, I foresee no trouble at all. In the kiosk, the official shuts the door behind me and again points to a piece of paper.

"Do you want the chassis number?" I ask. The form is not very clear.

"Huhmm."

"Ah, yes, I see. And they want the engine number too . . ."

"Huhmm."

And so we stumble through the form. I ask a question. He harrumphs. At the end of the exercise, he looks over the form and then vocalizes his first complete word of the morning. He ignores the letter from the rental company and states, "Proceed." I give him a smile and a cheerful farewell, but after the effort of that single word, he regresses to grunts again.

As we drive across the delta toward the Botswana side of the border, I spot a man in his mokoro poling his way through the channels of the marsh. A string of bream dangles from the tip of his pole. At the end of the bridge, two officials step into the road. "We have to confiscate all fresh foods. There's been an outbreak of fruit fly." I am familiar with the exercise of declaring meat at disease control points and one particular day has become part of our family lore. Travelling through a foot-and-mouth control point in Namibia, an officer once stopped Ma and Dad. They'd just returned from a farm and had an entire kudu pickling in biltong brine and a sheep butchered to taste. The legs of lamb were wrapped up and hidden under the front passenger seat. (You don't waste space when packing a car.) Dad was ready to confess, but Ma just said, "John, let me handle this." She rolled down her window and greeted the young officer.

"Môre, Tannie," he responded in Afrikaans.

"Good morning," Dad signalled that he was English-speaking. The young man changed to English for Dad's benefit.

"I'm checking to see if there's any meat in the car."

"Yes, there is."

"Like lamb?"

"Oh, it's more like mutton these days. Well-travelled and a bit long in the tooth. I'll show you." Ma reached for her dentures.

"Er, no, Tannie. I meant something like *boude* –" He searched for the English word. "Rump . . ."

"Ah. Why didn't you say so? I have two. I'm sitting on them."

"I would need to see them."

"If you insist." Ma reached for the hem of her skirt.

The officer backed off. "It's for the foot-and-mouth, Tannie. We can't let any fresh meat though the checkpoint."

"I see." Ma turned to the back where my older brothers were sitting. "Rob, can you pass the meatballs? The Oom wants to see them. They're fresh," she said to the officer. "Made them myself this morning."

Ma has always been skilled this way. She could massage the truth to wiggle out of a tight spot if you didn't choose your words carefully. She still cannot resist a pun. That young officer didn't stand a chance. He waved us through. "I didn't lie," Ma said as Dad drove off. "I was quite open about having meat in the car. And I *was* sitting on two boude. I even offered to show them to him."

The Botswana officials are not interested in massaging the truth. They head straight for the cooler bag and remove all the fresh fruit and milk. Then they make us drive through the required dipping trough to disinfect the wheels and the undercarriage. In the background, the man throws our food into the fire. "I can understand meat for foot-and-mouth disease," Sinead says. "But fruit flies? They can just fly over the border. You can't exactly stop them."

Our bakkie objects to the indignity of being disinfected and coughs and splutters all the way up the hill toward the Botswana border post. She shakes the last of the dip off her chassis and comes to a gentle stop in front of the customs office. The man in the mokoro spots us and waves the bream at us as we disappear into the building. A neatly dressed young man calls us over and asks us to complete the immigration forms. As I finish, I spot a vehicle registration form on the desk in front of me.

"That's kiosk two," he says, and grabs the form away from me. He leans to his left and deposits the sheet of paper on the counter on the other side of the divide. I shuffle over and complete the form. Kiosk One stretches and offers me some advice on filling in the form. When I'm done, he leans over again and intones, "Permits, kiosk three." The guy sitting behind the counter at kiosk three leans over and takes the completed permit form from kiosk two. I shuffle over one step to kiosk three. Kiosk Three is having trouble logging into his computer. Between not being able to log in and a printer issue, it takes him twenty minutes to type in my information. Then he hits enter. The data screen freezes and demands a login. There's a sudden flurry of interest from Kiosk One. He scoots his chair over to Kiosk

Three's computer and presses a button. We lose all our data and Kiosk Three starts all over again. The PC freezes once more. Third time's a charm and we print off the form.

While we're waiting for the form to print, I dutifully show him my cross-border form, without which I was told I would not be allowed to take the vehicle out of the country. He grunts and tosses it aside without looking.

"I'd like that back when you're done," I remind him.

"Why?"

"It's my proof that I have permission to take the vehicle across the border." He grunts and leaves the paper on the counter in front of him. I'm not giving up that easily. It cost me a bad meal in Katima Mulilo to get that permit. It appears he's less concerned about the formalities of international paperwork than I am. Eventually, I reach over and take the permit back. Kiosk Three glares at me. Ninety minutes later, we're on our way to Kasane. A lone warthog forages at the side of the road.

In Kasane, we have breakfast before heading out to the border post at Kazungula. There are trucks lined up rows deep at the border and I fear this could take hours. We enter the customs building. It's a confusing mix of interlocking queues and forms and transactions spread out over twenty minutes during which six hundred pula disappears into the hands of a customs official who lurks on my side of the counter. The money moves from official to official, but I do not see any receipts appearing. In the end, I emerge with my permit intact and my passport stamped and that's all I care about. We pass through the final security check and drive into Zimbabwe.

The road through Hwange National Park is a sombre drive: it is dry season, but the lack of rains in previous years has left this area desolate. It is duller and greyer than it should be. Sinead finds a place where she can rent a bungalow for even less than the campsite she found on the Internet. We check in and then take a walk through the town to Victoria Falls. The railway bridge that crosses the falls into

Zambia makes me think of Sol Plaatje's description of the falls — the first written account of Mosi-oa-Tunya, The Smoke That Thunders, by a black African. By then, Plaatje was nearing the end of an illustrious career. He had founded the first Setswana newspaper; he had been a founder of the African National Congress (ANC); he had written *Mhudi*, the first English novel by a black South African; he had co-authored a book on Setswana grammar and had translated several of Shakespeare's plays into his native tongue. Despite all these accomplishments, the sight of the Victoria Falls left him almost speechless. It was 1931, and he had been invited on the maiden train journey from South Africa to Kinshasa (then still Léopoldville) to attend the 1931 international exhibition in Katanga, Congo. Their train arrived at Victoria Falls at night and Plaatje was fortunate enough to see the lunar rainbows suspended above the falls, a sight that prompted him to draw the inevitable comparison to Niagara Falls, which he had seen during his sojourn in North America. That sight of moonlit rainbows above the powerful waters of Africa was enough, in his mind, to trump the sight of blocks of ice cascading over Niagara Falls in winter.

On our way through the town of Victoria Falls, hawkers descend on us. There is a feeling of desperation to their efforts as they express a willingness to trade anything from shoes to shirts as we walk down toward the falls. They try to flog rolls of Zim dollars to us, confident that tourists will pay more for the worthless curiosities than any exchange rate would offer.

It is hard not to lapse into superlatives as you watch a mile of water tumble down the gorge at Danger Point. You can see the cataracts stretching off into the distance. About halfway across, they twist out of sight and can only be viewed from the Zambian side of the river. The pall that has hung over my daughter for the past week has begun to lift and the homesickness dissipates in the mist. It is Sinead who insists we cross over to the Zambian side, offering an ulterior motive as an incentive. "I promised Elizabeth I'd send her a postcard from every country we visited. Zambia is on that list." So over the bridge we go in search of stamps. We walk through a gauntlet of hawkers and beggars to get to the bridge and the border post. From there, it is short hike to the Zambian Falls.

Despite several warnings about how uninspiring the Zambian falls are, they overwhelm me. The smaller falls and the lightened load of water accentuate the frailty of their surroundings. The cliffs and the thin cataracts have a wispiness to them that belies the power of the water. This is a place of wonders, where the rising mist clings to your soul. It is a perfect complement to the thunderous applause of the Zimbabwean falls.

We walk another mile along the dusty road toward Livingstone before we reach a hotel where a curio shop sells stamps. The heat on the Zambian side is almost unbearable. It is election time in Zambia and politics blooms against every wall and tree trunk along the road. After the elections, the hawkers will still gather at the craft market along the banks of the Zambezi and they will still wrangle a living out of the foreign tourists. As it has always been. It's a hot and dusty slog back to Zimbabwe. On the way back, Sinead suggests that I approach one of the hawkers and exchange some of my rand for dollars. "Then we can change the dollars into pula when we're in Botswana."

Back at camp, Sinead looks at the brochures from the reception. She counts our money again and finds a way to pay for a sunset cruise on the Zambezi. In the morning, we go for an elephant safari and then head back to Kasane in Botswana. Sinead babbles incessantly all the way back through the border post. My daughter is back.

During the Namibian War of Independence, South Africa and Namibia became pariah states for international tourists. Instead, tourists came to Botswana — and so did war-weary young soldiers and officers who drifted over the border for respite from the stress of the battlefield. These luxury lodges on the banks of the Okavango River were built for pleasure and their opulence is out of place amidst the goats and other livestock that roam the streets among the modest, slightly worn buildings in the rest of town. We find a place to pitch a tent out in the boondocks, but there are no amenities at all and besides, the campsite bookings have to be made at one of the hotels in town. We head back toward Kasane, but at the reception of the hotel, the thought of going back to the rudimentary campsite is unbearable. We take a room in the hotel.

"It has a bath!" Sinead yells as we put our bags down in the room.

Sinead soaks in the first bath she has had in weeks. When she is done, she crawls in behind the mosquito net and goes to sleep. I try to phone the credit card company. They insist on charging me collect, but the hotel management won't accept these charges. I give up, and fall asleep. In the middle of the night, the ring of the telephone drags me out of a tropical malaise. I clamber over Sinead in the mugginess of the night. Julie's voice is a wonderful thing to wake to. She has not managed to procure an alternative source of money for us, but she sounds hopeful. "I'll check in when we get to Gobabis. By then we will have reception on the cell phone again," I tell her before hanging up.

At six-thirty a.m., I tiptoe out to the bakkie to get a book to read. By the time I return to the room, there's been a power failure. Fortunately, by now the sun is up and we don't need the light any more. I open the balcony door and let in the cool morning breeze.

When Sinead wakes, we stock up on supplies at the local convenience store and then head to the gas station to fill up.

"We're out of diesel," the attendant tells me. It's the only gas station in Kasane and we are forced to make our way to Kazungula. I try the station at the turnoff to the road south. It's barely seven-thirty a.m. and already there's a queue at the pumps, but nothing's moving. A local farmer parks beside me.

"The power failures are common," he says. "I've just popped into town to pick up some petrol for my generator so that I can watch the rugby and cricket matches this afternoon." His tanned skin creases with emotion as he continues. "If there was soccer on today, they'd never do it!" He nods his head in the direction of a photo of President

Ian Khama in the convenience store. "It's become worse. I've been here thirty years and they've become unbearable." He speaks with a tone of condescension that verges on hatred.

I manage to attract the attention of an attendant. They're out of diesel too, he informs me. "But there's a lorry at the underground tanks," I point out.

"Petrol," he says. "But it doesn't matter. None of them can start pumping until we get the generator up and running." I look at the line of vehicles already waiting patiently. Our only other hope is the station beside the border post to Zimbabwe.

"Plenty of diesel here," the attendant at the border assures me. "But we don't have any power to pump it with." He disappears into a cage at the side of the admin building and digs into some machinery. I can hear a two-stroke Lister generator sucking and blowing as it tries to churn itself into life. There is no option but to wait. A bunch of truckers gather around me and start chatting. The guy in the eighteen-wheeler is on his way to the Democratic Republic of the Congo. An Indian man in a Toyota bakkie paces around impatiently. He's the manager at the Choppies supermarket in Kasane and needs gas to run the generator for the shop. "No power means no business!" He's visibly agitated.

"These outages can last days," he fumes. "They're more regular now. I fill my generator and it gives me power for two days. After that, business is gone. After that, we don't know what to do about power."

That's reassuring. We could be here for two days.

"Go look at the animals. It will be a better use of your time," he says and storms off. I would do that, but I don't have enough diesel in the bakkie.

We sit around and talk car fuel. "There's a petrol station at Panda-matenga on the road to Nata," says the long-haul truck driver.

"I thought that station closed down," says Mr. Marume, the butchery manager at the Kasane Spar. He's also here to get diesel for his generator.

"Call the shop," he tells his assistant. "Tell them we'll be a while."

"I can't," the assistant replies. "I don't have any more minutes." Mr. Marume is stuck here, like the rest of us. After about an hour, the generator splutters into action, but it can't generate enough power to drive the pumps. At least the cash register is working and the long-haul driver buys us a round of juices.

"How long?" I venture to ask.

"Today. Maybe tomorrow."

"Maybe lunchtime," the girl behind the counter says in an effort to instill some hope.

"You need a container," says the man in the Orange Wireless shirt. "Then you can pick some up at the side of the road."

"I'd say you should try Maun," says another man, "but you'll have to fill up at least once in Nata."

"Maybe Gweta."

"I've waited here for two days once," says the truck driver.

"That's what happens when you don't have competition," says the manager from Choppies.

"They always wait until the diesel runs out before they order more," says a local shebeen owner. "I've got cold beers in my store if anyone's interested."

And so we wait. My companions haul out some of their notes and we exchange currency until I have enough pula to tide me over for a few days. I have no diesel, but I have money. I check my gauges again. I know I have a spare jerry can full of diesel in the back, but my tank is almost empty. Between the two, there's probably enough to get me to Nata, but if there's a shortage there, I'm well and truly stuck. I weigh my options. Around me the throng of diesel-seekers thins and people head off in search of better luck elsewhere, or simply give up and go home to wait.

Across the road, the warthogs root around without any qualms. Today is just another day for business here in Botswana. I contemplate spending another day in Kasane, but we can't afford to. Not at the price they charged us the previous night. Around eleven a.m., a couple of Australians pull up at the station in an oversized Land Rover. The driver's head dashes from side to side in search of a gas attendant. They appear to have prepared for any potential emergency except a power outage. Their frustration is palpable.

"Fuck!" the woman says when I inform them that there is no power. "This is unacceptable!"

"We've paid good money to get here. We shouldn't have to put up with this shit!" opines the man.

"Where's the nearest bottle store?"

"It's a Sunday. There is no bottle store open here in Kazungula," I tell the woman, "but there is a shebeen just down the road. I'm sure they'd supply you with something to take away."

"But this local fella — a *white* guy — told us there'd be a bottle store open today." As if that would change things.

"The shebeen opens at three p.m."

"That's like a *black* bar, isn't it?" the man asks as the woman swears again.

"Unacceptable!"

"A shebeen is a local gathering place. It's whatever you want it to be. You want take-aways, they'll give you take-aways," I tell them and turn around. As I walk away, I hear them bitch about the condition of the roads in Chobe National Park — unacceptable, of course.

"Fuck you too!" they shout at me as they race off.

The mention of Chobe puts an idea in my head. Perhaps we could cut through the Chobe National Park and save some time and fuel. I talk to the attendant. "No, that's 4 × 4 territory," he says. Shortly after noon, he informs me that they don't expect any power until the next day. I look again at my fuel gauge. The needle edges up to half full, then drops suddenly to well below a quarter. It's difficult to tell which extreme is correct. We decide to take our chances on Nata. I empty the jerry can into the tank and head out. On the way, I stop again at the Engen station.

"We've got the generator working," the manager tells me apologetically, "but don't expect the diesel delivery for another eight hours at least. First the petrol, then the diesel," he says, pointing to the row of four tankers lined up at the supply docks. We leave. I stop at Pandamatenga, only to confirm that the station has indeed closed down. At the kiosk, someone tells me there's gas available just down the road. I look out carefully, but see nothing. We have barely picked up speed when I notice a man rolling a large blue drum along the side of the road. I slow down. "Diesel?" I ask him.

"No, petrol," he replies. "Second drum today. Business is good! The government is providing many opportunities."

The road deteriorates with every mile we traverse. At times, the surface is little more than a potholed track. Overheated cars are parked along the side of the road and the abandoned carcasses of innumerable more fill the ditches. An overturned, burnt-out eighteen-wheeler lies across the new road that is under construction beside the surface we're travelling on. A five-ton truck lies on its side and a group of men are loading the contents onto two bakkies. We crawl toward Nata.

About one hundred kilometres from Nata, we get stopped at another disease control point. Once more, we have to hand over any fresh fruit and meat and dance through the dip. I lack my mother's skill in such situations and we forfeit the supplies we bought in Kasane.

At Nata, business is booming. "We've been really busy today with the shortage up north," says the attendant. I feel a twinge of regret as we fill up our tank. My initial plans were to head south to Serowe and Mahalapye before heading west toward Ghanzi. The 1,175 Ovaherero survivors who, according to the Bechuanaland authorities, made it across the Omaheke stopped briefly at a place called Tsau in the northwest of Botswana. Then they continued their desert wanderings to the east until they reached the Waterberg region in South Africa. By then, their numbers had halved again. They settled on a farm called Palala and just as they began to grow roots, the dreaded Natives Land Act of 1913 was passed. One of the consequences of the act was that the Ovaherero could no longer own the land on which they grazed their cattle. Once more they packed their belongings and trekked back into Botswana, settling in Serowe until the negotiations for land at Mahalapye to the southeast were finalized. Maharero died in Serowe in 1923, but his descendants have settled in Mahalapye. Over the years, some of them have made attempts to be repatriated to their ancestral land, but even after independence their struggle to be reunited with their people in Namibia continues.

Now, with a rapidly dwindling bundle of cash in my pocket, I decide not to visit Mahalapye and instead head straight for Maun. We drive into Maun just as the sun sets. It is a sprawling African town. People and cattle move around freely and the traffic is a tangle of vehicles. A row of neat brick houses peeks out from behind the hedgerow of shacks that line the road. The diehard hawkers have set up supper stalls and people are lined up for business. We turn to the left, following the instructions of the GPS in search of a campsite. I am looking for the infamous Riley's Hotel, home of outlaws and ruffians and a few more respectable traders, smugglers and hunters. The sleek three-star hotel that confronts us is a far cry from its historic roots as a vagabond's resting place. The campsite has been closed down, "To keep out the ruffians," the guard at the gate tells me. I am saddened by the loss of what I had considered an institution in Maun. We follow the GPS trail across a narrow bridge to the Maun Lodge. It's booked full. We work our way from campsite to campsite. Full. Full. Full. Eventually, we find a spot on the outskirts of town. The campsite is a compound in the middle of a small town of shacks.

Sinead and I spend the evening reading and playing cribbage before crawling into bed. It's been a long day's travel, but the energy of Maun lingers in my bones until late into the night. I lie awake listening to the jackals and stray dogs from the township howl at each other as they criss-cross the campsite. Sometime during the night, one sniffs at our tent.

The oppressive humidity of the past few days has broken. Perhaps it is because we are no longer in the tropics and the drier desert air has penetrated the thickness of the morning air. Kalahari sand spills through my toes as I walk to the camp kitchen to fetch some water from the communal tap.

While I make coffee, two hornbills fight over a scrap on the ground. As I settle down at the camp table to catch up on my journal, a stray dog settles at my feet. There is something nineteenth-century about this moment: writing at my camp desk with a dog at my feet. I almost miss my pith helmet. The cur wanders off when I start making breakfast. As soon as she sees me settling back into my seat, she returns.

Across from us an older gentleman emerges from his tent. A Sonderend Steak — an Endless Steak — dangles from his hands. It's a crosscut of beef round, a sea of red meat with an island of bone in the middle. He fans the coals and throws the chunk of meat onto it.

"I'm damned if I'll let them take this from me," he announces his intentions. "They stopped me at the checkpoint yesterday and took all our meat, but my wife had this one piece hidden under the seat. We're heading to Tsau and I don't know if there's a checkpoint along the way, but I'm not taking any chances."

We leave around ten in the morning, as we have little planned for the day beyond reaching Ghanzi. The road is in good condition and we make excellent time until the inevitable happens: we reach a disease control point.

Sinead digs in. "No way, not a third time! I'm hiding the apples!" She leans back, grabs the bag of fruit and shoves it under her seat. By now I have the routine down: I greet the officer with a smile and I have my papers at the ready. I get out of the bakkie and walk over to the dip tray. I step in it and return to the bakkie to get the cooler box out.

"Do you have any shoes?" the officer asks. I assure him that I have given him all my shoes.

"I haven't worn my shoes since they were in the dip at Ngoma," Sinead mutters. Still, he makes Sinead unpack her bag and disinfect every shoe. Then he checks the fridge. Sinead had missed some of the fruit when she leaned back, but the man ignores the fruit and heads straight for the milk.

"No animal by-products," he tells us.

"But it's processed long-life milk," I counter. I too have had enough of this bullying. "We've taken this milk through two checkpoints and a national border without any fuss."

The man becomes officious. "No by-products." He takes the soy milk too.

"That's soy milk." Sinead reaches out to take it from him. "See? Made from soy. It's a plant." He is unmoved and his impatience starts to show. A carful of government officials have pulled up.

"Move over so these people can pass," he instructs us. I pack the food back into the bakkie at an easy pace, take the milk from the officer and return it to the cooler bag. He's distracted by the presence of the government officials and doesn't register what I've done. "Can I proceed now?" I ask as I close the door.

"Move on," he shoos me off. As we drive through the dip, Sinead notices how he lets the government officials pass through without making them get out of their car.

"Just because they're government doesn't mean their feet are any less diseased," she fumes.

We get to Ghanzi by lunchtime. My uncle was the district commissioner in Ghanzi in the early 1950s. Among the reels of old film in our house, there is a short sequence of him and my father on camels. There is one other reminder of his presence in Ghanzi: as district commissioner, he was responsible for developing roads and one of the roads here is named after him. Sinead and I decide to spend what is left of the day looking for Midgley's Road. The hotel attendant sends us to the Department of Tourism office. We're visitors and the Secretary for

Regional Tourism attends to us personally. However, when I ask her about things to do in the area, she stares blankly. "We are a government office. I don't know what there is to do in Ghanzi. I just co-ordinate tourism in the region. You should try the Tourism Information Office."

We head off to the Tourism Information Office. "There's nothing to do in Ghanzi," the desk attendant tells me with a smile.

"Any cultural tours? Trips to the pans?"

She shrugs. "This is an end-of-the-road town."

"Would you happen to know where Midgley's Road is?"

She thinks for a while, then she says, "You know, here in Botswana, people are not big on giving streets names."

"But this road was built and named in the pre-independence era, by colonials who took naming very seriously," I try a different angle to the problem. I take out my map and ask her, "Do you know where Sir Seretse Khama Road is?"

"It's just off to my left, a little bit down the main road."

A man shouts something from an office behind the reception desk. The receptionist listens to him, then turns to us. "There are some cultural dances somewhere in the district. There's also a San museum just across the road." The "museum" turns out to be a display of crafts for sale. Sinead and I head back to our lodgings, disappointed. Over dinner, I exchange my last pula for SA rand with one of the other campers. We contemplate staying over in Ghanzi for a second night, but decide that we could probably find more to do back in Namibia.

21

At the entrance to Gobabis we turn left, away from the statue of a Brahman bull that guards the town. This sleepy town just across the border from Botswana has been a cattle outpost since the earliest days of colonial trade north of the Gariep River. When the Boers packed up and left the Cape Colony en masse in the 1830s, the Cape government turned to this area to supplement its supply of beef. And before that, the ships calling at Walvis Bay had demanded beef. British sailors had a seemingly insatiable desire for red meat, and local traders reached as far as Owamboland in the north and modern-day Botswana in the east to feed that demand. The cattle that came from Botswana had to be driven across the Kalahari Desert, and the cattlemen soon learned that Gobabis, with its lush springs and abundant herds of game, was an ideal spot at which to recover from the rigours of overland travel. Nor was it only travellers who stopped here. Before hunters decimated the elephant herds in this area in the late nineteenth century, this was a crucial watering hole on their ancient migration route.

Judging by the sleepiness of the lunchtime crowd and the smell of cattle in their trucks, life is still the same in Gobabis as it was a hundred years ago. This is where truckers stop to refuel on their way to and from Maun, or before they tackle the new Trans-Kalahari high-way that follows the old elephant migration route north. During the Namibian Wars of Resistance, it was the last haven for Schutztruppe before their long march up and down the folded valleys around Gochas and Gross Nabas. Here, Jakob Morenga, Hendrik Witbooi and other leaders of the resistance frustrated the colonial efforts to end the war quickly after the Battle of Ohamakari. For us, it is a layover on the final leg of our journey back to Windhoek. Everyone, it seems, is here only to refuel and leave.

Behind us, the oversized replica of a Brahman bull stares resolutely toward the open spaces beyond the town, waiting patiently, it seems, for an opportunity to escape the confines of its pedestal. It takes us no more than a few minutes to complete the circle around the central business district and end up back on Church Street. We stop at the local pharmacy, where the young assistant waves her still-wet nails in the direction of the shelves with a bored irritation that suggests she too wants to exit this town and head for the excitement of the big city.

"What would you recommend as the first thing we do in Gobabis?" I ask her.

"Leave." We choose not to take her advice. The Brahman bull and the fact that it stands on an island in the middle of Cuito Cuanavale Street have aroused my curiosity. Changed street names are common in Namibia and the names of struggle heroes have replaced the names of colonial governors, but nowhere on our trip have we encountered any mention of battlegrounds. Except here in Gobabis. The oddity of the street name is even more marked amidst the names of Afrikaans literary demigods that still hang about the corners of some of the streets. I ask the shop assistant where we can find a place to stay.

She directs us back along Cuito Cuanavale Street toward the Brahman bull. "Turn left at the bull. The hotels are down there."

"Do you know when the name of the street changed?" I ask as we gather our purchases.

"Things change all the time here. Never noticed."

Some say the name of the town is a corruption of the Khoekhoegowab words ≠*khoa* and -*bis*, Place of the Elephants. And that certainly is the name used by Reverend Joseph Tindall when he arrived there in 1845 to set up a mission station. Elephant Fountain is also the name the explorer James Chapman uses in his diaries. After a life of trading, he settled in Cape Town, but the adventurous gene was passed on to his children. Charles Henry Chapman moved to New York and from there traversed the ocean on business until, on the fifteenth of April 1912, he lost his life on board the *Titantic*. His brother, William James Bushnell Chapman, became a trader like his father. He was a restless soul, and when the Dorsland Trekkers at Rietfontein packed their bags again to head north, he joined their trek and settled in Humpata. In 1928, he returned from Angola during the first mass emigration of Angola Boers, and settled in Gobabis. I had been reminded of James Chapman Senior's travels at Swartbooisdrift, when Eric Peters pointed to the name "James Chapman" on the stone cairn. "His grandson, also named James after his famous forebear," he explained, "guards his father's Trek diary jealously. Give him a call when you get to Gobabis. Tell him I referred you." Here was another reason not to follow the shop assistant on her exodus from Gobabis: the chance to pore over this handwritten holy grail.

Afrikaner memory has been tried in the last two decades as the names of the old heroes recede and make way for the names of the new heroes that decorate street corners. Inside some diehard homes, photos of the leaders of the Boer Republics and the diaries of their commanders still occupy special places along the walls and shelves. But outside, in the harsh African sun, even the name of this town is up for negotiation and debate. Oral tradition holds that the original name of the place was in fact ≠*khoandabis*, The Place where Elephants Come to Lick, not Place of the Elephants. The emphasis is not on the elephants at all, they say, but on the salt licks at the edges of the fountain where they gathered.

Linguists maintain that it is not as simple as that. There is no evidence, they say, to tie the name of this place to elephants or salt licks at all, and the name is most likely a compound creation derived from a combination of *goba* and *-bis*, rendering it The Place where People Came to Argue, or the Place of Strife. There is validity to this line of thinking too, for the Gobabis district was often at the core of land disputes in pre-colonial times. James Chapman Senior gives a hint of the turmoil in account after account of trying to obtain permission from local leaders to move cattle through their territory, of paying tributes and of moving the ever-impatient herds around to avoid the outbreaks of cattle lung sickness or sporadic wars among the leaders of the Nama, the Witbooi, the Ovaherero, the !Naro, the Germans and the Afrikaners.

In his treks from Walvis Bay to Lake Ngami, Chapman repeatedly passed through Gobabis. His first observations of the Rhenish mission station at Gobabis in 1861 are of the "kind welcome, supper and warm bed provided me by the good Mrs. Krapohl." The church itself was a temporary building, but he notes that a larger, more permanent structure was being built. On his return from Lake Ngami in 1863, Chapman writes that Gobabis "has a more pleasing appearance to me than it had before. The large white church with its cross and steeple contrasts vividly with the blue range in the background. The place is dotted all over with warm colours, mat huts and white waggon sails. The deep valley has acacia forests dividing the villages, and what added to the ample aspect of civilisation was the presence of 6 missionary families here . . ." This is as lyrical as Chapman gets. For the most part, his diary consists of factual accounts of his day's travel: distances between places, accounts of his struggles negotiating passage, the effects of cattle lung sickness, etc. Wandering through the debris of his trade talk, it is easy to miss the reference to "villages" when speaking of this place he calls Elephant Fountain. But despite his kind remarks about the missionaries, his overall impression of Gobabis is that it is a town where beggars from these surrounding villages cluster around visitors to the mission.

The main road through Gobabis is Church Street, but it no longer leads to the Rhenish mission, which is long gone. In its stead, an elegant Dutch Reformed Church graces the centre of town. But the town is still as carefully manicured as it appears to be in Chapman's description. Freshly painted white buildings with black roofs line the neatly swept streets. It is a stark contrast to the chaos of a place like Maun across the border in Botswana, where the bustle of the city, the smell of smoke, the images of unruly children fishing in the lakes by the roadside and the old truss bridges linger long after you've left. Yet, as one moves away from the centre of the town, toward the fringes where the various townships are situated, the paint on the houses in Gobabis starts to peel and cottage white gives way to greens and blues. The neat brick walls that surround the homes of the town's core make way for rundown wire fences and makeshift chicken coops. Where the tarred streets end, the ruts left by years of erosion have begun to reclaim the roads. These settlements are the descendants of the villages James Chapman described, and now, like then, they are separated from the town itself, if not with acacia forests, then by the unruliness of poverty and lingering inequality.

It was the Germans who defined separate living areas for the people of Gobabis when they officially declared it a town in 1894, but it was merely a formalization of what already existed. Back then, people came to Gobabis to trade and to look for work at the mission station, much like the stragglers who arrive here today come in search of employment or to find a place to trade their cattle. The poorest of these migrants settle in Epako, the black township that was officially created in 1949. On the way into Gobabis, it is easy to look past these shacks to the affluence of the town that lies beyond. If visitors do venture into these slums, it is as part of a guided township tour, where one can observe, meet a few carefully chosen locals, and then retreat to the safety of the centre of the town. Even the town's Brahman bull has its back turned on these slum-dwellers, and it stares dolefully beyond the confines of the town. It seems to recall the bygone days when the people of this land could graze their cattle in the expanses of the Omaheke, where the fleeing Ovaherero died by the thousands as they made their way across the desert into Botswana.

This is arid territory, despite the deceptive lushness of the veld that has driven successive generations of cattle owners into the area — from Jonker Afrikaner and Amraal Lambert to the cattle traders and the Dorsland Trekkers who settled just south of here, at Rietfontein. The dry beds of Nossob River and its tributaries, the White Nossob and the Black Nossob, scar the earth in Namibia's Omaheke Region. The Black Nossob, which flows past Gobabis, has not had any water in it since 1989. In a country where ephemeral rivers run like interweaving scars across the landscape, such prolonged stretches of drought are not unusual. Farmers and communities grow to rely on the fairly stable supply of underground water to see to their needs at their favoured watering holes. And it is at one of these watering holes that we end up in our search for a place to stay. At the reception desk of the Big 5 Central Hotel, I hear the noise coming from the overcrowded bar where, shortly after eleven in the morning, alcohol is flowing more steadily than the Gariep River in flood. "They're here for the annual *skou*, the agricultural show," says the pasty-faced manager through the glass partition. "They're still setting up, but I've had a sneak peek at the stalls. Stay a day or two extra. For your daughter's sake. You have to take her to the show. Cattle to make your heart bleed.

"We have a camping spot available in the back, but you're a bit late for the rooms. The *skou*, you know." I take the spot on the lawn in the backyard and as I bend down to pick up our bags, he leans over conspiratorially, "*Gebruik die middel toilet en stort.*" He grimaces as he continues, "*Die een links is vir die werkers.*"

I have already turned to walk away. "You've got a funny look on your face," Sinead says. Her Afrikaans has improved sufficiently while we've been travelling through Namibia to understand the first part of his sentence. "He wants us to use the middle bathroom, but what does the rest mean?" I should have no difficulty translating the sentence for her, yet I find myself thrown off balance, unable to respond. Such a simple sentence.

I feel tired. Die een links is vir die werkers. The one on the left is for the workers. If only meaning could reside in the literal transcription of the words. If only I could take that statement at face value. But instead, I have to explain to my daughter, the born-free, the raw face of apartheid and how she is about to live it.

How do I explain to my child that all I can see is the black door in my childhood garden, the one to the right of the coal room? The chilly late-night autumn air has raised the hairs on my arms and the first hints of frost nibble at my bare toes. I have left the warmth of the spare room beside the garage that once may have served as servants' quarters or a workshop, but is now my bedroom. Outside, I stand on the frost-covered lawn outside the black door. I need the toilet, but the doors to the house are locked. Opening that door will change me forever. I stand outside until cold and desperation force me to enter. There is no light and I leave the door open despite the cold: I fear the claustrophobic darkness that envelops me. The floor is covered with a swirl of autumn leaves and I dig my toes into the crack in the cement floor.

Afterwards, I return to my bed. I lie awake, waiting for something to happen, for I have transgressed a cardinal rule of my society: I have used the workers' toilet. I have relieved my diarrhea in the same space as a black man. In the nights that follow, I test these waters again. And again. Nothing visible has changed. The road out of prejudice starts with a visit to the workers' toilet in the back garden.

How do I tell my daughter that, as a matter of principle, she needs to use the toilet on the left, but that the door is locked? And the key she holds in her hand won't open it.

I turn around slowly. The slits of the duty manager's eyes stretch to their full size. He quickly shifts the conversation to more pleasant things, like the prize bulls that will be exhibited at the upcoming show. "The animals go on display to the public in two days' time. There will be plenty of activities for the family too. You really should try to stay a few more days to attend the skou," he insists. His psoriasis has flared up and his neck is a ball of red flowers. Behind him, a black police truncheon dangles from a hook on the wall.

◆ ◆ ◆

In town, we have lunch before visiting the tourist information centre. As we walk out into the road after lunch, a young couple greets us with a gregarious "Enjoy your stay in Gobabis!" They deliberately flash the shiny rings on their fingers as they wave at us, their happiness obvious. "Congratulations!" I call back, guessing this to be the right response. They laugh and entwine their bodies as they head off down the street. All along the verges of the street, men and women recline in whatever shade they can find. These are not beggars; they are workers on a lunch break. Two men playing owela in front of the municipal offices laugh and shake their heads at the young lovers before turning their attention back to their game. James Chapman, that intrepid trader, noted how on one of his trips through Gobabis, he left the town in search of the local leader, Amraal Lambert, so that he could negotiate for the return of his cattle. "I found Lamert [sic] very busy in a game with his children and servants." He goes on to explain his understanding of the rules of owela and remarks that it is more difficult than backgammon, which it resembles.

Chapman was right about the challenges of owela, but he was wrong in assuming that it signified that Amraal Lambert was lazy. Like the two men by the roadside, he may simply have been treasuring a moment with family and friends. We watch the two men play for a short while: they become vociferous and animated as they thrust their hands toward the board and pull back. Owela is about intimidation as much as it is about skill. They glance at each other. Their rivalry in this game is real. We watch them parry and prod for a while before meandering back to our bakkie and heading out to find the local museum.

The gate to the museum is locked and as we wait for the curator to make her way up the pathway toward us, I glance over at the open spaces at the edge of the town. A little way off down the hill, there is a cluster of acacias inside a fenced-off area. I am still admiring the copse when the curator speaks. "I was just finishing my lunch." She waves us in. At the entrance, she picks up the item she's crocheting and follows us into the main display room. She hovers as we make our way around the room, the hook darting in and out of the yarn. "We're still setting up, really," she remarks from a respectful distance. A handful of display cases are already set up, but toward the back of the room I can see an array of boxes, stacked or half-opened. A story waiting to unfold. The display cases reveal the usual collection of family ephemera handed to the local curator over the years: Coins and crocheted craftwork side by side with service medals. I stop to examine one of the crocheted items. It is a fancy placemat, done in a delicate thread. The lacy double filet stitches in the centre of the work are tight and uniform, the result of a deft hand flicking the barbed hook along its course around the small mat. Tight, even knots. At the outer edge, I notice a slight variance in the colour and texture of the yarn, where the original must have frayed. The reparation has been done by a less deft hand. The stitches are uneven and a missed picot along the edge leaves a lopsided finish.

The curator startles me as she leans over and whispers, "There used to be a separate German museum across the way. A private museum. But after independence, the people objected to those arti-facts being on display." She backs off to observe the impact of her words. I look up and she responds with a few determined stabs into the yarn. I ask her what is in the boxes. She parries deftly as she moves between me and the boxes: "Medals from the wars, mostly. The bulk of the items in that museum were sold off to private collec-tors and the remainder were given to the national museum. Some were given to us here. Mostly the items depicting family life among the German settlers. Colonial stuff. It's not that I don't want those things, but what we need is a museum that belongs to all the people. That is what I am trying to achieve." She stabs at the yarn again and pushes us toward the door with the firmness of a marshal at a rally. Back in the foyer, she asks me to sign the register. But my eyes have caught sight of an opened box in the corner: the hilt of an old officer's sword and an assortment of assegais peek out of it. I try to get closer to have a look, but Madame has again slipped between me and the object of my gaze.

Back at the hotel, Sinead busies herself in the tent while I wander the premises. The manager has just come off duty and has poured himself a drink. He lumbers from one group of patrons to another, bantering with them about the cattle and the stalls at the show grounds. The barman puts a Tafel Lager down in front of me and I enjoy my beer while taking notes on the day's activities. After a while, the manager reaches me.

"What are you writing?" I explain that I'm just taking notes about the day's activities.

"Ah, a writer. Did you go to the show grounds?"

"No. We went to the museum instead." He's clearly bored, but perks up when I mention looking for a restaurant in Cuito Cuanavale Street.

"Ja, now there's a fuck-up," a man beside me chimes in.

"How so?"

"That name. Pressure." He stabs a finger at the roof. "From higher up. But we're pushing back. That's why it's the only street name in the city centre that's changed. We've let some of the back streets go, and the township streets, but the town has remained unchanged. It's not who we are."

In the corner of the pub, the regulars have gathered for a game of darts. They wave in our direction and the manager excuses himself. I finish my beer and return to the campsite to make supper. I am busy chopping onions when the security guard walks over for a chat. "Philippus Basson," he introduces himself, "one of Jakob Morenga's people. My father was from Okahandja — one of Maharero's people — but my mother and her family have lived here in Gobabis for generations." I am intrigued. Jakob Morenga emerges from the colonial record as one of the most fearless and tireless opponents of the Germans. His father was Omuherero, his mother Nama, a fact of history he used to his advantage as he established his power base in southern Namibia.

In 1904, he had led the Bondelswarts people in their uprising against the colonial authorities. When the Bondelswarts were given a generous peace settlement, Morenga refused to accept the terms that were offered and retreated to ||Khauxa!nas, the fortress built by Jonker Afrikaner and his people in the late 1700s. From this inaccessible fortress, Morenga continued to frustrate German efforts with guerrilla-style attacks throughout southern Namibia. As soon as the Germans made any advances, Morenga and other leaders would erode these gains with carefully planned attacks. When Morenga's people were finally defeated in 1906, he gave himself up to the Cape authorities and was imprisoned there rather than submit to the Germans. After the Germans declared peace in March 1907, Morenga was released. He immediately returned to Namibia with four hundred followers to resume the fight. This time, the Germans did not allow him to escape. They pursued him into British territory and killed him in battle at Eensaamheid Pan.

Morenga may have lost the war and his life, but the memory of his resistance lives on. I want to ask Philippus how his family fits in with the Morengas, as Jakob's stronghold lay far south of Gobabis, but he has already launched into another story: "I drove Buffels into Angola for the SWATF."

Philippus Basson hits his stride as I finish cutting the onions. He stands upright, tapping his baton, the one from the office wall, against his shoe as he talks. His eyes have dulled slightly, but it could just be the fading light. I begin to dice some tomatoes and he leans over to tap a switch on the side of a pole with the baton. Slowly, floodlights wheeze into action to cover the lawn in a surreal whiteness. His eyes become impenetrable. "Ja, it was back in 1976, Baas." He describes several forays into Angola, a gunfight. But I hear little of what he has to say. His stories are no different from the ones I've heard in the pub. What sticks is the word *Baas*.

I have not heard that term used without dollops of sarcasm for many years. It is a term that defines the power relations of the apartheid era. Baas: Master.

"My name is Peter," I tell Philippus.

"Ja, Baas," Philippus responds and continues to regale me with his army exploits. I invite him to join us for dinner, but he declines. Gradually, he runs out of stories, excuses himself, and wanders off on his rounds. After supper, I check some facts: the Buffel Infantry Mobility Vehicle was only introduced in 1978, and the SWATF was formed in 1980. Philippus Basson's stories of the 1976 invasion of Angola are fabrications, gleaned from endless evening rounds that take him past the bar where the white patrons reminisce.

When Philippus returns later in the evening, I probe him about the stories. He becomes vague and evasive. I ask about his family. He tells me how this job allows him to send his children to a good school. Slowly, I edge the conversation to the liberation struggle. Philippus holsters his ever-swinging baton and says firmly, with a glance over his shoulder, "*Hier praat ons nie oor sulke dinge nie.*" Here, we don't talk about such things.

As Philippus turns to resume his rounds, he assures me that he is there to protect me. I sit in the floodlit backyard reading a book and, as ever, jotting down notes. In the background, locals seat themselves on the patio in the back garden. Toward midnight, one of the bar patrons tries to reverse his bakkie out of the narrow garden, but the cars hinder his efforts. He unleashes a string of abuse at the hapless Philippus, who is blamed for any number of ills, including allowing the cars to park there. I walk over and tell the driver that if I move my car, he will be able to get out. He glowers at me and again blames Philippus. I point out that I have been watching patrons move their cars about against Philippus's directions. The man begins to open the door, but I lean against it purposefully. He shuts the door firmly and revs his engine impatiently. I move our bakkie, allowing the drunken patron to wiggle his way out of the backyard. Philippus retreats to the shadows and I crawl into the tent for the night.

Sinead and I wake early the next morning to meet a tour guide outside the front of the hotel. Today, Peter-Hain Uakii Kazapua will take us to a local San community for a walk through the bush. On the way through the hotel, I notice that our bakkie has been washed. As we walk past the reception, I see the baton back on its hook. Philippus has clocked out. Outside, Uakii is already waiting. He is the only black tour operator in a town dominated by white business. He is a friendly young man who talks widely and knowledgeably about local history. Throughout the day, he shifts effortlessly between Afrikaans, English, Otjiherero and !Naro, as the occasion demands. He grew up in an era when black people needed European names, he reminds us on the way out to the farm. "My parents said that if they were going to name me in a European way, they would give me a name that demonstrates reconciliation and that we can all live together here. So they chose the name of a person who fought to make such a world possible: Peter Hain."

Uakii tries hard to combine both the old and the new. "You can't advertise cultural tours as 'showing the way people live today' when the people don't live like that anymore!" he says emphatically. "The best we can do is give a snapshot of a moment from the past. You have to separate contemporary lives from an awareness of cultural history." In front of us, a small group of huts and a fireplace appear from among the bushes. A group of elderly San amble over. It is barely eight a.m. and they're ready for work. Uakii introduces us, asks for permission to visit from Ara, the eldest man in the group. Ara acknowledges us and offers a quick prayer to the ancestors in !Naro.

"Are you ready?" Ara asks as he finishes his prayer, and sets off at a blistering pace despite his age. Some way off, he looks back, surprised. "Are you coming?" he enquires. He's a showman who, throughout the walk, is very aware that his role as mediator is also that of actor.

"We are dressed in work clothes today," Ouma, the oldest of the women, says as we set off after Ara, and she points to the bare bodies that surround us. "This used to be everyday dress for our people, but now it's only work clothes. When our children get back from school, they take off their clothes. They also have to learn the old ways. It's important that they learn our language and our old ways."

Ara waits for us. "Today," he tells us as we draw nearer, "we are looking for *veldkos*, the plants of the area, and assessing their usefulness." We walk in a wide loop, stopping at plants that have medicinal value, plants used for shamanistic practice, plants for flavouring food. There's *gemsbokwortel* for diarrhea; stuff for backache; *uintjies* for beer. There's the bowstring plant, *hardegras*, for making a straw to suck water from the nook in a tree. *Tulp*: the upper part kills, the lower part cures.

"And this plant?" Ara asks me. I recognize *Boscia albitrunca*, the white stem acacia that I know best by its Afrikaans name, *witgat*: white-arse. I know too from family lore that Afrikaner families on the Great Trek and during the Depression used to make coffee from the roots. I share this information with Ara. "I am surprised our traditional knowledge has made it into Afrikaner culture," he says. "You people seldom trouble yourselves with our ways."

"There is more of your culture in ours than you can imagine," I tell him. "And more than many Afrikaners care to acknowledge." He laughs.

Uakii remarks pointedly, looking at me as he speaks, that Ara was a tracker in the SADF. On the way to the farm, he and I had talked about the San trackers the infamous 32 Battalion had used up in the north. After the war, the trackers were discharged and relocated — some to remote areas in South Africa; others to farms in Namibia. The people no one wanted, people who continue to live on the peripheries, like the black soldiers who served in the SWATF. The

Namibian president has made it quite clear that Namibians who fought in SWATF or in the South African forces will not be considered veterans under Namibian law, and thus do not qualify for pensions or veterans' benefits. Families still remain split as fathers and sons discover that they fought against each other in the war. Ara bends over to pick up some animal droppings. "Male or female?" he asks. I don't know. "Female droppings are round; male ones have pointed tips," he says and focuses his eyes on Uakii.

One of the younger women steps in to relieve the tension of the moment. "My daughter dances," she says.

"That's because her titties are still pert," Ouma throws back a retort. "Tourists don't come to see droopy tits. It's when they start to droop that we close them up," she says, pointing to her own modestly covered upper body. "*Ons ken nie skaam onder ons mense nie!*" We don't know shame among our people. She laughs. "We are not scared of our bodies or of old age like you." She claps her hands and starts to dance, reaching out to draw Sinead nearer. Sinead shies away and Ouma's body crinkles with pleasure at the reaction she's received.

As we walk along, Ara finds more spoors. He invites Sinead and me to test our knowledge of the veld. When we don't know, he presents us with riddles. "What little child is not afraid to walk alone in the veld?" he asks when Sinead cannot recognize an all-too-human footprint we see in the sand. She thinks for a while before she makes the connection. "A baboon."

"What spotted creature would make such a mess of the branches?" he wonders as he looks at the destruction below the tree. So many questions; so few answers. So much to discover.

As we near the end of the walk, Ouma squeals with delight. She starts digging in the red sand. I bend down and smell the sand. Uakii joins me on the ground and takes a small amount and puts it in his mouth. I follow suit. The wet sand has a rich smell and the taste is a complex blend of root and moisture. There is a hint of berry. Beside us, Ouma has gotten down to her shoulder into the hole and Ara, whose arms are longer, joins her. Finally, they emerge with a kambro root. Ouma wipes the sand off and breaks it open with a snap. The root is very fleshy and the liquid is refreshing. I find that the root itself has a slight peppery taste to it, but the sweetness of the liquid lingers longest.

"It tastes a bit like a watery carrot," Sinead says. Ouma smiles. When we've had enough kambro, Ouma puts the unused portion of the root back and replaces the sand. "You take only what is needed from the earth and return the rest. We have to look after the earth so that it looks after us."

As we approach the homestead, Sinead and Ouma almost step on a small night adder. Both of them jump back and Ara descends on the creature with determination. "It is too close to our homes," he says as he pounds at it with his walking stick, "but it will make a good snack." As we cross the road, he sees another trail. "A mamba — moving that direction about half an hour ago."

"When we see tracks like these, we say, 'Snake, pass before me where I can see you,'" Ouma says. "We only fear those that pass behind us, those we cannot see."

For the first few miles, we drive back to Gobabis in silence. After a while, Uakii and I resume our conversation about roots. He grew up in Rietfontein, a small town northeast of Gobabis, he tells me. His father was a farm labourer and just down from their house were some Dorsland graves. As a young boy, Uakii would visit these graves and listen to the stories about the Dorsland Trek. "It is part of my history now too," he says. "Afrikaners think that is their story, but it is mine too, you know. We have to share our stories. It was these stories and the stories I heard from my !Naro nanny that made me interested in the history of the Omaheke."

"We've been to a number of graves on this trip," I say. "Mostly, they've been graves of colonial soldiers and Trekkers. Up at Swartbooisdrift, Sinead and I went to the Dorsland Trek memorial. There was a guy from Gobabis there — Eric Peters." At the mention of the name, Uakii shoots a glance at me.

"He doesn't seem your type."

"True," I reply, "but he said some interesting things about the Dorsland Trek. He and the other members of his family try to make a pilgrimage to Swartbooisdrift every year to see the stone cairn the Dorsland descendants built there 'to preserve Afrikaner memory in this land,' as he put it."

"I know about the Afrikaners and piles of stones. Some years ago, an Afrikaner researcher, John Joubert, was murdered in Rietfontein while doing research on the Dorsland Trekkers. Afterwards, a group of Dorsland descendants approached me because they wanted to build a memorial to him. They wanted to know if it would be appropriate to build an ombindi. You know, we Ovaherero erect ombindi, piles of stones, to honour our ancestors. They wanted to know if black people would mind. It was the first time Afrikaners around here had consulted us on anything. I told them we are all people of stone here: We bled on the same rocks as children. We share a history of stone and we share the same ancestors. We're in this country together, I told them. It's all of our history, all of our ancestors. Go do the right thing. Build an ombindi."

Since we've strayed onto the topic of graves and memorials, I ask Uakii a question that has bothered me since our visit to the Commonwealth War Graves Site at Aus. "The maps all indicate major battle sites and German military graves, but where are the Ovaherero, Witbooi and Nama soldiers buried?"

"It is strange," he muses. "I can only tell you about the colonial graves. There had to be bodies of Morenga's people here, yet we don't know about them." Back in Gobabis, Uakii does not turn at Cuito Cuanavale Street. Instead, he heads past the church toward the copse of acacias I'd seen from the museum. "I want to show you something before I take you home." We enter a deserted lot and he parks his bakkie on a small rise overlooking a bed of reeds. "There is the spring where people used to gather to discuss matters of communal importance in the days before the Europeans settled here. That is where they argued. This is also the spot where our leaders, like Morenga and Witbooi, gathered to strategize their resistance to the Germans."

We watch the sun set over the reeds. "Imagine," Uakii dreams, "a few campsites over here and a statue of elephants drinking at the fountain. To remind us of the animals that also once visited these waters."

"A monument for cattle and a monument for departed elephants on opposite sides of the town. Quite appropriate," I remark.

Uakii chuckles. "We need to honour all histories, remember. The good and the bad. But seriously, if we develop this place, remember our past appropriately, maybe we can stop young people from leaving Gobabis. I just need to get the Chamber of Commerce to approve a permit. But we're arguing at the moment."

Uakii waits for the sun to set completely before taking us back to the hotel. I stop by the bar to settle my bill. While the duty manager attends to business, I order a beer and dial the number Eric Peters gave me. James Chapman does not answer the phone so instead I leave a message. "You're looking for Old Man Chapman?" the manager says as he walks in to give me my receipt. "He's visiting family in Windhoek. A heart of gold, let me tell you. And so many stories to tell. He knows all of our history."

"There's only one history now, and it's not ours!" a man booms from further down the counter.

"*Daar het jy dit!*" says the manager and raises his glass to his snaky eyes. "There you have it!"

22

There is frost on the lawn when we wake up and the tent is stiff as I crawl out and set about the task of making an early morning cup of coffee. Moist red granules of Kalahari sand press through the grass and cling to my knees. In the neighbouring yard, the silhouette of a stray cat rummages through the skeletal remains of cars that cover every available space in the lot. "I've been trying for years to get him to move them, or at least put up a decent fence," Snake-eyes lamented when we crossed paths at some point during our stay. "But it's a small town and you have to work with your neighbours all the time, so there you have it." The sun has barely reached over the barbed-wire fence when a homeless man emerges from one of the rusty husks and tries to slink off before anyone notices him. He freezes when he sees me. I smile and hold out a sandwich from the pile I have prepared for our lunch. He nods his thanks and shuffles over furtively. As I hand it to him over the fence, he holds out a mug. The kettle has just boiled and I make him a cup of coffee. "*Ek moet loop,*" he says nervously. "*Die man van die hotel sal die polisie roep.*" I have to go. The man from the hotel will call the police.

As the rising sun settles in on the centre of town, Sinead and I head down Cuito Cuanavale Street in search of more battlefields and graves near Gochas. Soon, we find ourselves driving along the fringes of the Kalahari Desert. The tips of the dunes rise above the vegetation on the right; on the left, dense copses of camelthorns line the course of the Auob River. I struggle to imagine that this is where some of the most brutal battles of the Wars of Resistance took place. The colonial governor, Theodor Leutwein, may initially have had qualms about General von Trotha's methods, but by September 1904, he was in agreement with the general and the German authorities that it was no longer about the Ovaherero alone and that this was the time to settle the "native question" once and for all. As the fugitive Ovaherero drifted from poisoned watering hole to poisoned watering hole in the Omaheke, von Trotha took personal command of the forces in the south and set about the systematic task of *Vernichtung*: destruction.

The GPS is sulking again, indicating roads that don't exist, or pointing us to areas in the veld by the roadside, with no clear directions on how to get there. "Do a U-turn," it intones. "Turn left in two kilometres; turn left again." In other words, another U-turn. We go around in circles. The two maps we have on standby are not much help, either. The official map doesn't list any war memorials in this area and the car rental map offers only the vaguest of clues. A star near where the C15 and the C23 meet suggests that there is a war grave site here at a place called Lidfontein. At the crossroad just north of Stampriet I turn toward Lidfontein. The GPS loses its signal. There is no town in sight, so I stop at the first farmhouse I see. I park the bakkie at the front door and Wilma Badenhorst emerges from the house to greet me. "Excuse my clothes," she says as she dries her hands on a dishcloth. "Danie and I have been tailing the lambs and marking their ears." Her clothes are flecked with blood and she wipes a stray droplet off her eyebrow. I in turn apologize for interrupting what is clearly a busy day for them and offer to assist, if they'd like me to. "I grew up in sheep country," I tell her. "I can hold a lamb, if need be. But first, can you tell me where we can find Lidfontein?" I show her the map. "It's meant to be a town, by the looks of things."

Wilma smiles appreciatively at my offer to help with the tailing. Then she replies cagily, "This is Lidfontein." I explain that I am looking for graves.

"We haven't had anyone looking for a while, but grave hunters come in waves. A few years ago, I considered sprucing up the place, or opening up a tea room here at the house," she muses, "but then the traffic dried up. Maybe I should rethink this."

"Would you be willing to direct me to the graves?" I enquire.

"The graves are very neglected," she tells me. "And besides, you won't get anywhere in *that* bakkie! I'll ask Danie to take you when he gets back. Would you like some coffee while we wait?"

We take her up on her offer. "We're almost done," she continues as she pours the coffee. "It's the rains. It brought the early lambs with it. And the ticks. So we're dipping and dosing too while we're out in the veld." We continue to talk about farming. Unlike the war, these are things I understand. As we chat over a cup of coffee and some rusks, Wilma warms to us. Strangers are one thing, but people who know farming are extended family, she tells me. "You're just one of us." That's when Danie calls to tell her he's stuck in the veld with a puncture. She needs to bring the spare. "I've got to run down into the end of the *huiskamp*, the home paddock," she tells me. "I might as well take you myself."

We drop off the tire with Danie and Wilma instructs one of the labourers with him to hop into the back where the tire was. These are warm-hearted people who will readily offer a complete stranger a meal and a cup of coffee, but old habits die hard. Habits like not letting farm workers sit in the cab with them.

We slip and slide our way through a mile or so of fine Kalahari sand before stopping at a small dune. "The graves are on top of this mound," Wilma tells me. Sinead decides she's seen enough graves for a lifetime and opts to stay in the bakkie while we walk to the cemetery. Along the way, several empty liquor bottles have pushed through the sand. "Ja, the old man who rented this place had a bit of a problem,"

Wilma remarks. "He rented from my father and when he passed, we decided to come and use Lidfontein as our base." The remains of a fence poke out from the sand in places, and bits of barbed wire are still visible. From what I can see, the only recent visitors to this place have been the porcupines. There are diggings everywhere. Wilma was right: the graves are very neglected and the headstones are crumbling to the point where they are barely legible. I can read the name of a Lieutenant Giesselmann Mees on one of the headstones. Beside him are two or three unmarked graves. A short way off lies a headstone made of marble. The name is clearly legible, but the date of death on this one is 1937 — long after the war. As with so many of these plots, military and civilian graves lie side by side. Here, there are only a limited number of places that will allow one to dig a hole in six feet of the country. This is inhospitable territory and when the earth gives you a space, you take it.

We can just discern the date on Giesselmann Mees's headstone: 29 November 1904. By that time, Hendrik Witbooi and the other Nama leaders had been harassing farms in the south of Namibia for months. Throughout 1904, German-language newspapers had published threats that, despite the peace treaties that had been signed in years past, the Nama people would meet a similar fate as the Hereros if they resisted disarmament. Witbooi, who read German fluently, was understandably alarmed at these reports and he knew he had to act in the interests of his people. He and other Nama leaders began to raid farms and to set up ambushes to harry the German patrols as they headed south to execute their new strategy among the Nama. The Germans were meticulous about keeping records of their battles and their fallen. Lidfontein, the records show, was attacked on the twenty-eighth of November 1904, and Giesselmann must have been one of the casualties of that engagement. And yet, Wilma tells me as we walk back to the car, she has been unable to find any concrete information on these graves. According to the records in the National Archives of Namibia, Giesselmann Mees does not exist. Where other

German soldiers who died in the battles in this area have been buried at the cemetery in Gochas, Giesselmann lies alone on a farm in the Kalahari. All the other war graves we have seen show the Reich's Cross, yet only a rifle and the German inscription hint at Mees's military background. Giesselmann Mees has now become just another unclaimed body. At least he has a name, I muse as I get back in to the bakkie, unlike the thousands of Ovaherero and Nama bodies that lie buried in the shallow desert sand, waiting for the wind to reveal their resting places.

We head back to the farm and arrive just as Danie pulls up. He looks harassed. He is sullen until he hears me speaking Afrikaans. His demeanour changes and he invites us in. "Two local farmers ran a regular gravesite tour a few years ago, but then they stopped. I never found out why. The farms around here are littered with them." He makes a few phone calls to track down the farmers, but without success. Danie and Wilma invite us to stay for lunch, but we have a long way to go still before sundown, so we turn down their offer and thank them for their generosity.

From Lidfontein, Sinead and I take the C15 south and estimate the distance to the next site of interest. We know we are heading somewhere south of Stampriet, but the rest is pure conjecture. We drive for about fifteen kilometres and when we pass the entrance to the farm Gross Nabas, I stop. Although the map indicates that there is a settlement here, I have learned from my recent experience. After the night attack on Lidfontein, war records show that Hendrik Witbooi had headed south, deeper into the Kalahari. That December, he and his ally, Simon Koper, suffered heavy losses at the battles of Naris and Koës, but managed to regroup in the Auob Valley near Gross Nabas. For two days, from the second to the fourth of January 1905, Witbooi and Koper turned the tables and inflicted heavy losses on the Germans at the Battle of Gross Nabas before fleeing south once more. A little way north of the farm gate, hidden in a dip by the roadside, stands a memorial plaque commemorating the battle.

From Gross Nabas, we head toward Gochas, looking for the second battle site that is marked along this road. This time, there is no farm sign to help us out, and we miss it. The map simply lists "War Memorial 1905" with no geographic co-ordinates. The GPS splutters and pants, but doesn't offer any useful assistance.

We decide to head past the turnoff to Gochas and explore a stretch of road that promises more war sites. We are not disappointed. Right after the Battle of Gross Nabas, on the fifth of January 1905, a German patrol rode into an ambush just south of Gochas and again suffered heavy losses. Witbooi and his soldiers disappeared before German rein- forcements could arrive. The heavy fighting in the region continued until April 1905, after which the war gradually settled into an uneasy stalemate. The Nama commandos would attack farms and ambush German patrols; the Germans would force the Nama troops into battle, but were then unable to pursue them effectively in the harsh terrain when they fled. The constant marching and fighting took a toll on everyone. German troops lacked local knowledge of the underground wells and food supplies in the area and relied solely on supplies and rations. During an ambush or a battle, it became impossible to replen- ish their supplies and several accounts tell of soldiers who fell into thirst-induced delirium. Nama soldiers relied on their knowledge of the land and their agility to stay ahead of the Germans. This tactic worked well for the soldiers, but since Von Trotha's proclamation included women and children, it meant that entire communities were constantly on the move. When the Germans sued for peace in July 1905, Hendrik Witbooi, who over the past decade had supported the Germans in some of their military endeavours, wrote to Karl Schmidt, "I was right there with you many times during your peace, and have come to see in it nothing but the destruction of all our people."

The winter of 1905 was harsh and drier than normal, forcing the Witbooi people out of the desert in search of water and food, only to be confronted by the same dilemma that had faced the Ovaherero in the north: the Germans had occupied the wells, or had poisoned them. At Aminuis, Hendrik Witbooi sent the women and children to the well bearing a white flag, but the Germans turned them away without offering them access to water. Kurd Schwabe, a German officer, describes scenes in which women and children wander aimlessly from well to well, pleading with the Germans for water. "It is here," he writes, "that the fate of the Witbooi people was to be fulfilled." Schwabe uses the word *Auflösung* to describe the effect of these events. It is a slippery word that can be translated simply as "resolution," as in the resolution of the war, but there are other, darker undertones to this word, including "elimination."

Under a massive weaver bird nest near the memorial for the Battle of Gochas, we see yet another sign, "Gefecht bei Haruchas, 3 Jan 05." Sinead and I have a quick lunch at the weaver tree before heading into Gochas itself. It is no more than a little spittle on the map, with a gas station and an outsized graveyard. We fill up the bakkie with diesel before heading off to look for the war graves. They are easy enough to find, but getting close to the graves proves more challenging. There is a tall security fence around the graves and a heavy padlock to prevent unwanted visitors. I look around and head for an official-looking building nearby. The sleepy attendant rubs his eye and directs me to the Village Council office.

The lady behind the counter at the Village Council office has a short pixie haircut and a temper to match. She barks at the gardener who had kindly escorted us in: "I don't do keys!" Then she turns her wrath onto a customer who has walked in bearing a form she wants to hand in. She snaps and scowls her way to the counter and grabs the paper from the woman. All the while, she avoids my eyes. The gardener wipes his hands on his overalls and walks into a cubicle. He can't find the key there and I help him rummage through a bunch of keys in a box taken from under Pixie's desk. She scowls at us at regular intervals, but still offers no assistance.

"Let me try one more place," the man in the overalls suggests and walks across the road to a workshop. There he finds the errant key and hands it over. "I'll meet you there in a little while to collect the key."

For every German soldier who lies buried in this cemetery, hundreds of Nama bodies lie in unmarked graves. I look around for clues, anything, anything that can lead me to a deeper understanding of these atrocities, but there is nothing. I sit on the edge of a grave in the winter sunshine, watching children walk by on their way back from school. A boy and a girl pass a soccer ball between them as they walk. I am empty and exhausted. The mid-afternoon shadows begin to lengthen and we have plenty of travelling left to do. I lock up again and return the key.

From Gochas, we head for Witbooisvlei in search of the ruins of a German police outpost. Again, we manage to find our way to a crossroad. We drive west for a bit, searching for an entrance. By now, the sun is low in the sky and we decide to give up our search for the day and head into the setting sun toward Mariental. At Mariental, we flip a coin to decide whether to sleep there, or whether to press on to Rehoboth. Rehoboth wins and soon the monotonous drone of the tires lulls us both into a tired silence.

We spend the night at a campsite along the banks of the Oanob Dam, a project that was completed in 1990 to address the chronic water shortages in Rehoboth. In the morning, we make pancakes on the gas stove as we watch an assortment of sugarbirds and finches trill their way into the day. Our ultimate goal for the day is to reach Waterberg, but first we want to visit the Rehoboth Museum. We park our bakkie in the recently swept, spacious front garden of the museum and knock on the locked door. When there is no response, we walk around to the back and enter a cobbled courtyard with a Roman fountain in the middle. A side door stands open and I peek in through the doorway. A woman stirs a stove full of pots, but when she sees us, she ambles over to the door and squeezes past me without saying a word. She heads through the archway into the back garden and a short while later returns with another woman in tow.

"Sorry," says the woman who has been summoned, "I'm the only one here and today is gardening day. We try to keep it pretty around here." I look around. The garden is indeed well kept and it is, by her own admission, the pride and joy of her twenty-five-year reign as curator of the museum. She holds a finger in the air, one that says, "Wait here until I return." The finger stays in place in front of our eyes as she disappears around the corner. It seems as if she can extend her reach forever. Then the hand disappears and I hear a door open.

"I love small-town museums," I confide to Sinead.

"Me too." We settle in to wait for the return of the curator.

Small-town museums seldom aspire to present visitors with the carefully curated exhibits one finds in big-city museums, where they consciously attempt to place historical events in a global context. Rather, they tend to navel-gaze, offering interpretations of the local context. Yet it is the eclectic artifacts gathered from the community that make them interesting in ways that the larger museums can never be — the elder's top hat that was traded for a farm, the assortment of rifles and buggies and horsewhips, the needlework cases and doilies, and swords sticking out of flowerpots. Throughout, the hand of the curator looms large. Then sometimes, quite unexpectedly, you stumble upon something that threatens to unsettle the fabric of the universe. The air of such possibility lurks in the shadows of Rehoboth. In 1908, Eugen Fischer spent four months doing field research here. Today, Fischer's name is associated more with the eugenics research conducted by a one-time student of his, Josef Mengele, than with his own work, but in his day, Fischer's own contributions carried a fair deal of weight. When he published the findings of his research in Rehoboth, it compelled the German government to ban interracial marriages throughout its colonies.

By the time Fischer arrived in German South West Africa, the Wars of Resistance were over and the trafficking in human remains that had flourished during the war was a thing of the past too. In

Rehoboth, Fischer repeatedly asked the government to be allowed to exhume some bodies so that he could take the skeletal remains back to Germany with him for further analysis. The colonial government in Windhoek refused and Fischer left town without his specimens. He arrived in Swakopmund and booked into his hotel to wait for the Woermann Line vessel that would take him home. It was during this layover that he heard about some Topnaar graves in the desert. Descendants of the Nama who were among the first traders with Europeans along the coat, the Topnaar still observed many of the ancient burial rituals. Not one to miss out on an opportunity to conduct research, Fischer immediately arranged for a trip into the desert, leaving his own account of the events:

> I searched eagerly to find traces of the graves. Two Cape Boys served as my carriage driver and digger; I wanted to avoid using native Nama or Herero, since they would probably have found it too painful that — for scientific reasons that they would not have understood — we disturbed the peace of their buried com-patriots . . . Suddenly we stood before the melancholic image of the burial ground. A number of flat rocks . . . were placed deep in the sand, in uneven rows, so that only about 20 centimetres reached out of the sand. The pale, gray, deep-hanging sky . . . set the appropriately eerie mood for us shivering men. The dead were only about half a metre deep in the sand, lying in a supine position with their feet towards the water . . . With closed eyelids there was a serene peace about the hollow Nama faces.

Then he returned to his waiting ship and sailed for Germany. Later, in 1914, he petitioned the colonial governor directly for more human remains.

You have to grant it to Fischer, he was the master of understatement. He had good reason to believe the Nama or Ovaherero would have been upset. After all, the Wars of Resistance that had just ended came about in part as a result of grave robbing. Lieutenant Ralph Zürn was in charge of the garrison at Okahandja when the Ovaherero forces attacked on the twelfth of January 1904. The exact sequence of events that led to the incident that ignited the Wars of Resistance is a bit murky, but even the colonial farmers acknowledged that Zürn had played a role in bringing it about. Maharero subsequently referred to the genocidal war as "Zürn's War." There is evidence to suggest that Zürn had been involved in incidents of grave robbing and had desecrated Ovaherero graves.

As it happened, Fischer was eventually to lay his hands on the bones he had so desperately wanted while he was in Rehoboth and later at the outbreak of the First World War when he pleaded with the colonial administration to send him some skulls for his laboratory in Dahlem. After the Okahandja incident, Zürn was relieved of his duties and sent back to Germany. He took with him an Omuherero skull that he gave to his friend, Felix von Luschan, an avid collector of all things bone from around the world. On his death in 1902, von Luschan's collection was donated to the Frederick William University, now the Humboldt University in Berlin. When the Kaiser Wilhelm Institute of Anthropology, Human Heredity and Eugenics opened in Dahlem in 1937, Fischer became its first director. Finally, Fischer had unlimited access to Namibian skulls, skulls taken from the Swakopmund and Shark Island Concentration Camps, as well as his own corpus of photographs from Rehoboth. And of course there were also the Topnaar remains he had stolen on his way home. A picture of Fischer at his desk in Dahlem shows him staring intently at the image of a woman from Rehoboth while in the background a man gazes into the depths of the laboratory.

Our guide has returned and unlocks the door to the display room. She leads the way. The centre of the room is empty to allow larger groups to gather, while the edges of the room are crammed with local ephemera. She positions herself between us and the exhibits. Her jean shorts and pale orange T-shirt contrast the dour Puritan clothing that peeks out from behind her. Her hair is pulled back into a ponytail that threatens to come undone as a result of her labours in the garden. She wipes her hands on her apron and scratches her forehead with the back of her wrist, the long, graceful fingers of her right hand twisting as she contemplates her opening lines.

As she gathers herself into the rehearsed pose of public speakers around the world — feet apart, back straight, dropped shoulders and opened chest — she stares at a point slightly to the left behind us, then launches into her spiel. "Hi, I'm Agathe. You can walk though by yourself, or I can guide you," then immediately proceeds to lead us through the exhibits. Browsing, evidently, was never really an option.

"Do you know anything about the history of the Basters?"

It's another complicated story of people on the move. During the late 1860s, a community of mixed-race people at De Tuin, a mission station not far south of the Namibian border, requested the British colonial government to grant them leasing rights of the Crown land they were living on. When the government refused, citing the concerns of other settlers in the region about a mixed-race community near them, the community packed their belongings and trekked north in search of freedom and the ability to govern themselves.

"*Dis onse Groot Trek*," Agathe tells us. "It's our Great Trek. Just like the Boere s'n. The original three hundred Trekkers bought the land at Rehoboth, and they'll defend it, just like the Boere did at Blood River."

The easy analogy to a foundational myth cited by the most ardent advocates and defenders of apartheid troubles me. By the time I try to interject to tell her that such ready comparison of these two events is highly problematic, she's well into describing the next stage of the journey. "They settled first at Berseba in the south of Namibia, but they were only allowed to stay there for two years. After that, the Basters trekked further north and settled here on this empty piece of land."

Terra nullius has been the favoured argument of land-grabbers for a very long time. Again I want to interject to point out that such uncritical identification with the arguments of the empire can only get one in trouble. Again, she's too quick for me, so I scribble a note to myself to raise the issue with her later. She sees me writing. "What are you writing down?" she demands. "I see you taking notes while I'm talking." As she speaks, her hands settle along her diaphragm and she draws herself up to the full extent of her six-foot frame.

"I'm keeping a diary and working on a book, so I make notes about the people I meet and the things I see before I forget them," I say. "I was making a note to talk to you about . . ."

She cuts me off. "Okay. It's just that I've had reporters here and they never listen to me. Then they go and do their own thing. But you're not a reporter, so okay, keep writing." She breathes deeply and she lets her hands slide away from her diaphragm. They hang by her side for a moment before she continues. "I'll tell you, Rehoboth is a religious community. There are seventy churches and ten schools. This is a community founded on strong religious principles. The Bible has been our guide from the very beginning. Genesis 26:22. Rehoboth is land the Basters bought from the Namas. This is our land. It belongs to us. We bought it. It is ours."

Rehobothers are happy to tell you how the town got its name, for it speaks to how it came to be part of Namibia. The Book of Genesis tells of the time when Isaac left the house of Abimelech in the land of the Philistines in search of a place he could call his own. On their third attempt at digging a well in the Valley of Gerar, Isaac's shepherds succeeded and no one quarrelled with them over it. Isaac therefore named the place Rehoboth, which translates as "Now the Lord has given us room and we will flourish in the land." These were allegedly the words uttered by Kaptein Hermanus van Wyk, their leader, after he had negotiated with Abraham Swartbooi for the purchase of the land. Witbooi and his people had lived here, but during a conflict with the Ovaherero, they had left the region and settled to the north. The Ovaherero too had returned to Okahandja, thus providing Hermanus van Wyk with the opportunity he sought to procure land for his people.

Although the terms of the sale were agreed upon, the sale never actually went through. In the interim, the Basters had built a church and a home for the resident missionary. They drafted a constitution and they elected a governing council. In 1876, Swartbooi threatened to take his land back; in 1882, he attacked Rehoboth. The residents of the Gebiet defended their territory and so, through successful defence of the land rather than purchase, the Basters gained a claim to ownership of the land. Rehoboth became their patch of paradise. At least, that was the idea. Hard as the people of Rehoboth tried to maintain their neutrality, outside events kept intruding. When the Germans arrived, they negotiated a treaty and Rehoboth became, at least in name, a German protectorate, while maintaining its independence. Soon a German magistrate arrived. Then the rest of the colonial administration set up shop in Rehoboth. But still the Baster council persevered in their efforts to remain independent.

We have inched toward a large display cabinet in the corner by the window. "The Basters too have their own *Geloftedag*, their own Day of the Covenant," she tells us. I quickly explain to my Canadian-raised daughter that on the sixteenth of December 1838, a group of Boer Trekkers had made a Covenant with God to commemorate that day in all eternity if God granted them victory in the Battle of Blood River. Agathe scowls at me while I interrupt, then picks up her story. "On the eighth of May 1915, the Basters had to defend Sam Khubis. For all our history, we had remained neutral as the battles raged around us for this land, but when they came to take ours, we stood firm. Like the Boere, we asked for God's help and made a Covenant. And so, every year, we hold *Geloftefees* just like the Afrikaners. They too were just people searching for their own place in the sun."

Sinead turns to me in confusion. "Who is Sam Khubis?"

"You mean where?" I have learned from my previous experiences in the room, so before I continue, I turn to Agathe. "Can we have a minute to look at the photos?" She retreats to a respectful distance and while we look at the photos, I explain to Sinead. "It's a place called Tsamkhubis, where the mountains lie in a circle to create a natural fort. By the way, she's wrong about the neutrality thing," I point out. "Remember the Reiterdenkmal in Windhoek? It had the names of Basters who died fighting for the Germans. During the Wars of Resistance, the Basters fought on the German side, but their pact fell apart in the First World War. They refused to fight the South Africans for fear of losing their land and fled to Tsamkhubis. When the Germans attacked, they made their Covenant. After a day of fighting, the Germans suddenly stopped firing at them and then retreated. The Rehobothers considered it a miracle and felt the God had heard their prayers. In fact, the Germans retreated because a South African force had arrived to assist the besieged people."

Agathe feels we've had enough alone time and turns our attention to the clothes and handiwork in the adjacent corner before shuffling us toward the exit. At a display case containing more recent photographs from the community, she stops. "That's our Kaptein, Hans Diergaardt. But I didn't vote for Diergaardt," and again she stretches herself to her full length in a combination of indignation and pride, "because he wanted independence for Rehoboth." During the apartheid era, from 1984 to 1990, the government had granted Rehoboth nominal independence, just as they had a number of Bantustans in South Africa, and Diergaardt was Rehoboth's chosen leader at the time.

"With independence, Rehoboth became part of Namibia. We kept our kaptein but lost our land. Other people had to give up their kapteins, but gained ownership of the land in the conservancies. Now they want ours." Hans Diergaardt became a member of the Constituent Assembly of Namibia, but dreams of independence and control over the land lingered inside his head. Less than a month after Namibian independence, he engaged in a standoff with the new government, blocking the road through Rehoboth. In order to help defend Rehoboth, should it come to that, Diergaardt made an alliance with the Afrikaner Resistance Movement in South Africa, a militant white supremacist group that continues to advocate for a white homeland. Eventually, Diergaardt backed off. Agathe tries to explain the complexities underlying the events, but she becomes flustered and animated as she insists on the righteousness of Diergaardt's actions, even as she repeats how she could never vote for him because he advocated independence. "We're one Namibia now," she shrills. "We can't have those old ways anymore."

Agathe is a complex personality and it's a challenge keeping track of her constant vacillation. One moment she's pure Namibian; the next she's defending Rehoboth's right to independent governance. Sinead gives up and wanders off to one of the exhibits. Without permission. I follow her and manage to peek at a picture of Baster soldiers during the Second World War before Agathe bustles us out of the door. As with almost everything about Rehoboth, the town's relationship to World War II is ambivalent. Most Rehobothers fought with the Allies, but some, like Ernst Dahms, were studying in Germany when war broke out. He may not have been Aryan enough to be part of the new Germany, but Hitler had no compunction about drafting him into his army. Dahms died in battle at Königsberg.

Agathe locks the door behind us. Her flip-flops slap the floor as she walks resolutely across the passage to open up the other room for us. She stops in the doorway and turns to us, again raising her finger in the air. "I never got married," she booms, "because I won't let a man tell me what to do. They all said a woman must marry and have kids. I wanted a job. So I became curator here at the museum. I bring school children through here all the time. Visiting the museum is a compulsory field trip." Where the other room offered the most intimate details of a community's history, this room has the air of a school laboratory about it. "Back at Sam Khubis," Agathe picks up her story, "we made our own Gelofte and we honour it still. That's because we are a nation founded on Christian principles. God created man, and science and evolution just create problems. Namibian law says we have to teach evolution in the schools. So I made a plan: I created this display," she waves at the surrounding displays with a sense of pride in her achievement. "Here we can show the children evolution and then the teachers don't have to talk about it in school. It becomes part of their museum visit, which is also in the curriculum." The plan is stunning in its guile and simplicity.

Underneath posters of the big bang and the planets, there is a picture of the fossilized jawbone of *Otavipithecus namibiensis*, the Miocene hominid found at Mount Aukas in northern Namibia. Nothing more than a fragment of the jawbone remains. I count the teeth (four molars, a stub of a canine and some incisors) and wonder what secrets these teeth hold about life in the Miocene Age. Agathe is impatient and wants us to leave. She shoos Sinead toward the door as she talks.

"Otavi Man was the first inhabitant of this country. The rest of us are all settlers, including the Khoisan and the Nama. So you see, when the Basters arrived here, this was *niemandsland*, no-man's land." Agathe remains consistent in her ability to surprise. "They, the Basters, settled this land," she emphasizes the point, "and they paid for it. It is ours."

Since we are discussing bone, I attempt to engage her in a conversation about Eugen Fischer's research. "Back in 1908, just after the war, a man called Eugen Fisher came here to Rehoboth," I venture. "Do you know anything about him?" Agathe looks blank. "He stayed here for four months, taking pictures and measuring skulls."

Agathe has latched onto something familiar. "Skulls? No, no one worked on skulls. Not here. That's not *onse mense* — not our people. That's Herero stuff. We had nothing to do with the war." She looks imploringly at the door, as if to inform us that the sun is high and she still has beds to weed before it becomes unbearably hot.

23

For nearly sixteen thousand kilometres, our bakkie has behaved impeccably. Now, halfway to Okahandja on our way to the Waterberg, she flags. As I try to pass a big truck on an open stretch of road between Rehoboth and Windhoek, the bakkie splutters and coughs. The engine loses power dramatically and I fall back. There's a pop as the exhaust backfires and a cloud of black smoke billows from the back. We have become *that* car. The thick black smoke trails behind us to the next garage, where I fill up and check all fluids and filters. Everything seems fine, but I buy two pints of oil just in case. Sinead and I have lunch and then get back onto the road. We still have about three hours' driving ahead of us and the gates of the rest camp at Waterberg close at six. I'm hoping to check in and have enough daylight left to stretch my legs on a short walk. My body aches from the cumulative effect of driving for weeks on end and I can identify with the bakkie's protests at the thought of moving. Happily, it seems as though a rest and some attention was all she needed, for she's in high spirits again and we get to the Waterberg in the late afternoon. We head straight through to Okakarara to put in diesel. The bakkie responds with a satisfied purr on the way to the rest camp.

At the turnoff to Waterberg, I offer a ride to a woman who is standing by the roadside. As we stop, she gathers a swathe of parcels and runs to the car. "Thank you! Thank you! I would have been so late if I didn't get a ride soon!" She is on her way to work at the Waterberg Rest Camp.

As has become routine here in Namibia, we communicate using a mixture of Afrikaans and English. I ask about the Battle of Ohamakari, the Otjiherero name for the Waterberg. She points back to the farm we passed on the way to Okakarara. "No, not the guest farm," I say, "I want to know about the battle. Against the Germans."

She shakes her head. "No, no fighting here. We welcome everybody."

I try again. "What does Hamakari mean?" I deliberately leave the question vague to see whether she will return to the guest farm, or whether she'll talk about the battle and what it means to live right beside a place of such historical importance. She simply shrugs her shoulders and says, "*Ek weet nie.*" I don't know.

We drop our passenger off at the staff entrance and head up the hill to our chalet. Slowly, the landscape emerges from memory. Toward the end of 1990, Julie and I took a weekend off and drove up to the Waterberg with Andreya.

"When Mommy and Andreya and I were here," I tell Sinead as we drive past the swimming pool. "Andreya forgot her towel at the pool. I came back to fetch it, but a leopard had jumped the perimeter fence of the rest camp and was drinking from the pool. I had to sit in the car for a long time before it moved and it was safe to fetch the towel. Mommy worried herself sick while I was gone." She still does. Since the fiasco with the credit card, she has been texting me constantly to update me on the current state of our finances. "Enjoy yourselves. Don't worry." And then follows a text with a dollar amount. I look at it and I do worry. About my wife who has had to perform miracles in order to get us back to Windhoek, and about Andreya who isn't here with me this time, and I miss them both as we drive up the mountain toward the rocks that have turned a deep gold in the late afternoon sun.

I think there is something in our genetic makeup that compels us to return to places we have known, to come to terms with the past, to find a measure of understanding and closure. "Can you live with your choice?" my brother asked me on the evening before I made my objection to conscription public. Here at Waterberg, at the end of our trip through Namibia, I know for certain that I can, that I have. I am at peace with my decision.

A troop of baboons walks through the camp in the early evening, scavenging for anything that has been left out. They have no respect for boundary fences and enter the camp at will. They linger outside our chalet and try to open the baboon-proof garbage cans. Throughout the night we hear them fussing and grumbling, calling to each across the rest camp. We sleep in, then start the day with a leisurely breakfast. I have coffee; Sinead has tea. We have no fixed plans. After breakfast we set off on a hike up the Waterberg. In places, the boulders give way to patches of red sand, as if to remind us that this is still Kalahari, Omaheke, despite the lushness of the surroundings. The world is aflame with luxuriant yellow, green and white lichens clinging to their backdrop of rusted ironstone.

We stop at a point where the hiking paths cross and look out over the valley. "I have walked this path before," I tell Sinead, "with your mother and sister. We walked that way, under the overhang over there and then down in a circle back to the camp." I point to a path that runs parallel to the top of the mountain along the edge of the cliff.

"Let's go the same way, then." Sinead and I follow the path until we reach a dead end. The faint remnants of a walking trail that has been closed for many years run into the dense undergrowth that continues down into the valley. The bush is as impenetrable as it has ever been. Accounts of the Battle of Ohamakari note that in places the bush was so thick that when the Germans attacked the Ovaherero, they were forced into hand-to-hand combat in some areas, for there wasn't enough open space to fire a rifle. We will not be able to follow that path to retrace the steps of the past. Today, we will have to find a new pathway and I let Sinead guide me. Back at the intersection, we meet up with two women who have come down the mountain. We hear them speaking French until they round the corner and spot us. They switch to English. "The path runs up the mountain and then down again in a circle. We have come from the top now. Which way leads home? To the rest camp?" They stumble through the English words. Without hesitation, Sinead responds in French, explaining to them how to find their way home. Then she turns around and leads the way up the mountain.

Up, up, up we go. Into the gorge and over the wooden bridges that run along the steep inclines until we reach the sign that says "No Trespassing." We follow a path that leads to the left, through the bush, looking for a way down, but we just push further along the edge of the plateau until we arrive at a ravine. There is no way out except to go back the way we came.

I stand there looking out over the escarpment. It is the perfect vantage point from which to imagine a battle unfolding. General von Trotha had arrived in Namibia on the eleventh of June 1904. He made his way straight to Okahandja, where he met with General Leutwein. When Leutwein asked for a measure of clemency for the Ovaherero, von Trotha responded, "I shall annihilate the revolting tribes with streams of blood and streams of gold. Only after a complete uprooting will something change." Von Trotha built up his army over the winter months and planned the attack. Gradually, he moved troops up north. The Ovaherero followed the approach and set themselves up against the natural defences of the mountains.

"What's that hill over there?" Sinead asks. She's pointing at the mountain directly beside us.

"That's the Waterberg Plateau, where the dinosaur footprints are," I tell her. "See that narrow gorge between them? The Germans hid behind the mountain to prevent any Ovaherero from escaping through there. Just south of the plateau is another mountain, Little Waterberg."

"Yeah, I see it."

"Another group of Germans blocked the narrow gorge between them, while a third group under command of a Colonel Deimling pushed through and attacked the Ovaherero soldiers who were encamped just east of the mountains, over there toward the foot of the plateau, at a place called Omuveroume."

While Deimling and his men prepared for battle to the west behind Little Waterberg, von Trotha and the main column of soldiers set up their camp directly south of the mountain. Two companies of Germans moved to the east to block off any escape in that direction. Having surrounded the Ovaherero, von Trotha and his soldiers moved north toward the mountain during the night to capture the watering holes.

"But how did the Germans communicate with each other if they split their troops like that?"

"Aha. During the night before the battle, a group of German soldiers gathered up here on the top of Greater Waterberg, about where we are standing now. Their job was to set up a heliograph station from where they could relay messages to the troops below. They were meant to direct the movement of troops from up here."

"How many soldiers were there?"

"There were about 5,000 Ovaherero soldiers and 1,488 German soldiers." It strikes me as an odd coincidence that the number of German soldiers who had arrived by ship tallies with the year that Bartolomeu Dias sailed around the southern tip of Africa.

"But if the Ovaherero had guns and outnumbered them by that many, how did the Germans win?"

"Well, the Germans brought with them twelve machine guns and thirty-six cannons. Throughout the battle, they used the cannon to bombard the Ovaherero soldiers and the camp where the women and children were. The machine guns were used to mow down approaching soldiers."

The first day of the battle was tough: von Trotha tried to capture the watering holes, but Ovaherero troops fought them off. By the end of the day, the Ovaherero has almost managed to break through the cordon to the east. Communication from the helio station must have been ineffective, because the German sections were cut off from each other. Moreover, Colonel Deimling had ignored one of von Trotha's key instructions — to join the main force in the south after he had broken through the gorge between the plateau and Little Waterberg. Instead, he advanced to the Waterberg Station, directly below us in the area of the rest camp.

"During the night, the Ovaherero began to flee to the east, where they had managed to weaken the German attack."

I continue my story even when Sinead starts fidgeting and looking around at the scenery. "About two hundred kilometres east lies the Kalahari Desert. The Ovaherero wanted to head through there and across the border into Bechuanaland, which is what Botswana was called in those days. Only about 1,175 Ovaherero eventually made it to Tsau."

I imagine the confusion of the battle. Troops from both sides milling around and the cries of the women and children as the bombs fall among them. Then the silent nighttime retreat between the enemy lines. From Waterberg, the Germans pursued the Ovaherero mercilessly, hoping to exact the complete victory that had eluded General von Trotha at the Waterberg.

"I do care about the story," Sinead says when I'm done. "But after my obsession with the Holocaust when I was younger, I can't do this stuff anymore. It's too hard to hear." I understand.

We sit for a while. "I'll never understand it," Sinead says after a long silence.

"Primo Levi, a survivor from Auschwitz, once wrote about the Holocaust that it is one's duty *not* to understand it. We return to these moments of intense horror in order to be part of a larger conversation. But understand? Never, says Levi. It is our lack of understanding that keeps pushing us back into the dark places of our souls."

My words cascade over the cliff's edge. There are no more battle cries coming from below, no more chants. There is only the stillness of midday. I sit down and feel the heat of the sun seep into my body. My legs become one with the rock under me. I revel in its roughness and marvel at how my muscles fold into the uneven surface. There is no height up here, only an immense sense of comfort. Slowly, my heart turns to African stone. My feet bend to the shape of the land. The boulders invite me to step into them and to test their security.

I tug at the rock with my hand and feel it gripping me. I pull back. The rock releases my hand with traces of its redness flecked onto it. We are blood brothers, I muse, for I have grazed myself on this rock many times and given my blood to it; now it returns the favour.

Bloedsake. Blood matters. I think of Banie in the Place of Stone, Uis, and of Willem Goliat, our guide to the prisoner of war camp in Aus. They were right after all, this trip is about bloedsake.

We retrace our steps. At the crossroads, we choose to circle away from the camp. As we round a boulder, I spot some scat on the rocks under the overhang. Bits of bone, bleached white by the animal's stomach acids, cling to the scat. I scrape at the scat with a stick and watch the whiteness fall apart and become one with the surface. A gust of wind blows the powdered bone and lifts it into the air, where the spores mingle with the air and the soil, become one with the earth again.

All that remains is to return to Windhoek, return our bakkie and the gear. "Can we go and visit the cheetah farm in Otjiwarongo on the way home tomorrow?" Sinead asks. I do the calculations in my head. "If we get on the road as soon as the gates open in the morning, we could do it. It'll be a long day."

Otjiwarongo lies northwest of the Waterberg, behind the plateau, right in the heart of Namibia. At the farm, researchers spend much of their time educating farmers and the public on cheetah behaviour. There's a wonderful display on the evolution of the cheetah and the genetic bottleneck it emerged from in ancient times. At the end of

the exhibit, just before we exit, there's a list of the names of the reha-
bilitation centre's patrons. One name catches my eye instantly: Jane
Katjavivi. Jane is an acquaintance from 1990 and I recently finished
reading her own moving account of her life in Namibia, *Undisciplined
Heart*. I have consciously avoided seeking out old acquaintances from
that time. I wanted to look at the country through a stranger's eyes,
but on seeing her name, I decide to call Jane when I get to Windhoek.

Along the highway back to Windhoek, we pass the turnoff to
Mount Etjo. "Mount Etjo," I say to Sinead, "where peace finally came
to Namibia. The various parties to the War of Independence had
reached an agreement in New York, but it was broken the first day it
came into effect, the first of April 1989. For nine days, there was
fighting between the South African troops and PLAN soldiers re-entering the country from Angola. Some people think the mass graves
at Eenhana are a result of that battle, but some of the soldiers who
were stationed there say they're from even earlier, from around 1986.
Anyway, after those nine days, they had to renegotiate the terms of
the transition here at Mount Etjo."

"It's weird," says Sinead. "It seems as if people spend more time
after the fact blaming each other or figuring out what happened or
what caused the war and making complicated treaties. Wouldn't it be
simpler to just talk and not to go to war in the first place?"

24

We are seated on the espresso bar patio in the Post Street Mall in Windhoek when Wolfram walks past. He is the owner of a bookstore in the Kaiserkröne mall, where we have just celebrated our return to Windhoek by buying books to read on the flight back to Canada. It's a delightful poky dugout filled with treasures. Untidy piles of books old and new jostle for space on the tables and shelves and Wolfram readily offers suggestions while you browse. He stops when he sees us, leans on the railing and begins to lament the drop in the standard of living in Windhoek, measured largely in the decline in book sales over the years. "People don't read anymore!" Wolfram blames it squarely on the city; I suggest it's a worldwide trend. He's ground down and morbid about Windhoek; I am revelling in the excitement of the city. It may have to do with the fact that we have spent six weeks on the road, travelling through remote places and that the city feels luxurious after weeks of camping. I let the sound of the conversations in the street — French, Portuguese, Russian, English, German, Afrikaans, Otjiherero, Khoekhoegowab — cascade through my head. Soon, I will return to the dullness of hearing only English around me. The city smells of boerewors and mahangu and vetkoek and bunny chow mingled with German *gebäk*. Vendors at the craft fair take their

lunch breaks and devour fish and chips and boerie rolls on the side-
walk, while in our enclosed patio space, we have baked potatoes
covered in creamed spinach and feta cheese. Right beside me, a man
plays his guitar and points to his bowl. A child sleeps in a patch of
shade while the mother minds her stall; two men play owela.

Besides spending time in Wolfram's bookstore this morning, we
have visited the Owela Museum and the National Art Gallery. I begin
to tell Wolfram about some of the more interesting pieces currently
on display. He shrugs. "I miss the galleries of Europe. You just haven't
been here long enough if you still find this exciting," he says as he
takes his leave. "It wears off soon enough." At least we agree on the
first part — I haven't been here long enough. I doubt it will ever wear
off. I love the soil and the sand and the warmth and the people and
the slant of the sun on the Alte Feste and the makalani palms that
grow around the town and the stone, oh God, the stone with its reds
and browns and black black heart and the fool's gold shimmering on
the surface of the streets. And the townships and the shebeens and
the music and the open air markets. I love every bit of it. I love the
resilience and the fact that after all the warfare that characterized
their past, they can still laugh and forgive. I love the desert and its
starkness and the beaches and the fog and the mist and the people:
a Nama smile, an Owambo beard, otjikaeva headdresses, the beading
in an Ndonga woman's hair, the ochre loveliness of the Ovahimba
women. I love the fact that skin and bones and soil can combine into
such immense beauty. I love that the sun has turned my white skin
into a permanent dun and that I am able to see the colours of the soil
on my own body.

After lunch, I run over to the Ministry of Home Affairs and
Immigration and enquire about my passport application. "You have to
have a fixed Namibian address," the man on the other end of the counter tells me. "The youth hostel is not a permanent address. We have
not been able to process your passport application." I am too exhausted
to fight. Namibian citizenship is my birthright, I know, but the irony

of my situation makes me burst out in laughter: It seems as if I am doomed to be the eternal traveller in search of my homeland.

Sinead wanders through the craft market. She's smartened up and bargains like a pro. As the shops begin to close, we meet Jane Katjavivi in the courtyard at Garlic and Flowers, the little restaurant right beside the National Theatre of Namibia. As with people who have not seen each other for a long time, we spend the first part of the conversation getting reacquainted. The conversation treks across a wide-ranging list of mutual interests and obsessions — publishing, writing, our children, and, finally, Namibia and, inevitably, the skulls.

I tell her about our visit to Shark Island and our round trip to sites from the various wars of the past. "They've turned it into a monument now, I believe," Jane cuts in. I watch the horror on her face as I tell her it is still operating as a campsite. "We suffer from such cultural memory loss in this generation," she whispers. "We need that as a monument to help people remember."

"I'm not so sure, Jane. When we were at Omugulugwombashe, I probed the nurse on duty about the monument there. The most she could do was to tell me, 'It's something to do with soldiers.'"

Jane does not seem surprised. "When Margie Orford was teaching Kaleni's book, *Meekulu's Children*, which details the horrors of the War of Independence, the students refused to believe that such things happened. And that was only ten years after it happened!"

Perhaps, after all, those girls in Lüderitz were wrong: we do need to remember.

"*Tears of Courage*," Jane breaks my thoughts, "is a series of interviews with the wives and widows of the people who fought at Omugulugwombashe. Read it." She turns to Sinead, "You know, I've lived here for more than twenty years and I've travelled all over the place, but I've never been to see the monument at Omugulugwombashe. Do you know what the battle was about?"

Sinead nods her head. "Daddy told me, and I read the inscription."

"You know the skulls are being returned," Jane remarks.

I nod and finish my sip of beer. "I saw a recent notice in the newspapers. And I know that Peter — your Peter — was instrumental in getting them returned while he was in Germany."

"Yes. Perivi is in Germany at the moment, filming the return of the skulls. It's taken six months to organize the official return. The Germans seem terrified of what a bunch of Hereros might do to Hamburg." Perivi, Peter and Jane's son, is an up-and-coming young filmmaker in Namibia. He is one of the delegation of sixty-two Namibians who have been selected to go and give the skulls a traditional ancestors' blessing and attend the handover ceremonies.

"They'll be back in two weeks," Jane continues. "They'll house the skulls in the Owela Museum before they are interred properly. They still have to decide where to place the remains. In the meantime, they're having a vote on that monstrosity on the hill." She points in the direction of the large monument that is being built beside the Alte Feste, where the Reiterdenkmal used to stand.

"They've moved the Reiter, but they still haven't done anything to honour the Ovaherero who died in the genocide." Jane is visibly upset when she talks about this period in Ovaherero history. Peter's aunts were both survivors; in fact, the older aunt was imprisoned right here in Windhoek. For the Katjavivis, proper recognition of the atrocities is personal. "Anyway, the debate in parliament at the moment is about changing the name of the monument they're building to include the Nama and Ovaherero. Peter, as Chief Whip of SWAPO, has to steer the debate. It's lasted a week."

"It seems at this point as if they'll build another monument for them. It would be appropriate if it were in Okahandja, where the returned skulls should also be laid to rest."

"My hometown," I remark.

"Really? Do you have a Namibian passport?"

"Not anymore." I tell Jane about getting my passport in 1990 and losing it and not being able to apply from outside the country.

"So did you apply now?" It's not a question.

"Yes," I reply. It is not a lie, but I omit the details of this afternoon's discussion with the people at home affairs. Perhaps I did learn from my mother after all.

Jane has to fetch Peter from Parliament. "Next trip, Angola," she tells Sinead as we get up to leave. Sinead nods and laughs.

◆　◆　◆

In the morning, I walk past the knee-high sword lilies where they stretch their blades to reach the rays of the early morning sun. Soon, the slender sheathed tips of the leaves will unfold and reveal their spiked flowers, but for now, they stand tall and bulging with life. In the bar, a new group of young folk have gathered for breakfast. We linger, for there is no rush to get to the airport. When all the others have left the lapa and have headed out for their day's adventures, I turn to Sinead. "There's one more grave we need to visit."

"Are we going to the Heroes' Acre?" Sinead wants to know.

"Not today," I tell my daughter. "Today is personal."

She's unsure about going on another long day trip, but gets into the bakkie and directs us to the old municipal cemetery. We wander among the children's graves, gradually noting how the years recede as we move in behind the caretaker's building. Some years there are only a few names; in others, the sunken bodies of a single year take up an entire plot. Eventually we stumble across two tiny cherubim seated at the top of a black marble slab. The name on the tombstone confirms that this is indeed the place we have come to find: John Midgley *† 5–1–1953. The brother I never knew. As I did before departing Windhoek in 1990, I stand at the foot of the grave, running my foot over the red dust on its marble surface. How does one mourn someone one has never known? How do you begin to imagine the potential of these bones beneath you? How do you piece together a face, a smile, a voice from nothing but day-old narrated memories? A fleeting glimpse. How long do you need before you truly belong?

I know flowers will wilt in the Namibian sun. Here, things of more permanence are required, so before we leave, I kneel down and place at his feet a small pile of stones: one from each of the places his siblings have scattered to around the world. Something to tie me to this place in my absence. Sinead has moved in behind me. She puts her arms around me and leans her head on my shoulder.

ACKNOWLEDGEMENTS

It takes a village to raise a child. Thank you to everyone who helped raise this one. Michael Luski offered many useful suggestions during the conceptual stages. My first readers — Kimmy Beach, Leslie Peterson, Lauri Kubuitsile and Myrl Coulter — provided me with many good suggestions along the way. My editor and publisher, Noelle Allen, picked up where they left off. The book is richer for her input. Ashley Hisson took on the important tasks of copy-editing and proofreading.

I can never express fully my gratitude to my family — there would be no story to tell without them. My daughter, Sinead, has been part of this book from beginning to end. She was the best travelling companion I could have had.

Namibia is a land born of war. I am deeply honoured to have people on both sides tell me of their experiences in the War of Independence/ Border War. Willie Haacke, now retired from the University of Namibia, set me straight on aspects of Khoekhoegowab. Rina Sherman generously offered insights into Ovahimba transborder culture and aspects of Otjiherero grammar. The definitions of Otjiherero words that appear in the glossary are taken from her website: www.rinasherman.com.

Jane Katjavivi helped more than she'd know. Her enthusiasm for the idea when I contacted her after eighteen years was what convinced me to make the trip. She shared her knowledge of Namibia and Namibian literature with me generously.

I read many books and articles in the writing of this book and I cannot list them all. Lu Carbyn lent me his personal collection of Namibiana for my research. I spent a day in the National Archives in Windhoek, looking at photos of the concentration camps. I have tried, as far as possible, to verify dates and times and places that were mentioned in the conversations I had with people. For that, and for aspects of Namibia's history reflected in *Counting Teeth*, I relied primarily on the following books: Klaus Dierks's *A Chronology of Namibian History: From Pre-historical Times to Independent Namibia*; Jan-Bart Gewald's *Herero Heroes: Socio-Political History of Herero of Namibia*; David Olusoga and Casper W. Erichsen's *The Kaiser's Holocaust: Germany's Forgotten Genocide and the Colonial Roots of Nazism*; and Marion Wallace's monumental study, *A History of Namibia: From the Beginning to 1990*. I take full responsibility for errors that have emerged from my misreadings of their facts.

All the books in the Archives of Anti-Colonial Resistance and the Liberation Struggle series were most useful for helping me to understand the lives of those who were closely entwined in the Struggle: Ellen Ndeshi Namhila's *Tears of Courage: Five Mothers, Five Stories, One Victory*; Helao Ndadi's *Breaking Contract: The Story of Helao Vinnia Ndadi*; and Lydia Shaketange's *Walking the Boeing 707*.

There are a handful of quotes in the book. Kurd Schwabe's quote on page 235 about the fate of the Witbooi people comes from Marion Wallace's *A History of Namibia*, page 169, and the wording of the von Trotha's decree on page 38 comes from page 165. Eugen Fischer's quote about robbing Nama graves on page 238 is taken from Casper W. Erichsen's article, "Skullduggery and necrophilia in colonial Namibia," which is located at: http://www.africavenir.org/news-archive/newsdetails/datum/2012/03/19/skullduggery-and-necrophilia-in -colonial-namibia.html.

The omatandu cited on page 38 is taken from page 164 of *A History of Namibia.*

Finally, the research for this book was facilitated by a grant from the Alberta Creative Development Initiative.

ABBREVIATIONS

ANC — African National Congress

CANU — Caprivi African National Union

ECC — End Conscription Campaign

FAPLA — *Forças Armadas Populares de Libertação de Angola*, the Armed Forces of the Popular Liberation Movement of Angola

FNLA — *Frente Nacional de Libertação de Angola*, the National Front for the Liberation of Angola

MK — Mkhonto weSizwe, the Spear of the Nation. The armed wing of the African National Congress (ANC).

MOTH — Memorable Order of Tin Hats

MPLA — *Movimento Popular de Libertação de Angola*, the Popular Liberation Movement of Angola

PLAN — People's Liberation Army of Namibia, the military wing of the South West African People's Organization (SWAPO)

SADF — South African Defence Force

SWAPO — South West African People's Organization

SWATF — South West African Territorial Force

UNITA — *União Nacional para a Independência Total de Angola*, the National Union for the Independence of Angola

UNTAG — United Nations Transition Assistance Group. UNTAG was established to assist the Special Representative of the Secretary-General of the United Nations to ensure the early independence of Namibia through free and fair elections under the supervision and control of the United Nations, and to carry out a number of other duties. Independent Namibia joined the United Nations in April 1990. UNTAG was operational from April 1989 to March 1990.

A NOTE ON TERMINOLOGY

In *Counting Teeth: A Namibian Story*, I have had to refer to various peoples and languages and in each instance, it has necessitated a specific choice on my part.

In the Western world, we have come to use the terms *Herero* and *Himba* to designate everything from two related groups of people who inhabit Namibia to their language and to preface their cultural institutions. While this has developed as acceptable practice in Western discourse, it is problematic: Himba, for example, does not mean anything related to designating a human being — it could mean "here," like the French "*ici*," or "to sing" or "to beg," depending on how you write it and the context in which it is being used. Herero is a blanket term that refers to several people who speak a language properly known as Otjiherero: the Ovaherero, the Ovahimba, the Ovakuvale, the Ovacaroca, the Ovadhimba, the Ovahakahona (also written Ovahakaona), the Ovatjimba (and then there are also the Ovatjimba-tjimba), the Ovagambwe, the Ovatwa, etc., all form part of the Otjiherero-speaking groups who live in parts of Botswana, Namibia and Angola.

The common language they speak, Otjiherero, is a tonal language that is made up of some twenty-one noun classes that each include defined sets of nouns. The prefix *Otji-* designates *-herero* as a language (the prefix can also be used to designate places, as in Otjiwarongo). The prefixes *omu-* (*sing.*) and *ova-* (*pl.*) are used to designate people. It is therefore correct to speak of Ovaherero and Ovahimba when referring to the people as a whole and to refer to their language as Otjiherero. When referring to one person only, you would use the singular forms, *Omuherero* or *Omuhimba*.

However, in urban worlds, people — including urban Ovaherero — tend to say Herero for both Ovaherero and Omuherero, just as they say Himba when they mean Omuhimba or Ovahimba. Likewise, people speak of Herero Day when referring to a major cultural event.

Where people have used Herero in conversation, or in reference to official designations, I have maintained that usage. In all other instances, I have opted for the correct terms: Omuherero, Ovaherero, Omuhimba, Ovahimba and Otjiherero.

Similar problems arise with the use of the terms *Nama* or *Damara*. Nama can refer to Khoekhoe people, or to the language, Khoekhoe-gowab and to First Peoples, known variously as Bushmen, Khoi, San, Khoesan, Abatwa, or by their individual names, like Haiǁom or !Naro. Where possible, I have been specific in my usage, or have tried to pay deference to the names preferred by the people themselves. Since almost all of my references to the Nama people are in the historical context of the Wars of Resistance of 1904 to 1908, I use Nama to refer to the people but I refer to the language by its contemporary name, Khoekhoegowab. Likewise, Damara can refer to both a language and a people. Although the language the Damara speak is also Khoekhoegowab, I do use Damara to reflect regional usage among the Damara people.

GLOSSARY

abbavel — a cloth wrapping used for carrying a baby or small child

Afrikaner — Afrikaans-speaking white South Africans

Ag nee, my kind — Oh no, my child

agama — common name for species of lizard in the Agamidae family

assimilado — African subjects of the Portuguese Empire who had received a European education and who had been schooled in European values

bakkie — pickup

biltong — cured meat delicacy

Boer — a South African of Dutch descent; Afrikaner

boerbrood — cottage loaf; literally "farmer's bread"

boeretannies — Boer women

boerewors — farmer's sausage

boerie rolls — hot dogs made using boerewors

bollas — hair buns

braai — barbeque

Buffels — mine-protected infantry mobility vehicles used by the South African Army

bunny chow — a loaf of bread filled with curry; possibly derived from a corruption of "bun" and "atchar"

Deutsche Kolonialgesellschaft — the German Colonial Society

Ehi rovaherero — this land belongs to the Ovaherero

ekori — a traditional headdress

equestres — equestrian class

flâneurs — wanderers

gasthauses — guest houses

gemsbokwortel — *Tylosema esculentum* or morama bean; a traditional
    food plant from the Kalahari Desert, also used to treat diarrhea

Kaokoveld — the coastal desert of northern Namibia and southern
    Angola

karakul — a Middle Eastern breed of sheep

karos — blanket or cloak made from cured leather

kaserne — barracks

kisklere — Sunday best; literally "coffin clothes"

knobkierie — a short club with one knobbed end, used as a weapon

kraal — cattle enclosure made from sticks

lapa — thatched enclosure

leguaan — monitor lizard

mahangu — pearl millet

mancala — a count-and-capture board game

moerig — cantankerous

mokoro — a dug-out canoe

nachtreste — remains of the night

Ombepera i koza — The cold is killing me

ombindi — a stone cairn

omuhona — boss, chief, leader, rich man; *pl.* ovahona

oshanas — shallow depressions inundated seasonally with water

oshikundu — traditional drink made from fermented mahangu

otjikaeva — headdress worn by Ovaherero women

otjize — red ochre unction used by Ovahimba women and sometimes
    men. It is made from ground red iron oxide stone, cow fat or
    butter and a mixture of perfumed plants, with ash added to
    provide a darker colour for certain applications

oupa — grandfather

outjina — traditional songs or praises sung by women

ovahona — see omuhona

owela — a Namibian version of mancala

padrão — a large stone cross inscribed with the Portuguese coat of
arms that was placed as part of a land claim by numerous
Portuguese explorers during their Age of Discovery

panga — machete

Prester John — the legend of Prester John told of a Christian king
who ruled among the pagans in the Orient or Africa

reiter — equestrian soldier

rue — street

s'n — an Afrikaans contraction of the Dutch "zijn," which indicates
possession

Schutztruppe — the African colonial armed force of Imperial
Germany

Schutztruppe Denkplatz — war memorial for Imperial soldiers

shebeen — an informal drinking house; pub

skelm — thief

Sperrgebiet — Forbidden Territory

stoep — stoop, verandah

tannie — aunt

Thixo, Siph'uxolo — Lord, grant us peace

toyi-toyi — a southern African dance used during political protests

trockenposten — drying out post

troepies — troops

uintjie — any of a variety of plants belonging to the genus *Cyperus*

vetkoek — fat cakes

vlei — a shallow depression filled with water, mostly of a seasonal or
intermittent nature

vygies — any of the species of succulent plants in the taxonomical
subfamily Mesembryanthemoideae